THE SPELL OF JAPAN

COURT AND GATE, SHIBA PARK, TOKYO (SEE PAGE 42)

The Spell of Japan

Isabel Anderson

Orchid Press

THE SPELL OF JAPAN
Isabel Anderson

First edition, The Page Company, Boston 1914
Second edition, Orchid Press, Bangkok 2018

Orchid Press
P.O. Box 19,
Yuttitham Post Office,
Bangkok 10907 Thailand
www.orchidbooks.com

Copyright © Orchid Press 2018
Protected by copyright under the terms of the International Copyright Union: all rights reserved. No part of this publication may be reproduced in any form or by any means, electronic or mechanical, including photocopying, recording, or by any information storage or retrieval system without prior permission in writing from the publisher.

ISBN: 978-974-524-206-7

TO THE MEMORY OF

MY FATHER

WHO WAS THE FIRST TO TELL ME OF

THE LAND OF THE MILLION SWORDS

JAPANESE PRONUNCIATION

In general, single vowels have the same sounds as in the Continental pronunciation of Latin. The diphthong *ai* is like *i* in fight; *ei* like *a* in gate; *au* like *ou* in bough. The consonants are sounded as in English, except that *g* is always hard and in the middle of a word is like a prolonged and very nasal *ng;* and z before *u* is the equivalent of *dz*. When consonants are doubled, both are distinctly enunciated. Syllables are pronounced lightly and with nearly uniform accent as in French, but vowels marked long are carefully lengthened.

INTRODUCTION

The term "Spell," as applied to a series of books treating of various countries seems instantly to conjure up before the vision the most romantic and attractive episodes in their history, the most picturesque and fascinating aspects of their geography, the most alluring qualities of their inhabitants. Under this ample and elastic term, Romance has been able to weave its iridescent glamour, if possible enhancing the charm of the reality, like a delicate veil over a mountain view.

The fortunate authors have been enabled to take journeys as it were on Solomon's magic carpet, the aerial vehicle of the Imagination, and to depict ideal conditions based nevertheless on solid foundations of Truth.

Occasionally Fate seems to idealize reality: a novelist could hardly conceive a more fortunate setting for a romance than the Court of an Oriental Potentate, or find a happier source of vivid experiences than would spring from the position of an open-eyed American woman suddenly transported to such a scene as the wife of an ambassador sent to some exotic Empire. Fiction in such a case is transcended by actual fact and there would be no need of inventing opportunities of inner observation: every door would stand open and the country would be revealed in its highest perfection.

In this respect Mrs. Anderson's "Spell of Japan" differs perhaps from most of its predecessors in the series of "Spell" books. Her husband was appointed by President Taft in 1912 Ambassador Extraordinary and Minister Plenipotentiary to the Court of His Majesty the Mikado, and the whole time of their sojourn in Dai Nippon was filled with experiences seldom vouchsafed to foreigners. They witnessed functions to which they were admitted only because of their official position; they were granted every facility for seeing aspects of Japanese life which ordinary visitors would have infallibly missed, and they became acquainted with the very flower of Japanese civilization.

Introduction

Mrs. Anderson took copious notes and she has utilized these in the preparation of her most delightful and illuminating volume. It is so naturally and unostentatiously written that one almost forgets to be amazed at the intimacy of the pictures: one enters the Imperial palaces and attends Court functions as simply as one would go to an afternoon tea at home. Then perhaps suddenly comes the realization of what a privilege it is to be admitted to see through her keenly observant eyes the penetralia so jealously hidden from the general throng.

The book therefore is rightly entitled to carry the title of Spell, for it shows Japan at its very best; it makes one understand the glamour which the courteous manners, the elaborate customs, the harmonious costumes, the perfect Art everywhere displayed, cast over all those who have been fortunate enough to visit the Land of the Rising Sun.

Mrs. Anderson's book cannot fail to serve as a new and important tie of friendship between the United States and Japan; it will be hailed as an eminently fair presentation of Japanese ideals, and will from its authoritative accuracy and its admirable spirit give great pleasure to all in the best circles of the Empire and serve to do away with many prejudices which ignorance has disseminated among our own people. It could not have breathed a more conciliatory and friendly spirit, and its simple and engaging style cannot fail to win golden opinions for its talented author.

NATHAN HASKELL DOLE.

FOREWORD

My recent residence in Japan, when, we lived in the Embassy in Tokyo, has served only to enhance the Spell which that country has cast over me since I first crossed the Pacific, sixteen years ago. What beautiful summer evenings were those on the Southern Seas, when the moon was full! As we sat in the bow of the *Doric* and sang to the music of the *eukalalie*[1] we gazed into the water glistening with phosphorescence. The mornings found us there again, listening to the swish of the waves as the boat slowly rose and sank on the long Pacific swell. We watched the flying-fish, and the schools of leaping porpoise, and the tropical birds with their long white tail-feathers sailing in the blue sky.

The excitements and interests on the steamer were many and varied. On Sunday, while Christians were singing hymns, Chinese and Jews gambled at fan-tan, Filipinos and Japanese wrestled on the steerage deck, and Chinese and Hindus knifed each other. Among the passengers were missionaries with large families, and wayward sons shipped to the East; in a single group we saw an opium smuggler, a card sharp, and the ever-present commercial traveller.

As we neared Japan a huge turtle floating on the smooth surface of the water appeared to have come out expressly to greet us and wish us long life and happiness, for that is what he represents to the Japanese. We are grateful to him, for it is true he was a good omen; we were on our honeymoon, and Japan cast its Spell about us then and still holds us in its toils, for we have returned again, and yet again.

As Japan consists of five hundred and eighteen islands it is often called the Island Empire. In the days of mythology and legend it was named The Country in the Midst of the Luxuriant Reed Plains; later it was The Mountain Portal, while during the Middle Ages the Chinese called it The Source of the Sun, or The Land of the Rising Sun—Hinomoto. Finally it

---

[1]   Hawaiian guitar

Foreword

became Nippon Dai Nippon—Great Japan. But it has still other names, such as The Land of the Gods, The Land of a Million Swords, The Land of the Cherry Blossoms, and The Land Between Heaven and Earth.

Notwithstanding the changes of recent years, the picturesque "and enchanting Old Japan that men of letters have written about so delightfully still survives in many ways. The enormous bronze Buddha at Kamakura sits calmly looking down upon us, as always. At Nikko the avenue of cryptomerias is still wonderfully fine, while the huge blocks of stone in the long flights of steps on the wooded mountain-side bring up a vision of the armies of coolies who placed them there to remain through the ages. The bronze tombs are the same, only more beautifully coloured with age, and the wood-carving and lacquers of the glorious old temples have been kept bright and new by faithful, loving hands. The Inland Sea is just as mysterious and ever-changing, while Fuji is worshipped to-day as it has been since the beginning of all time.

So much has been written—and well written—about Old Japan, that in the language of the Japanese, "The Rustic and Stupid Wife is loth to give to the Honourable and Wise Reader these few poor notes." It is not so much of Old Japan that I will write, however, but rather of New Japan, of social and diplomatic life, of present-day education, of motor trips, and politics, of bear-hunting among the Ainus, and of cruising in the Inland Sea.

Notwithstanding our four visits to Japan, on all of which we kept journals, I wish to say that I have begged, borrowed or stolen material from travelling companions and others; I desire to acknowledge my special indebtedness to Mr. C. J. Arnell, of the American Embassy, who kindly contributed the chapter on bear-hunting, to Major Gosman, also of the Embassy Staff, who gave me notes on motoring, to Mrs. Lucie Chandler, who allowed me to use her conclusions in regard to education and missionaries, to Miss Hyde for the loan of her charming wood-cut, and to the *Japan Magazine*. Much of my information, besides, came from my husband's journals. I wish also to thank Miss C. Gilman and Miss K. Crosby, who have done so much to help me in getting this book together.

I. A.

Weld, Brookline,
MARCH FIRST, 1914.

CONTENTS

JAPANESE PRONUNCIATION VI
INTRODUCTION VII
FOREWORD IX

I	OUTLYING JAPAN	1
II	HISTORIC KYOTO	16
III	FIRST DAYS AT THE EMBASSY	28
IV	COURT FUNCTIONS	45
V	LIFE IN TOKYO	61
VI	THE GROWING EMPIRE	73
VII	A YEAR OF FESTIVALS	86
VIII	CULTS AND SHRINES	102
IX	NEW LIGHT FOR OLD	119
X	PROSE, POETRY AND PLAYS	134
XI	AMUSEMENTS	153
XII	BEAR-HUNTING AMONG THE AINUS	173
XIII	MOTORING AND CRUISING	185
XIV	FLOWERS, INDOORS AND OUT	212
XV	THE ARTIST'S JAPAN	228
XVI	SAYONARA DAI NIPPON	244

BIBLIOGRAPHY 249
INDEX 251

LIST OF ILLUSTRATIONS

	PAGE
Court and Gate, Shiba Park, Tokyo (see page 42)	ii
Map of Japan	xiv & xv
A Korean Couple	3
A View of Seoul	7
The American Consulate. Seoul	11
"We passed...strangely laden horses."	15
The Tomb of Mutsuhito	18
The Funeral Cortege	20
Hideyoshi's House and Garden	22
The American Embassy, Tokyo	30
Japanese Servants	32
"Secret."—Wood-cut by Miss Hyde	36
Shiba Park, Tokyo	42
The Coachman and the *betto* of the American Embassy	47
The Moats, Imperial Castle, Tokyo	49
The Late Emperor	57
"Little girls with littler girls on their backs"	71
A Rice Field	83
Display of Dolls, Dolls' Festival	92
Display of Armour and Toys, Boys' Festival	96
Grand Shrine of Ise	104
Cloisonné Work	108
Eastern Hongwanji Temple, Kyoto	110
The Honden, Iyeyasu, Nikko	114
Off Miyajima	116
Miss Tsuda's School, Tokyo	123
Red Cross Hospital Buildings	129
Armour and Weapons of Ancient Warriors	138
A Japanese Stage	150

Geisha Girls at the Ichiriki Tea-house, Kyoto	155
An Actor of the Present Day.	159
Mr. Arnell and Mr. Arnold in Japanese Play.	163
A Wrestler..	167
The *No* Dance..	169
The Hunting Party..	175
Mr. Arnell, and Ainus..	179
Kagos (sedan-chairs) for Mountain Climbs..	183
The Buddha of Kamakura..	187
Fuji from Otome-Toge	189
"Looked wisely at some presents which we had for him."	191
The wonderful avenue of cryptomerias..	193
Lake Biwa.	195
Ama-no-Hashidate.	199
Ancient Temple near Nara.	201
A View of Matsushima.	205
Japanese Junks.	207
The Great *Torii*	209
A Japanese Flower Man	214
Ike-bana or Flower Arrangement.	218
"The table decorations... are especially interesting."	220
A Japanese Garden, Tokyo	224
A Carved Panel.	230
The Castle of Himeji.	232
View of Mount Fujiyama.—Print by Hokusai.	236
The Little Apes of Nikko.	246

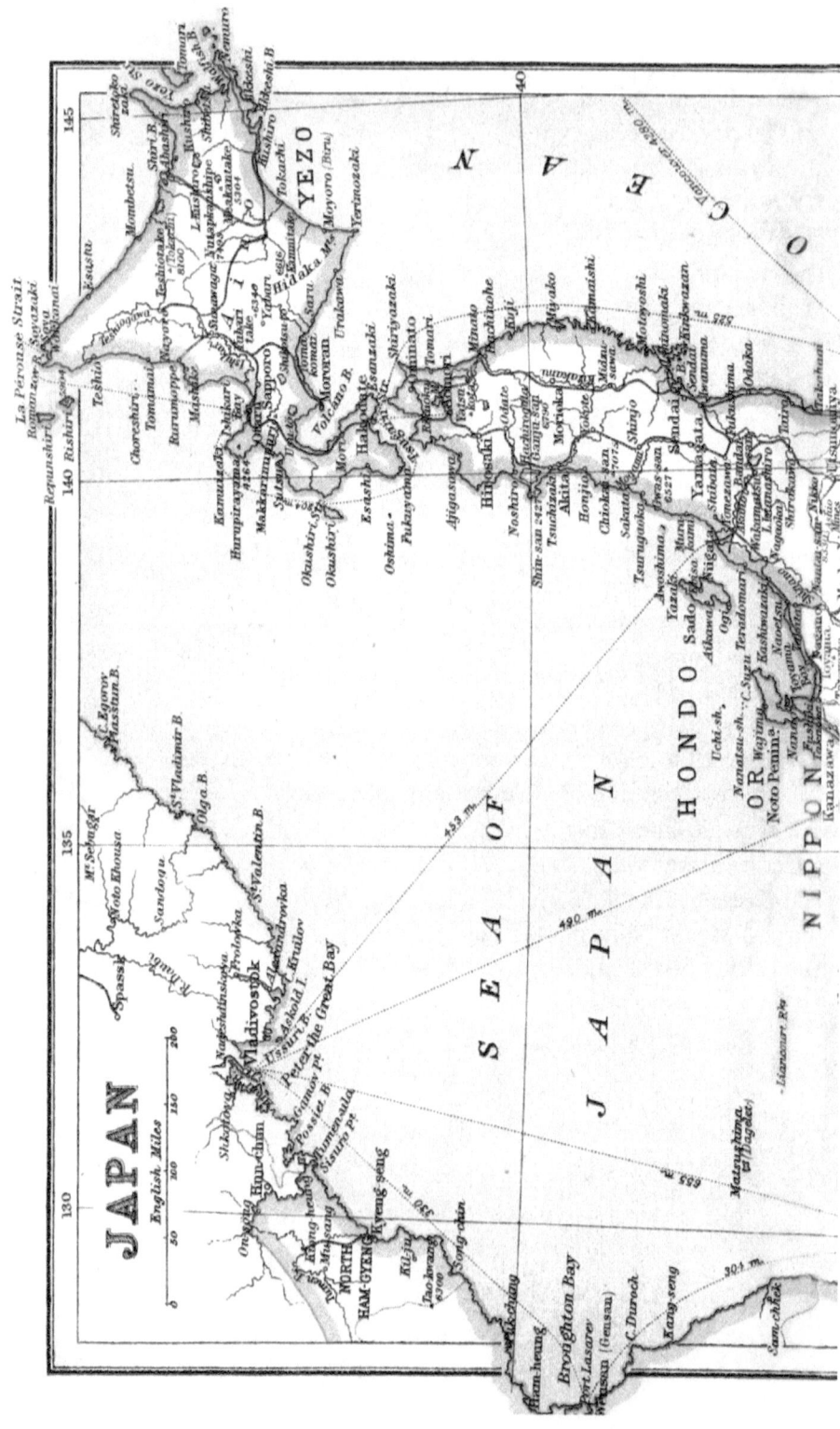

MAP OF JAPAN

THE SPELL OF JAPAN

Chapter I

OUTLYING JAPAN

OUR last sight of Brussels, when we left it in early December, was a row of people, among whom was the Japanese Minister, waving good-bye to us at the Gare du Nord.

"We were starting for the Far East, for my husband had been transferred from his post in Belgium to that of Ambassador to Japan. This promotion was very pleasing to us, for Eastern questions were vital, we liked the Japanese people, and no country could have been more interesting to us than the Land of the Cherry Blossoms. It was our fourth visit to the Orient, and, strange though it may seem, when we reached Korea, the "jumping-off place," we said to ourselves that we began to feel at home.

A quick run across Germany and Russia brought us to Moscow, where the great Chinese walls reminded us that we had reached an outpost of the Occident, a city which had once been occupied by the Mongols. When the Siberian Express pulled out of the station, we felt that we had really said farewell to Europe and our faces were turned toward the East. We crossed the vast plains of eastern Russia and western Siberia—monotonous expanses of white, only relieved by the Ural Mountains, which at the southern extremity of the range, where the railroad passes over them, are not really mountains at all, but hills.

Beyond the Obi River we rose from the level steppe to the foot-hills of the Altai Mountains, a forest region interspersed with open stretches of good farming land—a country so much like our own West that it is sometimes called "the new America." We passed immigrant trains filled with Russian peasants, and the old road over which the exiles used to march before the railroad was built, and saw cars with barred windows, like those of prisons, in which convicts are transported.

The thermometer went down, down, as far as forty degrees below zero, but the cars on the Trans-Siberian were kept as warm as the tropics. The drifts grew deeper, and there were days and nights of endless snow. In the hilly country around Lake Baikal we saw some fine scenery. Low hills and high cliffs covered with larches border its eastern and western shores, but to the southward, a huge mountain wall, lofty and snow-clad as our Californian Sierras, closes in around the lake.

In comparison with our fast American trains this "express" moved so slowly that we feared we should be old, grey-haired men and women before reaching the end of the journey. It was a welcome sight when Kharbin at last appeared, and we knew we were nearing Manchuria. Most Siberian towns that we had seen consisted of low wooden buildings, but Kharbin contains many substantial brick structures.

It is supposed to be nine days from Moscow to Kharbin, and fourteen days from London to Tokyo direct, via Vladivostok. We were eighteen days from Brussels to Kyoto, but we stopped off at Seoul. Our route was through Korea, which, as everybody knows, is now a Japanese colony, because my husband wished to see it on his way to his new post. Passengers for Vladivostok left the train at Kharbin, but we were to continue on southward toward Changchun, where we expected to find Osame Komori, a Japanese whom we had known for many years, and who was to be my husband's interpreter.

We had already received the following letter from Osame:

"Dear Excellency:

"My honourable sir, allow me the liberty presenting you this letter. I meet you Changchun. My gratitude is higher than Fuji and sacred as the Temple of Ise. Your kindness to me is as deep as the Pacific Ocean. Your letter was like sunshine in my life, your news gave me the life from death. . . . I am total wreck by fire. We had storms lately turning the beautiful Fuji like silver capped mountain, but grain still presents carpets of red and yellow. About gold lacquer you write. I made several enquiry when it will be accomplished. I kick Y. urgently to finish

A KOREAN COUPLE.

it. . . . My baby has grown well and often repeat the honour of your last visit.

"Best wishes I remain,
"Your Faithful Servant."

Osame was better than his word, for he met us at Kharbin instead of Changchun, bringing with him supplies of various sorts, which he thought might be acceptable.

After leaving Kharbin we passed through Manchuria, a flat and low-rolling country, in places somewhat roughened, where streams have cut their way. The black earth is carefully cultivated as far as the eye can see, and at this season it was all in furrow. Little primitive carts with shaggy ponies crossed the landscape, laden with bags of the bean which is the great product of this section. Every now and then we passed small fortified guard-houses of stone and brick, with the sentry at his post, for protection against the brigands who sweep down from the mountains and try to carry off even parts of the railway.

At Changchun we were assured that the Japanese Government wished us to be its guests, and we found compartments reserved for us on the Pullman train. From this point we were escorted by Japanese officials, who were sent to meet us and give us all the information we could ask about the country. They told us with bows that the train would be run on a faster schedule than usual in our honour, and sure enough, we soon were speeding over the excellent road-bed at a good rate.

As we went on, the snow began to disappear, and the sharp mountains of Korea came in sight, with little villages tucked away in the ravines. For Chosen, the Land of Morning Calm, as it is always called in Japan, is a country of mountains. Granite peaks, deep gorges and fertile valleys are everywhere in the interior, and the rugged, irregular eastern coastline, of which we had a glimpse in crossing to Japan, winds in and out around the base of the ranges. Among the hills and groves that we passed were the mounds of buried ancestors. We were much impressed by the sturdy, well set-up appearance of the Japanese soldiers along the route, and the military bearing of their officers.

Here live the bear and deer, and the long-haired Korean tiger, so well-known to sportsmen. Foreign sportsmen are free to hunt among these hills wherever they will and they find it a strange sensation to watch for tigers on ridges from which they can look down on the thatched roofs of small villages, or to hear at night from their tent in the village the cough of the tiger seeking his prey on the hills. The wild pigs and hog deer, startled by this cough, flee in blind terror, and are seized by the tiger as they dash past him. In every village a horn-blower is on the watch at night, and when he sounds his horn, all the people beat their tiger alarms of tin pans to drive the animal away.

The Korean peasants eat the meat and drink the blood of a slain tiger in the belief that this will render them brave and strong. They make an all-powerful medicine from the long white whiskers, and use the tiny collar-bones as charms to protect them from any devils they chance to meet.

Although it was winter, both men and women were dressed in white cotton, which looked rather startling after the dark costumes of the Chinese and the fur coats of the Russians. White used to be the badge of mourning in Korea, but now it is the national costume. Various stories are told to account for its adoption. According to one of these, in the early part of the nineteenth century three kings died in close succession, and as everyone was obliged to wear mourning for three years after the death of a ruler, at the end of this period all the dyers had become discouraged and given up their business, and so white became the dress of the people. Now, when the men are in real mourning, they wear huge straw hats, and do not think it proper to speak.

Although white is still the national costume, the Emperor, some years ago, published an edict giving his subjects permission to wear other colours. The nobles wear a number of coats of the finest cream-coloured silk lawn, over which there may be an outer garment of blue. The white garments impose a needless burden upon the women of the lower classes, who are incessantly engaged in laundry work. The coats are ripped to pieces and washed in some stream, where they are pounded on stones, then after they are dry are placed on wooden cylinders and beaten with sticks until the white cotton has taken on the sheen of dull satin.

Korean men wear curious little open-work hats of black horsehair, which make them look very tall and slight and give them a dudish appearance. They present an especially funny picture when riding a bullock. The women, on the contrary, are wound about in white cotton to such an extent that they look rather Turkish, and they waddle as if bow-legged. Many of them are comical in green silk coats, with which they cover their heads without putting their arms into the sleeves. They were allowed to wear these garments as a badge of honour for their bravery in battle, or, as some say, that they might be ready at a moment's notice to change them into soldiers' coats.

It is said that the broad-brimmed hat sometimes worn by the men originated, several centuries ago, in the efforts of one of the emperors to put a stop to drunkenness. He decreed that all the men should have a light earthen-ware hat of the shape worn today, which was never to be taken off, except when they were lying down. The head was protected against the hard surface of this covering by a light padded cap beneath. As the rooms of Korean houses are small, not more than four men could be seated in one, if they had this peculiar headgear. When any one was found to have a broken hat, it was taken for granted that he had been in some drunken brawl, and he received the prescribed punishment.

On our arrival in Seoul, we were met by Japanese officials, and were also greeted by our Consul-General, Mr. Scidmore.

Seoul is charmingly situated in a valley surrounded by beautiful white-capped mountains, over which wanders the high wall that encloses the city. The old entrance gates are massive structures—great foundations of stone with arches cut through them, on which rise the double recurving roofs of tile. The old town with its narrow alleys and its filth has well-nigh disappeared. Under Japanese administration, the gates are no longer closed at night, for there is police protection, and parts of the city are lighted by electricity. The new streets are wide, clean and well drained. Although Korea is called the Hermit Kingdom, and said to be many years behind Japan, there are telegraph lines, electric cars, bicycles, even one or two motors, brick houses and a Railway Station Hotel. The Japanese portion of the town was gay with flags flying from bamboo staffs, in honour of the approaching New Year, and red and white lanterns swung along the ridgepoles.

One peculiarity of Korean houses strikes a Westerner as very strange. As their walls and floors are of stone or brick, it is possible to heat them in the same manner as the Chinese *kang,* that is, by fires built below. So, many of them are warmed in this way, the wood being put in from the outside through an opening in the wall of the house, and the smoke

A VIEW OF SEOUL.

escaping through a chimney on the opposite side. A network of pipes under the floors carries the hot air to every part of the building.

We visited the old palace where the dethroned Emperor and Empress used to live. It is rather Chinese in appearance, but not quite so handsome as the palace in Peking, which we had seen previously. The approach to it is by a broad way lined on each side with low, tile-roofed houses; this leads to the great *Mon,* the entrance gate, with double overhanging roofs towering above it. Inside this is a great court, next another massive gateway with two-storied upturned roofs, then another courtyard, around which are low houses, and a third gate, leading into the last court, which is approached by terraced steps of stone. Finally appears the audience hall, a building with recurving roofs of tile, beautiful carvings, and brilliant decorations in colour. Passages and courts lead from this to the pleasure pavilion, a large, open, two-storied structure with a heavy pagoda roof, which stands on a stone terrace, and is reached by three bridges with stone balustrading. Beside it is a tank where lotus grows, and near-by a park-like grove of quaint pine-trees.

In this palace, several years ago, Empress Bin of Korea was assassinated while asleep. The Emperor, however, dressed as a coolie, escaped to the Russian Legation, where he lived for two years. He afterward built himself a new palace in European style, where he resides now as a sort of prisoner, while his son lives in another palace, and the grandson is being educated in Japan. The Emperor is now known as Prince Yi the Elder, and his son as Prince Yi the Younger, while his grandson, who also bears the same name, is the last of the Yi dynasty, which has ruled Korea for five hundred years.

As we all know, Korea was involved in the two terrible wars that have been waged in the Far East in recent years. Japan needs Korea as an outlet for her surplus population, as a source of food supply and a market for her manufactured products, but still more does she need it as a strong country to stand between herself and Russian aggression. In the last decade of the nineteenth century the Hermit Kingdom was still under the suzerainty of China, and its government was weak and hopelessly corrupt. Japan refused to acknowledge this overlordship of China, and insisted that the Korean government must be reformed. China was asked to help in enforcing the changes, but refused to interfere. Neither China nor Japan would yield.

Finally the Koreans sent for Chinese troops, and then the Japanese attacked the Emperor's palace. A great naval battle was fought at the mouth of the Yalu River, in which the Chinese were defeated and five of their ships sunk. The Japanese army took Dalny and Port Arthur. Another naval battle ended in the surrender of the Chinese fleet and the suicide of the Chinese admiral. Togo and Yamagata, whom I once had the pleasure of meeting at a luncheon in Tokyo, and Nogi, were among the heroes of this war. By the treaty of Shimonoseki, in 1895, China agreed to pay an indemnity to Japan and to recognize the independence of Korea, and also ceded the Liaotung Peninsula with Port Arthur, and the islands of Formosa and the Pescadores group to Japan. No sooner was this treaty signed, however, than the Great Powers compelled Japan to restore Liaotung to China.

But within a few years, Russia obtained a lease of Liaotung, and the Powers made no protest. She soon invested immense sums in Manchuria—in building the Manchurian Railroad, in fortifying Port Arthur and making it a naval base, and extending the Chinese Eastern Railroad toward the Yalu and Korea. She made Kharbin her military base and filled Manchuria with soldiers.

Japan saw the necessity of protecting not only her freedom of trade, but her very existence as a nation, for Russia, from her vantage ground in Manchuria, had begun to take possession of the valley of the Yalu River, on Korea's northwestern frontier. Once this section was in her power it would be an easy matter to sweep down through the peninsula and across the narrow Straits of Shimonoseki to the Island Empire itself.

In vain did Japan try to open up negotiations with Russia. On one excuse or another, she was put off for months, while all the time Russia was preparing for war. Finally diplomatic relations were severed by order of Baron Komura, Japanese Minister of Foreign Affairs, and war was declared February 10, 1904. Baron Kaneko, in an address before the Japan Club of Harvard University, in April of that year, said that Japan was fighting to maintain the peace of Asia and to conserve the influence of Anglo-American civilization in the East.

After Admiral Togo had destroyed the Russian fleet, and the long siege of Port Arthur had ended in its surrender to the heroic Nogi, all the Japanese armies combined for the final struggle around Mukden, which terminated in the flight of the Russians from Manchuria. The treaty of peace, which was signed at Portsmouth, New Hampshire, gave Japan Port Arthur, a protectorate over Korea, and half the island of Saghalien, and provided that both nations should evacuate Manchuria. The protectorate over Korea has since become a sovereignty.

The Japanese Governor-General, Count Terauchi, is a very strong and able man, and under his administration many improvements have been made in Korea. This has not always been done without friction between the natives and their conquerors, it must be confessed, but the results are certainly astonishing. The government has been reorganized, courts have been established, the laws have been revised, trade conditions have been improved and commerce has increased. Agriculture has been encouraged by the opening of experiment stations, railroads have been constructed from the interior to the sea-coast, and harbours have been dredged and lighthouses erected. Japanese expenditures in Korea have amounted to twelve million dollars yearly.

The Governor-General gave us a dinner at his residence, a big European house, where everything was done in European style. The four Japanese ladies who received, however, were all in native costume—black kimonos, which they wear for ceremony only, and superb gold *obis,* or sashes. One of them was the Governor's daughter, Countess Kodama, who was very beautiful. I went in to dinner with the Governor-General, and had on the other side a Japanese doctor of the Red Cross, who had been much in America and was well acquainted with Miss Boardman, the head of our Red Cross here.

Our delightful luncheon at the Consulate must not be forgotten, for no more charming people could be found anywhere than the Scidmores. Miss Scidmore is the author of "Jinrikisha Days," as well as other books on the East. The remarkably pretty Consulate, which is owned by our Government, is an old Korean house, or *yamen,* built in a walled compound on the slope of a hill. Having only one story, it presented more the appearance of a studio than of a residence, but was made cozy with open fires and attractive with many beautiful curios.

The religions of Korea are Buddhism, Confucianism and Shamanism, all found there today. Shamanism is the form of worship of the more primitive masses. There are many Buddhist temples in Chosen. For instance, among the peaks of Keum-Kang-San alone, in the heart of the Korean mountains, there are over fifty monasteries and shrines, but all

THE AMERICAN CONSULATE. SEOUL.

more or less in a state of decay. Christianity was brought into the country by the Roman Catholics in 1777.

The American colony in Seoul numbers about five hundred, among them being many Methodist and Presbyterian missionaries. In regard to the recent troubles between these missionaries and the Japanese the accounts differ. The Governor was attacked by some Koreans, and, of course, ordered an investigation and the trial of those accused. Some of the Koreans asserted that they were tortured by the Japanese during their imprisonment, but in most cases this was proved untrue. The missionaries, having been the advisers of the natives in all kinds of ways, should not be too harshly judged for taking the part of those whom they believed innocent.

The results of mission work in Chosen are certainly very striking. I was told by an unprejudiced observer that the largest congregations she ever saw were in Seoul, and she was assured that, farther north, the numbers drawn into the churches were still greater. Even if we admit that some of these converts were won over by the hope of material gain, we cannot fail to see that all this work has had a humanizing effect, which is especially needed in this country.

Some of the best work of the missions is done in schools and hospitals—especially in hospitals. Hygienic conditions among natives not in contact with foreigners are frightful, and their ideas of medicine and surgery are most primitive. From mere ignorant attempts to aid alone there is tremendous physical suffering. The foreign hospitals have now won the confidence of the people, so that in the end they always make application there.

When we left Seoul, many Japanese officials were at the station in the early morning to say good-bye, among them being General Akashi, Count Kodama, and others. At every town of any importance, during our journey south, the mayor, the chief of police, reporters and hotel-keepers came to the train, presented their cards, and exchanged pleasant remarks with my husband. We were surprised to see how many of them spoke English.

Southern Korea is quite beautiful, with fine snow mountains and cultivated terraces, where rice is raised by irrigation. The red soil is very fertile, but the mountains are bare of trees, the Koreans having cut down the forests. As the Japanese have made good forest laws,

I : Outlying Japan

however, the trees will now be allowed to grow again. The whole trip through Korea was beautiful and most interesting, and in the south particularly we noticed that numbers of Japanese immigrants were settling in the country.

The colonial possessions of Japan include not only Korea, but part of Saghalien, Formosa and one or two groups of islands in the north. It was to Saghalien that the most desperate of Russian convicts were sent for many years. The southern half was ceded to Japan after the Russo-Japanese War. It has proved quite a valuable asset, inasmuch as it contains extensive forests of pines, larches and other trees of sub-Arctic regions, is noted for its fisheries, and abounds in sables, the fur of which is shipped to Japan. These last are perhaps not so fine as the best Russian sables, but they are of good quality, nevertheless.

Formosa, which I had seen on a previous visit to the East, lies to the southward, off the coast of China. About one half as large as Ireland, it consists in the west of a narrow, fertile plain, and in the centre and east of mountains, which descend to the coast in sheer precipices over three thousand feet high. Mt. Morrison, the loftiest peak on the island, is higher than Fuji, and has been renamed by the Japanese Nii-taka-yama, the New High Mountain. The ascent of Mt. Morrison discloses all the variety and luxuriance of vegetation seen nowhere except on a peak in the tropics. At the lower levels are palms, banyans, huge camphor trees, tree-ferns and rare orchids, and impenetrable growths of rattans; higher up are cryptomerias—giant cedars; still higher, pine-trees; and alternate tracts of forest and areas of grass land extend to the very top.

The word *formosa,* which means beautiful, was given to the island by the first Portuguese navigators who sailed along its coast. It is indeed one of the loveliest islands of the Far East. In the late afternoon, the day we passed by, the sky was a hazy grey and the island a delicate mauve. The sun disappeared behind the peaks, and the heavens became a glowing red, transforming the mountains into dark, flaming volcanoes. As darkness came on, the heat was so great that we slept on deck. The beautiful Southern Cross gleamed above the horizon, and the glory of the sunset gave place to the wonderful, mystic charm of a tropical night.

After having been occupied by China for over two centuries, Formosa was ceded to Japan in 1895. Here, as in Korea, Japanese administration has introduced great changes, and it is difficult to realize that railways and electric lights are to be found in this remote part of the earth. In return Formosa supplies Japan with rice, tea and sugar. It also produces nearly all the camphor used in the world.

The Chinese, during their possession of the island, inhabited only the western section, and had no power whatever over the wild Malays of the eastern half. These savages are head-hunters, and are difficult to handle, because they enjoy above everything else that most terrible and exciting game in the world, the game of taking another man's head. They dance war dances, and keep the skulls of their slain enemies as drinking-cups, from which they drink wine made from the brains of their victims. The Japanese have devised an ingenious scheme for keeping the head-hunters under control and conquering them. They have encircled the mountain peaks with a live electric wire, and have stationed guards at intervals along the line. The natives have learned the danger of this. Now the Japanese are gradually moving the wire higher and higher, so eventually they will have the savages pocketed, and will subdue them by starvation or otherwise.

After our brief stay in Seoul we bade farewell to the Colonies and turned our faces toward the Land of the Rising Sun itself, making the crossing from Chosen to Shimonoseki in a single night. This is far pleasanter than the passage from Vladivostok, which requires several days. In order to attract travellers, the Japanese have put their best cars and boats on this route. Our last glimpse of the Hermit Kingdom was a picture of jagged peaks rising in lofty precipices from a moonlit sea, their black masses outlined in solemn grandeur against the heavens.

"WE PASSED...STRANGELY LADEN HORSES."

Chapter II

HISTORIC KYOTO

It was a day's journey in the train from the coast to Kyoto. We ran through stretches of glistening paddy-fields, with their patches of bright green crops and rows of yellow straw-stacks, and then through long villages of tiny thatch-roofed houses, or by avenues of twisted pine-trees. We passed bullock carts and strangely laden horses, and people clip-clipping along on their wooden clogs, and arrived finally, late on Christmas Eve, at Kyoto, the ancient capital.

To our delight and surprise, we found that the thoughtful hotel proprietor had arranged a pretty Christmas tree in our parlour. So we had supper and exchanged gifts, although the hour was late, and felt that in spite of being so far from home we were having a real Christmas after all.

We stopped in Kyoto for the especial purpose of making a pilgrimage to the burial place of the late Emperor Mutsuhito, now known as Meiji Tenno. The emperors take their posthumous name from the name of their era; the present Emperor has chosen to call his era Tai-Sho, for instance, which means Great Righteousness. As L. wished to pay his respects, it was arranged that we should visit Momoyama, where the late Emperor is buried.

As all diplomats are obliged to wear Court mourning, we put on our deepest black—I had a crêpe veil and bonnet which I had been wearing for the mother of the King of Belgium. We went in a motor. The roads were excellent, and the people made way for us, so that we ran with speed and comfort, even through the narrow streets of the continuous village with their congested traffic.

The place chosen for the tomb of Mutsuhito is on a hill beyond Kyoto where there is a fine outlook which the late Emperor greatly loved. As we drew near, constabulary, who were apparently waiting for us, directed and stopped the traffic, so that we soon reached the broad new highway which had been made for the funeral. It is a wide

II : Historic Kyoto

gravel road winding around the base of the mountain to the low-lying buildings about the tomb. These are of the simplest style. Indeed, the entire burial place and shrine are in the Shinto fashion, very-plain in form and arrangement.

We were met by the Honourable Chief Keeper of the Tomb, a Japanese gentleman in a frock coat and top hat who conducted us into a pavilion at one side, where seats were placed at the head of a table. Here we sat for a few moments, and then, preceded by the Keeper, passed into the wide gravelled courtyard surrounded by houses and walls of plain wood. There are two "wash-hand" places at one side, between which a path leads to steps that ascend from the court toward the burial place. People are admitted to this courtyard, and at times over a hundred thousand have come in a single day to worship the memory of the late Mikado. Princes and ambassadors may go beyond this space, however, so we bowed and passed up another gravelled way to the Memorial Temple, in its simple Shinto style. Immediately above this, higher up on the hill, is the temple beneath which the Emperor's body is buried.

At one side of the Memorial Temple, in a small pavilion, three figures were squatting, immobile and expressionless. These were noblemen, dressed in ancient fashion. Here we found a mat on which we knelt for a while, then rose and bowed again toward the tomb, and then toward the figures in the pavilion, who bowed in return. After that we passed out as we had come.

It had really been a most impressive ceremonial, although so simple. As we had been received by his late Majesty in audience and at luncheon, there was something personal as well as official in the respect which we had tried to show by our pilgrimage. Afterward we heard that it had been greatly appreciated by the Japanese officials and people, who consider their Imperial family almost divine.

The funeral of the Emperor occurred several months before our arrival in Japan. From all accounts it must have been a very wonder of wonders. Special ambassadors came from every country as guests of the Japanese Government, and fine houses were put at their disposal. Mr. Knox, our Secretary of State, was conveyed from the United States in a man-of-war. Great pavilions in Shinto style were erected in Tokyo to accommodate the distinguished guests during the evening of the procession, and feasts were provided for them.

THE TOMB OF MUTSUHITO

II : Historic Kyoto

As it had been so long since an Emperor had died, special Shinto services had to be arranged. The funeral was at night. The music was very weird and sad, and the wheels of the funeral car, which was drawn by oxen, were made to creak as they ran along, as if writhing and crying in agony for the loss of the Great Emperor they were bearing to his resting-place.

High officials, officers, and priests, in old ceremonial costumes or modern uniforms, were in the procession, and the brightly decorated avenue, lined with soldiers and crowded with onlookers, made a weird picture in the flashing lights—one never to be forgotten, I should imagine, by those who were fortunate enough to witness it. After passing in this fashion through the streets of Tokyo, the body was put on the train and conveyed to Kyoto, where the procession was resumed to the tomb.

Of its reception in Kyoto, Terry, author of "The Japanese Empire," says: "To the distant crashing and the reverberating roar of minute-guns; the wailing of bugles and the booming of gigantic temple bells; to the sound of the wild minstrelsy of priests and bonzes, the pattering of a weeping, drenching rain and the sighing of a vast concourse of mourning people . . . the mortal remains of Mutsuhito . . . were laid tenderly in their last resting place."

A poem written by the late Emperor and translated by Dr. Bryan has recently been published. It is called "My People," and although so short is rather impressive.

> "Whether it rain or shine,
> I have only one care:
> The burden of this heart of mine
> Is how my people fare!"

Kyoto, sometimes called Saikyo, was the ancient capital, where the shoguns and mikados used to reside in the early days. It is a city of temples, where nothing under three hundred years is counted old, and although typically Japanese it seems somehow different from other cities. The tiny houses and narrow streets appear tinier and narrower here than elsewhere.

The hills to the east of the city are covered with old shrines and buildings, and the woods are full of temples, too. In the Chionin Temple,

THE FUNERAL CORTEGE.

II : Historic Kyoto

founded some seven hundred years ago, may be seen an umbrella left among the rafters of the roof by the master-builder during its erection. Tradition insists that it flew thither out of the hands of a boy whose shape had been assumed by the guardian deity of the temple, but the other explanation, while less romantic, seems more probable. Near this temple, on a small elevation among the trees, stands the Great Bell, the largest in the country. Not far away are many other interesting things, among them the Dai Butsu—the Great Buddha. There are also some sacred springs, a curious temple on stilts, and innumerable lanterns.

The two most important temples are the Eastern and the Western Hongwanji, which belong to the most powerful Buddhist sect. We went through the latter, which had some excellent paintings. The garden and houses belonging to this temple, which are six hundred years old, were built by Hideyoshi, the famous "clever boy," who from nothing at all became shogun. The Eastern temple is described in the chapter dealing with religions.

The approach to the Gosho Palace, once the abode of the mikados, is not very attractive, leading through a bare, flat park. Our interest was soon aroused, however, by the sight of one of the six gates of the palace, through which we drove, following the grey wall with its stripes of white and its tiles showing the sixteen-petalled chrysanthemums—both emblems of royalty. Another gate, perhaps a little smaller than the first, brought us to the immediate entrance. The building is comparatively new, the old palace having been destroyed by fire in 1854, but it is very large, covering an area of twenty-six acres.

Two officials greeted us at the inner gate, and, after politely asking us to remove our shoes, conducted us down the long, narrow corridor to what were probably waiting-rooms. There were three of these, decorated in sepia. From here we were led through another corridor, past the room with a dais at one end for the higher nobility, where the courtiers used to dine off the flat, red lacquer tables, to the Seiryoden—the Pure and Cool Hall—a room used for religious festivals, with marvelously coloured birds painted upon its walls. This hall received its name from a small stream of clear water which runs through a sluiceway near-by. Opening from this is a courtyard in which grow two clumps of bamboo, named centuries ago for the two ancient Chinese kingdoms, Kan and Go—Kan-chiku and Go-chiku.

HIDEYOSHI'S HOUSE AND GARDEN.

II : Historic Kyoto

To the right of the Seiryoden is a room which is reserved for special audiences, called Shishinden, or Mysterious Purple Hall. In the centre of this is a platform on which stands the throne, a great chair inlaid with mother-of-pearl. It is covered by a canopy of pale fawn-coloured brocade with outer drapings of red and purple, and is guarded by the two sacred dogs. The walls of this room are painted in panels representing Chinese sages, the panels being copies of the originals, which were painted in 888 A.D. and afterward destroyed by fire. Leading from the courtyard into the hall is a flight of fifteen steps, corresponding in number to the grades into which officials of government were divided. The higher order stood on the upper step, and so on down to those who were obliged to stand in the court. On one side of the steps is a wild orange tree named Ukon-No-Tachibana, and on the other a cherry tree, Sakon-No-Sakura.

From this hall we passed through more galleries, and through one particularly beautiful chamber with decorations of wild geese in sepia. At the end of a corridor, making a turn to the left, we came to some more waiting-rooms, decorated in blue and white—the most heavenly blue, surely pieces of the sky brought down from the kingdom of the gods by the first illustrious ruler! Here tea and cigarettes were offered us, and we were glad to rest and enjoy the view of the landscape garden with its miniature lake and islands on which were temples and twisted trees.

From this room we passed through more corridors to the entrance, where we bowed to our guide, put on our shoes, and departed, with a feeling of having been soothed and rested by the beautiful simplicity and solemnity of the Gosho Palace.

Once more out in the sunshine, we drove through the park into the streets of the city and on to the Nijo Castle. This palace, formerly belonging to the shoguns, dates from the early part of the seventeenth century. Its splendid iron-bound gates are fine specimens of Japanese architecture and carving. It is much more resplendent than the Mikado's palace, having been built in a spirit of rivalry to show the superior wealth and power of the Shogun. We were received here in the same cordial manner as at the Gosho, and after removing our shoes were taken into a small antechamber, which had two superb doors made of the cryptomeria tree with bronze studdings and hinges. Then followed a series of rooms, the first of which was set aside for the samurai and decorated with tigers with intent, awful eyes, crouching, rampant, even flying, on a background of glorious gold.

From these we passed into the rooms used by the *daimyos*, and on from room to room, every apartment having its golden setting, which was so rich and mellow with age that we seemed to be breathing in the creamy softness of it. In each of these suites were secret closets, where guards were stationed in olden times, unseen by the assembly. One chamber with its paintings of pine-trees was very attractive in its simplicity; the next delighted us with remarkable carvings; the following one, with its cherry blossoms and its ceiling, so pleased the late Emperor that he had it copied for the banquet-room of his palace in Tokyo. Still another apartment, with its bamboo decorations, rivalled those we had seen before, while the last one had a pathetic touch with its poor little cold and starving sparrows.

One door of especial note showed a heron, wet, cold and miserable, standing on the gunwale of a boat. The grain of the wood had been skillfully used by the artist to represent a rainstorm. The door had unfortunately been much damaged by vandalism during the regime of the Kyoto prefecture in 1868.

From a long series of rooms radiant with sunshine we entered others which had the moonlight for their setting—all so beautiful that it is difficult to express one's admiration. From this suite we were led finally back to the entrance once more, arriving there bewildered by the vast number of rooms, the length of the corridors, and the splendour of all that we had seen.

It was in this palace that the last of the Shoguns formally turned over his power to the Mikado, an event which marked the beginning of the new era for Japan.

Japanese history, with which Kyoto is closely identified, begins with myth and fable. No definite facts or dates are known, previous to the fifth century A.D. According to legend, the country was first created by Izanagi and his wife Izanami; from his left eye came the Sun-Goddess and from his right eye the moon, while a tempestuous god came from his nose. He was blessed with more than a hundred children, but, in spite of this, his wife, Izanami, died and went to Hades. Although their parents were divine, the children were only demi-gods, and came to earth by means of a floating bridge.

II : Historic Kyoto

The Sun-Goddess, Ama-terasu, was given partial control of the new realm. She appointed her grandson, Ninigi, and his descendants forever, sovereigns of Japan. Before leaving his grandmother's kingdom Ninigi was presented with a sacred mirror, sword and jewel. The mirror is shown at the shrine of Ise, the sword in a temple near Nagoya, while the stone has always been kept by the Mikado. Ninigi, accompanied by a host of gods, alighted upon a mountain in the province of Satsuma, and his son, Jimmu Tenno, finally made a conquest of Japan.

The Emperor Jimmu is said to have been the first human sovereign in the land. He rowed up through the Inland Sea with his warriors, overcoming and subjugating the savages whom he encountered. All this happened during the seventh century before Christ. February eleventh is the date celebrated as the anniversary of his coronation as Emperor, but, of course, not only the date but even his very existence, is uncertain. The present Emperor is believed to be a direct descendant of this first ruler.

Some think that Jimmu Tenno may have been a Chinese warrior, for it is true that during the third and fourth centuries A.D. vast hordes of Chinese and Koreans invaded the country, bringing with them the arts and sciences of civilization, as well as the religion of Buddha. The Ainus, who were probably the original Island people, began to disappear and are now found only on the northern island of Hokkaido—also called Yezo.

The first woman who seems to have taken an active part in Japanese history is the Empress Jingo (Singokogu). She is supposed to have lived in the third century A.D. and to have made a conquest of Korea, which she added to her other possessions.

The son of Sujin, "the Civilizer," became known as the Merciful Emperor, because he did away with the terrible custom of burying alive, with a deceased Emperor, his family, retainers, and animals. Instead, he substituted clay figures about the tomb. This is still the fashion, for such figures were placed inside the tomb of the late Emperor. They are also to be seen on the avenue leading to the Ming Tombs, near the Great Wall of China.

Kyoto became the seat of the mikados during the eighth century A.D. and was known as the Western Capital. From the twelfth century on, these descendants of the Sun-Goddess were rulers of Japan in theory only, however. In reality the power was held by a succession of powerful nobles—mayors of the palace, like the Carolingians in mediæval Europe—who were called shoguns.

The shoguns continued in power for nearly a thousand years, living at first in Kyoto but later—in the sixteenth century—removing to Tokyo (Yedo), which became the Eastern Capital. They never claimed supremacy, always affirming that they ruled the country simply by authority delegated to them from the Mikado. Any titles or honours which they wished to bestow upon themselves or their favourites were given in the name of the Emperor.

The Portuguese were the first foreigners to arrive, coming in 1542. With them were Jesuit priests, who, under cover of attempted conversion, were thought to be plotting a Portuguese conquest of the country. As a result of this discovery, in 1587, an edict was issued that all Christian teachers should leave Japan. Later even more stringent measures were taken for the destruction of the Church, and all proselytes were called upon to recant.

After this event two centuries and a half of peaceful seclusion, known as the Tokugawa Period, followed. The founder of this dynasty was Tokugawa Iyeyasu, a general of great genius who succeeded in bringing the other nobles to terms and in establishing a strong and effective central government. Bismarck is said to have described him as "a great man long trained in the school of adversity." Feudalism reached its perfection under his rule.

While the shoguns were in power they owned all the land in the realm. This land they leased to the daimyo, or barons. These in turn sublet to their vassals, the brave samurai, who formed the fighting class and gave military service to their lords for the value received. Merchants, traders, manufacturers, farmers, artisans and coolies, all owed allegiance to their immediate master, who stood next above them in the social scale.

During the Tokugawa Period art and letters flourished. The country was at peace, and well governed. The only foreigners allowed in the country were the Chinese and Dutch traders, who might enter the harbour of Nagasaki under guard.

To Americans the most interesting date in Japanese history is that of July 14th, 1853, when Commodore Perry appeared with his black ships, his big guns, and a letter from the President of the United States to the

II : Historic Kyoto

Shogun of Japan. (Foreigners did not realize that the Shogun was not the supreme authority.) Prince Tokugawa not only received the letter, which was contrary to national law, but in due time consented to the opening of certain ports to foreign trade.

Soon after this, the "open door" policy proving unpopular with the people, the country found itself in the throes of a revolution which resulted, in 1868, in the restoration of the Mikado to the throne of his ancestors and to the power which went with it. Prince Keiki Tokugawa, the fifteenth of the House of Tokugawa and last of the shoguns, retired in favour of the Emperor, Meiji Tenno. He survived the Emperor by over a year, dying in November, 1913.

Although the Imperial line was restored to power, their capital, Kyoto, was abandoned in favour of Tokyo, which has remained the seat of government ever since.

Chapter III

FIRST DAYS AT THE EMBASSY

SOON after Christmas we left Kyoto for Tokyo. After having been on the train eighteen days I looked forward with pleasure to being quiet once more.

At the station we found the members of the American Embassy Staff and some old Japanese friends waiting to greet us. There were nineteen in all on the Staff—a larger number than at any other American Embassy. As we walked down the platform to the carriage, the photographers took flashlight pictures of the party in quite an up-to-date American fashion.

We had a house ready for us on our arrival, as the United States owns the Embassy in Japan. Of course all our embassies and legations and consulates are considered American territory, but as almost all these are rented houses, the theory is rather absurd. Years ago, however, the Government felt that it was necessary to buy land in Japan and Turkey for embassies and in China for a legation, and this accounts for our experience.

Congress is not generous in anything which does not concern immediate home politics. It will not pay for embassies which compare with those of other nations, as a rule. The one appropriation so far suggested in Congress for the purchase of five or six embassy buildings is not sufficient to buy one suitable residence, so the Government would probably acquire, at best, only a second-rate house, which would make the American Ambassador second-rate in the eyes of the country to which he was accredited.

Granting that the Government did acquire a suitable house, however, it would require an increase in salary to keep it up. Diplomats are obliged to observe certain standards of living unless they wish to have their country looked down upon. For instance, in Vienna even the secretaries must drive in a carriage with a pair—a one-horse conveyance

III : First Days at the Embassy

is not considered suitable for diplomats. On the other hand, as there is no regular diplomatic service in America, the raising of salaries would attract a poor class of politicians who would seek foreign posts for the money that went with them. This happens sometimes in representations from other countries, but as they have a well-organized service it does not occur very often.

From the outside the Embassy in Tokyo looks rather like an American summer hotel—a large white house with green blinds, of no particular style and somewhat old and ramshackle. I was told that it had to be built of wood on account of earthquakes; it certainly had great cracks in the walls. It had been newly painted in honour of our arrival, and looked fairly well on the outside, comparing favourably with some of the other embassies: the English, German and Austrian are perhaps better, and the French are to build an ambitious new one. The Dutch and the Brazilians were our nearest diplomatic neighbours; the former have a very nice compound on a hill near-by, and although the house is not large it is filled with beautiful curios. Our own Embassy was shabby, but we found it rather nice and comfortable, after all; it was one of the few houses in Tokyo that had a furnace, which is a rare luxury in Japan.

The embassies are scattered about on commanding hills in different parts of the city, as the land was bought at various times by their respective governments. At one time Tsukiji was the only part down by the river where foreigners who were not officials were allowed to live, but I believe they may now rent houses in any section of Tokyo.

Our compound was on the slope of a hill in a district called Akasaka. It covered about two acres and contained, besides the Embassy and the chancery and the servants' quarters connected with it, a stable and two bungalows. One of the bungalows was for the First Secretary, the other for the First Japanese Secretary, who was not a Japanese but an American who had mastered the language.

The compound itself, in which all the buildings stand, is really a garden, with cherries and plums and twisted trees, an arbour of wisteria, and, of course, a little pond and bridge. The snow that came several times during the winter only added to its charm, making of it a place where sprites would have loved to dance.

The front door of the Embassy opened into a large hall with a staircase at one side. On the left was the Ambassador's private office,

THE AMERICAN EMBASSY, TOKYO.

III : First Days at the Embassy

which connected directly with the chancery offices, while on the right was a small reception-room with an open fire. I often received guests in this room for tea; it was done in green and had Japanese brasses and prints upon the walls. Opening out of it was another small parlour done in pink and white, with rows of books about; from this one entered a drawing-room with red brocade on the walls, heavy furniture, and a piano. This led in turn into a large dining-room, finished in white, with an enclosed veranda outside.

Up-stairs there were four bedrooms, a library, and a long enclosed balcony into which the sun poured all the morning. The bedrooms were large and barn-like, but with the aid of Japanese crêpes and rugs they came to look quite attractive.

The place which I liked best of all was a writing-room on the veranda. On a table covered with a blue and white Chinese cloth stood a small *hibachi,* a fire-box for warming the hands, made of hammered brass, with fantastic chrysanthemums and leaves. There were also a long Korean pipe and a shorter Japanese one, as well as a gun-metal box that we had bought in Kyoto, inlaid with a crouching gold tiger. On the wall were red and green prints. Pottery and baskets with plants in them, and a bowl of goldfish, completed the decorations of this little den.

A few stray pieces of furniture, rather the worse for wear, were the only things owned by the Government, but we had arranged to rent the furnishings of my husband's predecessor. Fortunately these were attractive things, so that the house was ready for use upon our arrival. It is much harder than one would imagine, even today, to get things in Japan for European houses. The foreign shops which had European furniture to sell charged well for it, and did not have much that was in good taste.

During the first few days we were busy unpacking our belongings— some old Japanese screens that had travelled round the world back to Japan with us, a few rugs, and our linen and silver. "We weeded out the things we did not especially care for in the house, and picked up here and there some interesting prints and curios. It was said to be the moment to purchase porcelains that were coming out of China, and as Jaehne, an American dealer in Tokyo, came back with some good things, we bought a few. With these, and with the enchanting little dwarf trees in bloom, the Embassy soon looked homelike and pretty.

JAPANESE SERVANTS.

III : First Days at the Embassy

We had already engaged in advance the Japanese servants. These live in the Embassy compound, and many of them are passed on from one Ambassador to the next. Their quarters are connected with the Embassy house, and they sometimes invite their relations to live with them, so that often fifty or more persons may be found there. As they both eat and sleep upon their mats and are very quiet, one would never know they were in the compound at all.

Watanabe and Dick, with the little maids, all wore Japanese costumes. Watanabe, the "head boy," or butler, had been in the Embassy for thirty-five years, and had entire charge of the housekeeping arrangements. He was head of the "Boys' Guild" of Tokyo, and an important person. Dick was the only one of the servants who had been in America, although the cook had been in France, and O Sawa, the maid, had been to China and the Philippines.

Every morning the cook sent up a French menu for approval. European food, as prepared by the Japanese, is really very good. Turtle, served in American fashion, is quite as palatable as our terrapin, and the "mountain whale," or wild boar, is a real delicacy. (In olden times the Buddhists were not supposed to eat meat, and because it was difficult for the people of the mountains to get to the sea for fish the priests allowed them to eat the wild boar on the hills, but called it "mountain whale!") Some of the meat used in the city comes from Australia, as does also the canned butter. Cows are few, but we were able to get our own milk and butter from a local dairy. My husband is very fond of Japanese food, and as I like it too, often of an evening when we were alone or had friends who also enjoyed it, we would have Japanese dinners at the Embassy, served upon the table but in the pretty lacquer bowls on little lacquer trays. Eels with rice and *soy* was a favourite dish.

I used to enjoy sitting in the den and listening to the street noises, they were so strange and interesting. There were the songs of men carrying heavy loads, and the bells of the men who, in the winter, run from temple to temple, almost naked, and have cold water poured over them, as a penance. There was the fanfare of the soldiers, too, something like that of the Italians, and the flute of the blind masseur, and the steady whistle of the man who cleans the pipes of smokers. The newsboys all wore bells, and the people selling wares often had little drums which they beat.

The Spell of Japan

When not listening to the sounds outside, I often used to sit and look into the bowl of glistening water where the goldfish lived, for they quite fascinated me, with their jawless chins, which they kept opening and shutting for food in such a greedy manner! The swish of their tails was like the grace of a trailing kimono worn by the ladies of long ago, while their fins suggested the sleeves of a *geisha* girl. Some of them had popping eyes that stared at you, some were so fat that they swam upside down quite comfortably. They would rush from one side of the bowl to the other, pushing their noses up close against the glass, as if they were eager to swim out of their lovely opalescent world. Many humans live in a world not very much larger than a goldfish's bowl, and never try to get out at all!

Of an evening one heard the notes of the *samisen,* an instrument like a small-headed banjo, made of catskin and having three strings. Japanese music is minor, and being in half tones, which our ear is not trained to appreciate, sounds very strange, and to many even uncouth. None of it is written—the songs are simply passed on from one to another. Although so many Europeans do not care for this music, I find it very fascinating.

But our ideas of what is beautiful are bound to differ. Watanabe caught a nightingale in the Embassy garden by means of a spider, and put it in a cage in the house. It had several notes, not all very pleasant, I must admit, but I suppose it was a compliment when he told some one, after having heard me sing, "Bird's high note just like Madam!"

In the silence of the night, one also heard the clack, clack of the watchman at a house near-by, who beat two sticks together so that his master might hear and know that he was keeping watch. Besides this, there was the squeaking of rats, the meow of our cat, or the barking of a dog. It must have been this same dog, by the way, who came to such an untimely end while we were there.

"Have you heard the news?" one of the secretaries asked one morning.

"Why, no—what is it?" I inquired.

"Perhaps you may remember that the Embassy dog barked so much that our neighbours complained and we had to give him away. Some *geishas* took him, but he still came back to visit us."

"Yes," I interrupted, "he comes back at night—I've heard him!"

III : First Days at the Embassy

"He did come back—but alas! he never will again. That is the news—we found him dead in the garden this morning. His funeral procession has just gone down the street, the *geishas* following the corpse in their 'rickshas."

"A dog's funeral! How funny!"

"Not so funny as something that happened not very long ago, when the local veterinary died," the Secretary assured me; "our Embassy dog was invited to attend his funeral. Of course we sent him, and he rode in state in the first 'ricksha behind the body, followed by other dogs of lesser rank, each riding in its master's carriage."

Occasionally there would be the tremor of an earthquake. But most of the shocks are slight—so slight that one doesn't often feel them. Having been born and brought up on made land in the Back Bay of Boston, where every team shakes the house, I did not notice one all the time I was in Tokyo. I had to take the tremors on hearsay.

Tokyo is considered cold in winter. It has a chill wind, but not so bad as the east wind in Boston. The climate might, perhaps, compare with Washington, but as the houses are so lightly built, and the people live upon the floor with little heat, the Japanese suffer a great deal from the cold. It had always been thought too severe in Tokyo for the Emperor, who as Crown Prince used to go to the seashore during the winter months, but this year, having become Emperor on the death of his father, he was obliged to stay in town.

Miss Hyde has perhaps the most attractive house and garden that I saw in Tokyo. The garden was small, but you entered under a *torii* gate, and found a bronze Buddha calmly sitting beneath a tree. Indoors, Miss Hyde had decorated some of the *shoji,* the sliding screens, with pretty, laughing Japanese children. Her wood cuts of these children, by the way, are enchanting. The day we lunched with her the table was charmingly arranged, with little dolls among the flowers carrying lighted egg-shell lanterns.

The different members of the Staff were very kind in welcoming us by dinners given in our honour. Each entertainment had a new feature introduced. Some of the "boys" are very clever in arranging miniature landscapes on the table, or dwarf box-gardens. Often electric lights are introduced among the flowers. Japanese fingers are so deft that the results

"SECRET."—WOOD-CUT BY MISS HYDE.

are marvellous. At one dinner to which we went, the guests found little lanterns with their names on them, and sat under a huge, wide-spread Japanese umbrella. On many occasions the place-cards were charmingly painted. One was repeatedly fascinated by the fairy-like scenes that were set on the tables. After dinner we often had music or bridge—every Saturday night a certain set met for bridge at the Italian Embassy, and on another evening at the Austrian.

One night, in the middle of a dinner, we heard great shouting outside. It sounded like a college cry in Japanese and ended up with *"Banzai Taishikwan!"* The latter word means ambassador. *Banzai* is often used as a toast—Good luck to you!—but literally translated, means, "Hurrah! Ten thousand years!"

At a dinner one evening, we met two Japanese ladies, sisters, who were dressed alike in black kimonos with white dots to represent a snowstorm—a design especially appropriate for winter; superb silver sashes embroidered with black crows completed their costumes. At this dinner an Italian tenor sang delightfully. For souvenirs we were given charming lacquer *saké* cups.

We ordered as mementoes for our dinners at the Embassy small silver boxes with the American eagle upon them. At Japanese dinners they often give you exquisite lacquer cups or black lacquer boxes with decorations in gold, tied with bright cord, or silver knickknacks made in artistic designs. They are sometimes put on the table in their boxes in front of you, or passed on a tray, uncovered, as is done at Court, at the end of the repast, so that you may pick out the object you prefer. It was said that the late Emperor himself used to design the tokens which were used on the Imperial table. The little souvenirs are admired and greatly treasured, both by the Japanese themselves and by foreigners, some of whom have really beautiful collections which are displayed with pride on the tables in their salons.

Shopping in Japan is always a leisurely affair. It is fascinating to go into the queer, pretty little shops with their soft mats, and to enter the attractive courtyards. If the dealer thinks you are sufficiently appreciative, he will take out of his *godown* or treasure-house a blue and white vase, or a peachblow, and will sit on the mat handling it tenderly while you drink a cup of tea or smoke a tiny pipe, as you choose. One may spend days in such a curio shop, discussing the beauty of a vase, admiring the bronzes, and finally, perhaps, settling upon a price! It is very exciting when the silken handkerchief is being unwound from some treasure, and you see the beautiful thing at last, for you never can tell whether it is going to be a little bronze or a piece of ivory, or smooth lacquer. We knew enough to make the dealer go deep into his *godown* before we began to talk or bargain, for they don't trouble to bring out their best things unless you insist. When you have seen the really good work you wonder how you ever looked at the *muki*[1] which was displayed at first.

After luncheon our drawing-room would fairly seethe with dealers, who came to show us their curios both old and new, which they laid out on the furniture or the floor, as it happened. They brought lacquer boxes and porcelains to tempt the eye, and innumerable wood cuts of doubtful quality.

Not only the old curios, but the modern articles made for foreigners, are very attractive, but dealers only make one or two of the same kind, so it is often impossible to duplicate even the simplest household things. Besides the silver tea and coffee sets, there are silk articles—stockings, handkerchiefs, and crêpes of all kinds, beautifully embroidered—while the modern porcelains are both charming and cheap. But one finds most of these modern things in America now. The old Japanese curios that are really good cost more than ever, and are every year more difficult to find.

The culture pearls are especially attractive, and only the Japanese produce them. The oyster must be three years old when it is opened and a piece of mother-of-pearl inserted. This causes an irritation, which forms a pearl in about four years. They are often coloured pink or blue by injecting chemicals, but as they are rather flat on one side they do not bring the prices of natural pearls.

It is possible to buy some furs which are rarely seen in America— the long-haired rabbit, the badger, and slippers made of monkey-skin. Wherever we went, we were advised to buy our furs elsewhere. China is, of course, noted for its skins—the long white goat and the leopard being among the best—but we were told not to buy in China because,

---

[1] Cheap articles made for foreign trade.

III : First Days at the Embassy

although furs were cheap there, they were not well cured. In Russia we were warned not to buy them because they were so costly, but to wait till we reached Germany, where they are both well-cured and inexpensive. I must confess that we bought in all places, however, and found them generally satisfactory. While the Japanese furs are not so cheap as the Chinese, they are cheaper than the Russian and are well cured.

The main shopping street of Tokyo, the "Ginza," is very broad and has the most prominent stores. Some of these look quite as modern as those on Broadway and are several stories high—a great contrast to the little wooden houses about them. One finds today in the city a great many wide spaces and parks that did not exist a few years ago, but, of course, many of the streets are still narrow and picturesque.

One lovely late afternoon, when there was a silver half-moon swimming in the sky, I went for a walk with Osame through the city streets, which are a continuous bazaar. We turned aside into little narrow ways, lined with bamboo fences with quaint gates, inside of which were glimpses of pretty gardens with gravel approaches and gnarled pine-trees, and of little houses with overhanging roofs that threatened to tumble over with their own weight. In front of the houses hung lanterns with characters which Osame translated for me. Here was the house of a "Teacher of the Tea Ceremony," there lived a "Teacher of Flower Arrangement;" each tiny dwelling bore the name of its owner—and often his telephone number!—on a little wooden slab tacked on the gate-post. It was all so typical and so characteristic—so different from a street anywhere else in the world. We came to a hill and passed up long flights of steps, coming to a temple on the summit which is as quiet and solemn as if it were miles from anywhere. Then we went down again, by another long flight of stairs, into a busy district, past many pretty tea-houses in which *geishas* live, and so out into the more respectable quarter of the Embassy. When my husband was here twenty-five years ago, much of this thickly settled part of the city was all paddy-fields.

Some of the signs on the streets, written in English "as it is Japped," used to be very funny, but the Government has tried to do away with the amusing ones, so that today they are seldom seen in the city, though one runs across them now and then in the country. "The efficacy of this beer is to give the health and especially the strength for stomach. The flavour is so sweet and simple in here if much drink," was one of them, I remember. A tailor of uniforms had on his sign, "Gold Tail Shop," while another shop assured the passer-by that "The tas [tea] are restful and for sharpen the minds." Cigarettes are driving out the native tobacco; a brand is advertised as being "very fragrant except a bad smell." One sign insisted that within could be produced "wine, beer, and others!"

The days at the Embassy passed very pleasantly. Afternoons and evenings were filled with social duties, but the mornings I was free to spend as I chose. Mrs. Caldwell, wife of one of the Staff, and I found the Japanese toys so fascinating that we could hardly tear ourselves away from the shops. Madame Van Royen, the American wife of the Dutch Minister, and I had several automobile rides together. Mrs. Caldwell and I played tennis and sang duets, and sometimes of a morning I would have a walk with one of the secretaries.

There was always plenty of sight-seeing to be done whenever we had any spare time. It was a happy surprise not to find more changes in the outward appearance of the country and of the people since my earlier visits. The hotels throughout the country are more comfortable, however, and the European food better. The *naisans* (maids) and *geisha* girls speak a little English now, which they could not do a few years ago. In many of the towns the streets are wider and are bright with electric lights, while electric cars and motors are quite popular, and even flying-machines are to be seen. The cities are more sanitary than they were, too, although even now an occasional case of cholera is discovered, and foreigners are still careful not to eat uncooked food.

The yellow journals of both America and Japan have been active in trying to stir up trouble between the two countries. When we were in Japan fifteen years ago, some of our papers said that foreigners were in danger there, but we never saw then, or while my husband was Ambassador, any rudeness or threat of violence. Lately, owing to the California trouble, I understand that some rude speeches have been made, and some writing has appeared on the Embassy wall. When we were there with the American Secretary of War on our way to the Philippines, no people could have showed greater good-will than the Japanese Government expressed in every way to our party, which represented the United States.

III : First Days at the Embassy

To return to the streets—although one sees many carriages and a few motors, the man-drawn jinrikisha is still the most popular conveyance; a few years ago there were forty thousand of them in Tokyo alone. The runners can jog along at a good six miles an hour, and can keep up the pace for a long distance. With a leader or pusher, or with three men, as many as ninety miles can be made in a day. As Tokyo is almost as wide-spreading as London, an automobile is a convenience in returning visits, notwithstanding the narrowness of the streets, in which people walk and children play. Pedestrians pay little attention to the warning of the automobile horn, perhaps owing to the whistles and horns of the dealers and the other noises of the busy streets.

There are some large new brick buildings in Tokyo, and a new railway station is being built. Some of the European government buildings are quite handsome, as well as very large and imposing—they would look big anywhere, whether one admired their architecture or not. There are also two large European hotels, and a good bank.

Shiba Park is not very far from the Embassy. People go there to see the Shiba Temples, which were built in honour of the sixth, seventh, and ninth shoguns. As usual, one enters through a *torii*, or gateway, into a paved courtyard, and takes off one's shoes before going into the temple.

In feudal times, when the Shogun came to worship the spirits of his ancestors, he alone ascended to the sanctum of the temple, the *daimyos* seating themselves next to him in the corridor below, while the rest of the nobility occupied the oratory.

The lacquer in these temples is perhaps the most beautiful that I saw in Japan, and the carvings are superb. In many places one sees the three-leafed asarum, which is the crest of the Tokugawa family, and the lotus, the Buddhist emblem of purity.

Behind the temples are the stone tombs with their bronze lanterns; the newest one bears the date 1877, and is the burial place of the present Emperor's great-aunt. Near the tombs can be seen the imprint of Buddha's feet, which must have been of phenomenal size!

One day we went over the Osaka Museum, which has probably more Buddhas than any other museum in the world. It is a private collection near the Embassy, and contains some superb red lacquers, all very well

SHIBA PARK, TOKYO.

III : First Days at the Embassy

arranged. It was interesting to note that the porcelains were tied to the shelves, on account of earthquakes.

One of the most popular resorts, Uyeno Park, which is well known for its temples and the tombs of the shoguns, is on very high ground and has a fine view. An immense stone lantern—one of the three largest in Japan—is there, and also an ancient pagoda and some fine cryptomerias. During the season people visit this park in hundreds to see the cherry blossoms.

The tombs of the Forty-Seven Ronins must be visited, so much has been written about the brave band, and their dramatic story is so often told in Japan. Under the huge cryptomerias on the side of a hill, one comes to the many stone lanterns surrounding a sort of court, where their admirers still place lighted incense sticks and leave their visiting cards on the dead heroes. By the path leading to the tombs the well where the Ronins washed the head of their victim still exists.

Briefly told, their story is as follows: In April of the year 1701, Asano, Lord of Ako, while in Tokyo with the Shogun, was asked to arrange one of the great State ceremonies. Now, Asano was a warrior, and knew little of such matters, so he questioned a nobleman named Kira, who was well versed in Court etiquette. It did not occur to Asano that he was expected to pay for the information, and when he failed to do so, Kira jeered at him, and one day insulted him by asking him to fasten his *tabi,* or footgear. Stirred to anger, Asano drew his sword and slashed the nobleman, without, however, killing him.

Unfortunately, this happened in the palace grounds. To fight in such a sacred place is a crime, and Asano was told that as a punishment he must perform *hara-kiri,* which he immediately did. Asano's castle was confiscated and his family declared extinct, so that his faithful retainers became *ronin,* or "wave men"—wanderers.

Oishi, the head retainer, consulted with forty-six of the most trusted of the band, and they swore vengeance on Kira, who had brought about their master's death. In time the forty-six became trades-people, while Oishi himself pretended dissipation in order to put Kira off the track. But they did not forget their oath of vengeance, and two years later, during a severe snowstorm, the Forty-Seven Ronins made an attack upon Kira and his retainers, and succeeded in vanquishing them.

As Kira was a great noble, he was given the privilege of performing *hara-kiri,* but he was afraid to kill himself, and so Oishi murdered him. As the Forty-Seven Ronins marched through the streets with the head of their enemy, the people came out of their houses and cheered. Oishi laid Kira's head upon the grave of Asano. Official sentence condemned all the Ronins to commit *hara-kiri*[2] and they have been worshipped as heroes ever since.

---

[2] *Hara-kiri* is an honourable form of capital punishment, and is also a popular method of suicide. The man who is about to die invites his friends to share in a farewell feast. Robed in white, he takes leave of them and enters a screened enclosure, where he proceeds to disembowel himself with a knife. A friend who acts as a sort of second stands by and with a keen sword puts an end to his agony by cutting off his head.

Chapter IV

COURT FUNCTIONS

NATURALLY, the most interesting event of the winter was our audience and luncheon at Court. We started from the Embassy at half-past ten in the morning. My husband was accompanied by his immediate Staff, in full evening dress, and all wearing mourning bands on their arms—the Naval and Military Attachés, of course, were in full-dress uniform. L. went off in a State carriage of gold and black, sent by the Emperor, with a Court dignitary to conduct him to the palace, and an escort of the Imperial Lancers on horseback, bearing pennants of red and white, the Imperial colours. Court carriages with the Secretaries and Attachés were next in line, each one having a coachman with cockade and golden bands on hat and livery, and two *bettos,* or running footmen.

I followed this procession in the Embassy carriage, with the Naval and Military Attaches' wives in other vehicles behind. The coachman and the *betto* of the American Embassy presented quite a fine appearance in their characteristic livery—navy-blue hats, mushroom-shaped and bearing the eagle, and coats to match, with shoulder capes piped with red, white and blue.

So we started on that wonderful drive through Tokyo. Down the steep descent from the quaint, lovely garden of the Embassy we drove, the *bettos* holding back on the poles to help the under-sized little horses. Two mounted soldiers fell in behind the official carriages as we passed down the broad streets. The *bettos* ran on ahead, and shouted out warnings to the pedestrians, who always fill the roadways where they are narrow, and scatter over them where they are broad. Men and women stood still and faced the Imperial carriage as it passed, uncovering their heads, and some even prostrating themselves on the ground; others came out from the miniature shops to gaze; jinrikishas and trolley-cars stopped, and people got out of them and stood respectfully; the tiny dolls of children even looked on in wonder, and the police stood at attention at the corners.

The Spell of Japan

For we were going to see the mysterious Mikado, Son of Heaven, Heir of Two Thousand and Five Hundred Years of Direct Descent from the Sun-Goddess. Hidden away there in his palace behind the ramparts and moats of ancient castles, strange and far away, he is still held sacred by his millions of people!

Every view was like a picture on a fan. We went on past the walled residences of ancient feudal lords; past the *torii*—the "bird-rest" gates at temple entrances—through which we caught glimpses of stone lanterns and the wide-open fronts of picturesque shrines. Again we passed tea-houses from which the twang of *samisen* was heard; and left behind us rows on rows of shops with wares of every kind exposed in front for trade. Everywhere the men and quaint little women went stumbling along on their clicking clogs, bowing low to one another; and every moment through some opening of wall or entrance we could see delightful little gardens of tree and stone and water arranged in a way both fascinating and fanciful.

"We came to the broad expanse before the first moat of the Imperial castle. Beyond rose the great stone wall, grey, moss-grown and impressive, of huge blocks like those of the Egyptian pyramids. The branches of the grotesque overhanging pine-trees bowed down to the still waters beneath, where the lovely lotus opens up its flowers in season and the great leaves lie idly on the smooth surface. At the corners of the wall rose the white, many-storied guard-houses, like pagodas with their curving roofs. We passed through the huge gateway with its heavy doors into a second wide space, which led to another moat and rampart of the ancient castle fortifications, crossed another bridge, and entered the sacred enclosure of the Imperial residence, with its imposing gate; and finally wound round a gravel road, bordered with great trees, to the palace entrance, a large covered porch, from which steps led toward the reception hall. On each side stretched the palace, built in old Japanese style, low and simple, in its wood colour and white.

Count Toda, Grand Master of Ceremonies, Count Watanabe, Minister of the Imperial Household, the Minister of Foreign Affairs, and other officials and chamberlains met us at the entrance. With little delay the bowing officials conducted the party through long corridors, laid with red carpets. Here more officials in gold-braided European dress were stationed at intervals. From the corridors we caught delightful glimpses

THE COACHMAN AND THE BETTO OF THE AMERICAN EMBASSY.

of large rooms with gorgeous decoration, and enjoyed the odour of perfumed woods. The ladies were left in one reception-room and the men gathered in another.

My husband was conducted alone to the Phœnix Hall, where he was to be received in audience by the Emperor. Taking a few steps along the gallery, which looked out into another delightful garden, he faced into a square, simple Japanese room, in the middle of which stood His Imperial Majesty, with his interpreter beside him, while at a distance behind and on either side were gentlemen-in-waiting. Etiquette required a low bow at the threshold and two others while approaching. The Emperor extended his hand, and made some inquiries through his interpreter. L. read a short speech, which was afterward translated by the interpreter, and handed his credentials and the letter of recall of his predecessor to the Emperor, who passed them to an aide at one side, and replied in a very low voice through the interpreter with a few words of welcome and assurances of the maintenance of happy relations. Then it was indicated that the Staff might be presented. They entered, making their three bows as they approached the Emperor, who shook the hand of each one, then they retired backward out of the room. After they had disappeared, His Majesty again gave his hand in token that the audience was over, and my husband made his bows and withdrew.

After this he joined me, and we were both received by the Empress in the Peony Hall, a small room with hardwood floors, wood carvings, beautifully decorated walls and ceiling, but no furniture. I followed L., courtesying at the door as he bowed, and again as the Empress gave me her hand. The ladies with me followed in our train, also courtesying.

Her Majesty talked through an interpreter, the conversation consisting principally of questions, such as—"How did you stand the journey across Siberia?" "Do you not find it very cold in Japan?" "Do you enjoy flowers?" The Empress is young, bright and very pretty. She was dressed in deep mourning, in European style, and her hair was done in the Western fashion. After she had spoken a few words to each one of us we courtesied and backed to the door. Their Majesties were kind enough to say they remembered us from our former luncheon at the palace during the reign of the late Emperor.

In the interval between the audience and the luncheon, the latter not occurring till half-past twelve, we drove back to the Embassy. Our

THE MOATS, IMPERIAL CASTLE, TOKYO.

"head boy" told us it was customary to have a glass of champagne upon returning from such a function, so we had some wine and biscuit, which the Master of Ceremonies and the officer in command of the escort were invited to share with us. Then we all went out and were photographed by all kinds of cameras levelled by an army of photographers—as. That seemed to be the custom, too.

When we returned to the palace, we were conducted into the vast Room of One Thousand Seeds, which, like the Peony Hall, had no chairs; but the ceiling was magnificently carved and there were beautiful panels and vases of flowers. Different members of the Imperial family came in, the men in uniform, the ladies in black European gowns and hats. As the luncheon was to be informal, frock coats were worn by the men of the Embassy in place of evening clothes. I was then presented to the Emperor, who was in khaki uniform, and seemed alert and interested in everything, and we followed Their Majesties into the large dining-room near-by.

This room was also vast and spacious, with glass on one side through which we looked out into the garden. The table was set in handsome European style for thirty or forty persons, and a number of servants in European liveries stood in impressive line behind. Their Majesties sat together in the centre of the table, with Prince and Princess Kan-in on their right and left.

Prince Kan-in, who was on one side of me, is a cousin of the Emperor, young and quite good looking. Having lived in France for nine years, he spoke French well. On the other side was Prince Katsura, who was at that time Prime Minister and one of the strongest and best-known men in Japan. Prince Katsura spoke a little English, but preferred German. His German was not much better than mine, so we did not have so much interesting conversation as we otherwise might have had. Prince Fushimi, now quite an old man, whom we had met years ago in Boston, was there, besides many others.

The luncheon was in European style and delicious. The table ornaments were exquisite orchids in silver dishes. During the meal the Emperor sent me several messages through one of the gentlemen-in-waiting, who acted as interpreter: "Do you have orchids in America?" "Are you going to Nikko this summer?" To my answer that I had been at Nikko, His Majesty replied, that his Summer Palace was at Nikko, and

IV : Court Functions

that he hoped we might go there again, as he felt sure we would each time see even more beautiful things. The Emperor proposed my husband's health by lifting his glass and drinking, and L. rose, lifted his, and drank to the Emperor. Then His Majesty pledged me, and I rose, and drank to him in return. At the close of the luncheon charming silver bonbon boxes in old Japanese designs, such as the *hibachi* and the *kago,* or sedan-chair, and bearing the Imperial crest, were offered us as souvenirs. We were each delighted to select one of these attractive mementoes.

After luncheon we returned again to the Hall of One Thousand Seeds, followed by the high officials of the Imperial Household. Here my husband and I conversed more intimately with Their Majesties. Conversation was carried on in a whisper through the interpreter, for Japanese Court etiquette requires that the voice be never raised while talking with the Emperor and Empress. Then the Imperial party withdrew, and the rest of us were left to pass out at leisure and view with interest and pleasure the rooms through which we were conducted, visiting the large, simple Throne Room on the way. So this extraordinary experience came to an end, and remains a dream, wonderful, seemingly unreal. The day after the audience we went over to the palace, and signed our names in the Imperial books.

The reigning Emperor is the one hundred and twenty-fourth of his line. It is said that he wishes to travel beyond his kingdom, but although the Japanese people themselves seek to be up to date and familiar with the ways of the Western world, many of them do not wish their ruler to be so, and therefore do not quite approve of his taking so much interest in foreigners. In his boyhood the Emperor went to school and seemed quite well and strong; it is said, however, that he is rather delicate now. Even then he was astonishingly democratic in his ideas. They tell a story that, when a boy, while out driving one day, he saw a man on the corner of a street selling cookies, and said that he wished to have some. Other cookies were made like them and given to him, but he refused them. Nothing would do but he must have those sold by the old man on the corner. In vain the attendants argued that those cookies were only made for common people, for human beings—members of the Imperial family are supposed to be divine—the boy said that if human beings and the common people could eat them, he could eat them, too. So the cakes were, finally bought, and no doubt he enjoyed them.

The beautiful new palace on the edge of the city, at Akasaka, is a fine building in good European style, much like the palace in Brussels. Here the garden parties take place. The present Emperor has never lived in it, preferring his Japanese palace on the same grounds, which he considers more wholesome, and where he lived as Crown Prince. Audiences are still held, as in his father's time, in the old palace, which has been done over somewhat since the death of the late Emperor.

After our audience and luncheon at Court, we were received also by several of the Imperial Princes and Princesses at their palaces. To these visits we went in our own automobile, our chauffeur and footman wearing caps with the American eagle and gold braid on the visor, and little shoulder-straps of gold that made them look suitably ambassadorial. Sometimes we took Osame on the box instead of the footman, so that he might straighten matters out in case of difficulty, as the footman and the chauffeur did not speak a word but Japanese. In his frock coat and top hat he looked quite properly funereal. My husband went in his evening dress, and I wore black. The houses were usually quite European, but were somewhat bare inside, with a little old-fashioned European furniture. As we entered, we were greeted by several officials-in-waiting in fine uniforms, and then were almost immediately received, quite in the same fashion as by the Emperor and Empress, except that we were asked to sit down.

One day the Prince and Princess Kan-in received us. The Nagasakis were in attendance and acted as interpreters. They spoke excellent English. We had known them before, and had found them especially agreeable. Mr. Nagasaki is Court Councillor and Master of Ceremonies, as well as Lord Steward to His Imperial Highness, Prince Kan-in. Prince Kan-in's palace is a large modern house with fine grounds, surrounded by a splendid old-fashioned wall and entered by a great old-time gate. It was rather cold and bare inside, but the Aide and the Master of Ceremonies in their gold regalia gave bright touches of colour.

The second princess who received us was the wife of Prince Asaka and daughter of the late Emperor. Again the officer in attendance had been educated in England and was a man of the world. As at Court, the women were in European dress and in deep mourning with jet jewelry. The conversation, as usual, was more or less about flowers, the weather and the journey.

IV : Court Functions

Later, we were received at Prince Higashi Fushimi's, whose house we found Japanese in style and especially charming. The room where we were received, however, had been arranged for the comfort of foreigners, as it contained a sofa, a table and chairs. Prince Fushimi, who is an admiral in the navy, was in London with the Princess at the time of the Coronation. Both spoke English very well. A card was sent to us as a return visit within half an hour after each diplomatic audience, as is required by Japanese etiquette.

An important function, which the Diplomatic Corps missed on account of the mourning for the late Emperor, was the New Year reception at Court. At this the ladies wear beautiful long court trains hung from the shoulders, such as are worn at the Court of St. James. I was told that the diplomats are first conducted to the Throne Room, a large hall, where two chairs are arranged upon a raised dais, much as at European courts. Here they march in the precedence of embassies and legations past the Emperor and Empress on their thrones, then past all the Imperial Highnesses, bowing and courtesying to each one. After this, in a smaller room they are served with tea, coffee and cakes, and receive lovely gifts as souvenirs. Finally, in still another room, they are received by Their Majesties and the other Imperial personages in a more special way.

Among Court recreations in which the Diplomatic Corps are invited to join, is the Imperial duck-catching party, held in gardens near Tokyo in the spring. By decoy ducks the wild birds are lured into little canals, on either side of which stand those who take part in the sport, holding large nets with long handles high in the air. All are silent and alert, and as soon as a duck takes flight, the netter dashes forward and, if expert, entangles a bird in the net. This sport is a combination of snaring and hawking, for if a bird escapes the hunter, it is likely to be killed by the hawk chained to the hunter's wrist, which is then set free. Afterward luncheon is served, a delicious duck stew being the principal feature, and the guests return home laden with the birds they have succeeded in catching.

The official celebration of the Emperor's birthday includes several imposing Court functions. When my husband was in Japan in 1889, earthquakes, reviews and events of all kinds were provided for His Imperial Majesty's thirty-sixth anniversary. First, they were treated to three seismic shocks within twenty-four hours, and of quite perceptible violence. Then there was the Grand Review of troops by the Emperor at the cheerful hour of half after eight in the morning.

My husband thus describes it: "Aoyama, the 'Champ de Mars' of Tokyo, is a tremendously large parade ground, which was simply walled in by the mass of plebeians that had turned out to do honour to the occasion. For the foreigners the 'high seats' had been reserved in the diplomatic tent next to the Imperial stand. The Emperor, followed by the Lancers and a gorgeous Staff, made a tour of the field, and then the troops passed in review before him. They were about ten thousand in number, and made a really excellent appearance; the marching and order were good, at times very good. The cavalry appeared rather awkward, but this was due to the brutish little horses more than anything else.

"In the evening there was the grand ball at the 'Rokumeikan,' given by Count Okuma, then Minister of Foreign Affairs, in honour of the Emperor's anniversary, which starts the social whirl of the capital for the season. It was an elegant affair, and from the good taste and good management, it might well have been in Paris. The grounds were beautifully decorated with lanterns and coloured lights, and the building was superb inside with bunting and flowers, the national chrysanthemum being used with excellent effect. The uniforms and decorations of the guests added brilliancy and movement. There were almost as many foreigners as Japanese, and nearly all the latter were in European dress, only a few ladies wearing the native costume. Those in European gowns carried them off exceedingly well, and danced waltzes and quadrilles in most approved Western manner."

The present Emperor's anniversary, as I have learned from a letter, was celebrated in 1913 in much the same way as his predecessor's more than twenty years ago—with one important exception, the three earthquake shocks were omitted! The day began with the review of the soldiers at Aoyama, after which congratulatory poems were presented to His Majesty by the Empress and the Empress Dowager.[3] The Emperor then received the Imperial Princes and Princesses, and entertained them at luncheon.

---

[3] The Dowager Empress of Japan died of heart disease at the Imperial Villa Nowazu, April 9th, 1914. She was the widow of Emperor Mutsuhito, who died July 30th, 1912. The Empress Dowager was born May 28th, 1858, and was married to the late Emperor in 1869. She was the daughter of a nobleman, Icliejo-Tadado, and was greatly beloved by the Japanese people.

IV : Court Functions

The birthday dinner in the evening was followed by the ball given by the Minister of Foreign Affairs, Baron Makino, at his official residence. Here were princesses of the blood in white gowns and superb jewels, Japanese ladies in kimonos, ladies of the Corps Diplomatique in European costume, priests in their varied robes, and diplomats and attaches in gorgeous uniforms. It was a brilliant scene. The rooms were lighted by electricity and decorated with a profusion of chrysanthemums and the Imperial crest in gold. Long clusters of wisteria depending from the ceiling sparkled with electric bulbs, and in the supper-room the guests were seated at tables under the branches of artificial cherry-trees blossoming in the Emperor's honour.

Some account of our previous reception at Court by the late Emperor and Empress may be of interest. It took place when we passed through Japan in the company of the American Secretary of War, Mr. Dickinson, on the way to the Philippines in 1910. At that time we crossed the Pacific to the Land of the Rising Sun.

News had been received while at sea by aerogram from the Embassy that the Imperial Mikado and the Empress would grant an audience and entertain at luncheon at the palace, but there was much doubt as to what this really meant, for the audience might be only for the Secretary and Mrs. Dickinson. So the pleasure and surprise were all the greater when, on arrival, it was found that those accompanying the Secretary were to be included in both functions.

The invitations, in Japanese characters, were handed to us with many others on our arrival, but had already been formally answered at the American Embassy. The instructions were the same then as they are today as to costume and etiquette. They indicated that the ladies were to wear high-necked dresses with trains and hats, and the men were to be in uniform or full dress. On the morning of the sixteenth (of July), we all met at the Embassy at eleven o'clock—as the audience was due at noon—and placed ourselves in the hands of the Ambassador.

Two Imperial carriages conveyed the important official members of the party to the palace, and the rest proceeded in vehicles hired for the occasion.

After the men of the party were presented to the Emperor, in the manner already described, they rejoined the ladies, and all were introduced to the lady-in-waiting, Countess Kagawa, and then conducted to Her Majesty's audience hall. Mrs. O'Brien, the wife of the Ambassador, preceded, making low courtesies; the ladies followed.

The Emperor, who was in uniform, appeared older than we had expected. Her Majesty was several years older than the Emperor, and had charming manners, but she did not smile. Expression, we were informed, is not considered aristocratic. Her hair and dress were in European fashion, and she wore beautiful pearls. She had no children—the present Mikado is the only son of Emperor Meiji by another wife.

Some stories that are told of the late Emperor show how much real strength of character he possessed. A few years ago, it is said, when a plot against His Majesty's life was discovered, the Prime Minister went to him and offered his resignation, saying that as this plot had been brought to light while he was in office (the first plot against any Mikado in the history of Japan), he felt that perhaps his administration had not been good. The Emperor, however, would not accept his resignation, saying that if the people wished to take his life, it must be his fault—it must show that he had not been a good ruler. Accordingly, he ordered only twelve of the twenty-four offenders to be put to death.

In his last illness, owing to the old belief that his person was too sacred to be touched, even the doctors were not allowed to come in contact with him, his pulse being counted by a silken cord about his wrist. The Empress was at his bedside when he died. The only person who ever entered his apartment, I was told, was Prince Ito, who came on some urgent affair of state in response to a telephone message from the Emperor himself. The Prince was admitted before the Mikado was dressed in the morning. Even on the greatest occasions, however, he was never really well dressed, because no one was permitted to fit his clothes, lest a mere human being should touch his person.

Yet the life of the late Emperor, secluded though he was within his palace walls, was freedom itself in comparison with that of the ancient rulers. In olden times, so Hearn writes, "His (the Mikado's) feet were never permitted to touch the ground out of doors, nor was he allowed to cut his hair, beard or nails, or to expose himself to the rays of the sun." His only excursions outside the walls of his palace were made in a large *norimono,* or palanquin, borne by fourteen men, in which, behind the latticed windows, he was able to catch glimpses of the outer world

THE LATE EMPEROR

while himself invisible. Even if he granted an audience, he was never seen, his person being completely hidden by bamboo screens.

The emperors of ancient days were allowed to have three consorts besides the Empress, also nine maids of high rank and twenty-seven maids of lower rank, all of whom were known as wives. In addition to these, he was at liberty to have eighty-one concubines. Only one of the wives ranked as empress, but the twelve next below her had each a palace near that of the Emperor. By way of contrast, it is said that the present Emperor has never loved any woman but the Empress. The Mikado's eldest daughter was in olden times appointed chief priestess of the Temple of the Sun, at Ise.

Somewhat in contrast with my husband's experiences were those of America's first Ambassador to Japan, Mr. Townsend Harris, as he has related them in his journal. After his arrival in Japan and many weary months of waiting at Shimoda, he wrote September 25th, 1857, "I am to go to Yedo (now Tokyo) in the most honourable manner; and after my arrival I am to have an audience of the Shogun, and then present the letter of the President!!"

"The manner in which I am to salute the Shogun," he adds, "is to be the same as in the courts of Europe, that is, three bows. They made a faint request that I would prostrate myself and 'knock-head,' but I told them the mentioning such a thing was offensive to me."

After two months spent in preparation for the journey, Mr. Harris with an imposing retinue started for Yedo, about one hundred miles away.

As a part of the preparation for his journey, "Bridges had been built over every stream," he tells us, "the pathway mended, and all the bushes cut away so as to leave the path clear." At one place the road had actually been *swept* only a few hours before the procession passed over it. All along the way the people stood motionless in front of their houses, and all the shops but the cook shops were closed. The magistrates of each village conducted Mr. Harris to the borders of the next, prostrating themselves in salute as they left. The Government had also ordered that there should be no travel over the Tokaido, the Eastern Sea Road, during his journey.

In Yedo the American Envoy was domiciled in the "Court" section of the city, and eight *daimyos* were appointed as "Commissioners of the voyage of the American Ambassador to Yedo." Another week was passed in receiving and paying visits of ceremony, and in arranging matters of detail. Mr. Harris received as a present from the Shogun seventy pounds of Japanese bonbons beautifully arranged in four trays.

On December 7th, at ten o'clock in the morning, our Ambassador set out for his audience of the Shogun. "My dress," he says, "was a coat embroidered with gold after the pattern furnished by the State Department, blue pantaloons with a broad gold band running down each leg, cocked hat with gold tassels, and a pearl-handled dress sword." He was escorted by the same retinue that he had had during the journey. He was carried in his *norimono* up to the last bridge in front of the audience hall, and before entering this building he put on a new pair of patent leather shoes. The Japanese, of course, went in their *tabis*. After a time he was led to the audience hall, past a number of *daimyos,* seated in Japanese fashion, who saluted by touching their foreheads to the mat. The Prince of Shinano, Master of Ceremonies, then threw himself on his hands and knees, and Mr. Harris stood behind him, with Mr. Heusken in the rear bearing the President's letter.

At a given signal, the Prince crawled forward on hands and knees, and as Mr. Harris followed and entered the hall of audience, a chamberlain called out, "Embassador Merican!" With the prescribed three bows at intervals, he advanced toward the throne, before which the members of the Great Council lay prostrate on their faces. Pausing a few seconds, Mr. Harris then addressed the Tai-kun—as he had been instructed to call the Shogun—expressing the good wishes of the President.

"After a short silence," says Mr. Harris, "the Tai-kun began to jerk his head backward over his left shoulder, at the same time stamping with his right foot. This was repeated three or four times.[4] After this he spoke audibly and in a pleasant and firm voice," expressing his pleasure in the Ambassador's speech, and graciously adding, "Intercourse shall be continued forever."

Mr. Harris then presented the President's letter, after which he withdrew, as he had entered, with three bows.

Mr. Harris' description of the Shogun himself is of interest: "The Tai-kun was seated in a chair placed on a platform raised about two feet

---

[4] I have been told that Mr. Harris *shouted* in delivering his address to the Shogun, who, perhaps, had never before heard any one speak above a whisper.

from the floor, and from the ceiling in front of him a grass curtain was hung; when unrolled, it would reach the floor, but it was now rolled up, and was kept in its place by large silk cords with heavy tassels. By an error in their calculation, the curtain was not rolled up high enough to enable me to see his headdress, as the roll formed by the curtain cut through the centre of his forehead, so that I cannot fully describe his 'crown,' as the Japanese called it. The dress of the Tai-kun was made of silk, and the material had some little gold wove in with it, but it was as distant from anything like regal splendour as could be conceived; no rich jewels, no elaborate gold ornaments; no diamond-hilted weapon appeared. . . . The Japanese told me his crown is a black lacquered cap, of an inverted bell shape."

Two years later Mr. Heusken, Mr. Harris' secretary, was assassinated, and his own house was burned. But Mr. Harris never wavered. Dignified, firm, self-respecting, he was always the kind, patient teacher of the Japanese in the ways of the outside world, winning from them the title which they love to give him—"the nation's friend." He was a great diplomat, but his was a strikingly human and Christian diplomacy. He laid the foundations for America's subsequent dealings with Japan so deep in the bedrock of justice and mutual forbearance that the superstructure has never yet been shaken. Our own personal experiences were pleasanter because Townsend Harris had led the way.

Chapter V

LIFE IN TOKYO

OUR diplomatic visits were made within two days of our arrival, as etiquette requires. My first visit was on the Doyenne of the Diplomatic Corps, Marchesa Guiccioli. The French Ambassador was Doyen, but as he was not married the Italian Ambassadress was the first lady of the Corps. When our diplomatic calls had been made and returned, we returned those made by the American colony in Tokyo and Yokohama.

During the winter the ladies of the Diplomatic Corps decided to have a day "at home" each week. The period of second mourning for the late Emperor had begun, and we all dressed in black and white. Dinners and calling among the diplomats continued, but the official dinners between the Japanese and the foreigners did not take place on account of the mourning.

The diplomatic dinners were always large affairs of twenty or thirty people, and quite formal, with the host and hostess sitting in foreign fashion at the centre of the table, the ends filled in with young secretaries. There were but few women present, for many of the diplomats in Tokyo were not married. Occasionally we found one or two Japanese at these dinners, but not often, owing to the official mourning. They might have been given in Europe or anywhere, except for a touch of the East in the costumes of the servants and the curios about the house.

To show how a Japanese lady or gentleman answers an Ambassador's invitation, I give literal translations of two responses which are quite typical.

"WORSHIPFULLY ADDRESSED.

"Having received upon my head the honourable loving invitation of the coming 25th day, I humbly regard it as the extremity of glory. Referring thereto, in the case of the rustic wife there being unavoidably a previous engagement, although

with regret, (she) is humbly unable to ascend; consequently the little student one person, humbly accepting, will go to the honourable residence. Rapidly, rapidly, worshipfully bowing.
"Great Justice, 2d year, 2d moon, 19th day.
American Ambassador,
Beneath the Mansion.
Honourable Lady,
Beneath the Mansion."

"WORSHIPFULLY REPORTING.

"Having received upon my head the honourable loving invitation to the banquet of the honourable holding on the coming 25th day, thankfully, joyfully, humbly shall I worshipfully run. However, in the matter of ——, although regretting, (he) humbly declines. The right hand (fact) upon receiving (he) at once wishes humbly to decline. It is honourably thus. Respectfully bowing.
"Second moon, 20th day.
American Ambassador, Mr. Anderson,
Beneath the Mansion."

Our first reception was attended by most of the diplomats, some of the American colony, and a few Japanese. In American fashion I had the ladies of the Embassy pour tea at the large table in the dining-room. There were over a hundred and fifty guests in all, many coming from Yokohama. On another of our days at home a huge shipload of tourists from the *Cleveland* arrived, which made the afternoon quite gay. They began to arrive half an hour before time, much to their dismay. It seems that they had been put into 'rickshas and their coolies instructed to take them to the Embassy, but when they got there they could not make the 'ricksha-men understand that they were early and wanted to drive about a bit until three. When my husband came down-stairs they had camped outside in the snow, which had fallen quite heavily the day before; he heard them talking, and, of course, asked them in at once.

One afternoon we entertained some American and English women. I was quite amused when a missionary's wife came up to me, wagging her head and looking very solemn about something.

V : Life in Tokyo

"I suppose you did not know," she said, "that the singer is a very naughty man."

"No, I didn't," I answered; "but I don't quite know what I can do about it—" and I'm afraid I wagged my head, too, as I added, "Don't you think we can reform him, perhaps?"

She must have seen the twinkle in my eye, for she laughed and said she didn't believe we could. We agreed that he sang very well indeed.

Our last big reception was held at the Embassy on Washington's Birthday. We had some souvenirs made in Japanese style, little black lacquer ash trays with the crest of the United States in gilt upon them for the men and fans also decorated with the crest for the ladies. A good many of the missionaries came, not only from Tokyo and Yokohama, but also from the interior.

On St. Valentine's Day I took some presents out to Watanabe's house, where I had asked all the children of the compound to gather. There were about a dozen of them, sitting on mats and making a very pretty group. They had put a carpet over the mat, so I did not have to take off my shoes, and a chair was procured for me to sit in. Then I told Osame to translate and tell them how, on St. Valentine's day, people in America send each other verses—sometimes love-verses, sometimes comic verses—but that as I couldn't write any in Japanese for them I had brought some little gifts instead. The children all bowed to the ground, and were very, very respectful—much better behaved than young people at home! They seemed to be pleased, and after giving each one his present I withdrew, telling Watanabe to give them tea and cake or whatever they wanted. But pretty soon he asked if they might come into the Embassy and thank us. So they filed in, bowing again, and sang a little Japanese song to my husband and myself, which was all quite touching. We showed them a toy tiger we had bought in Paris that would spring and jump when wound up, and a bear that would drink water, both of which delighted them greatly. After a while, bowing once again, they departed.

We made some very pleasant friends in Japan. Among others we met Baroness Sonnomiya, who is herself English but married to a Japanese. During her husband's lifetime she had great power, as she was the intimate friend of the Empress Dowager. There were also Dr. Nitobe and his wife, who were among the most delightful people we met. I enjoyed his books thoroughly, as well as his address before the Japanese Peace Society, which met at the Embassy.

This gathering had its amusing side, because the president of the Society had made most of his money selling guns! Moreover, before I realized that it was the Peace Society which was coming to the Embassy, I had invited the Naval Attaché's wife and an army officer's wife to pour tea! Just at that moment it hardly looked as if the cause of peace was making much headway in the world, for while we were talking about it, terrible battles were being fought in Turkey, the City of Mexico was under bombardment, and there was talk of fighting between Austria and Russia.

One day I called on Madame Ozaki, whom I had met in Italy when she was Marion Crawford's secretary. Her mother was English, her father Japanese; she is very pretty and writes charming stories. After living in Europe for a number of years she returned to her father in Japan and taught school, finally marrying Mr. Ozaki, one of Japan's most conspicuous politicians today. When I called on her I found her dressed in European style, but she had the true Japanese reserve; in fact was much more Japanese than I had expected after her many years abroad. Her house was partly European, but when the *shoji* was thrown aside, the little maid who received us bowed to the ground in true native fashion.

Madame Ozaki did not speak of politics, although her husband had just made an attack on Katsura, who had been for the moment overthrown. It was said that she had received threatening letters warning her and her husband to flee to England.

At this time of political upheaval a curious article appeared in the paper to the effect that three men had attended their own funeral services, which they wished to hold because they were about to start on a dangerous expedition. It was suggested that perhaps they might be going to take some prominent man's life, but nothing happened, so far as we knew, until spring, when Mr. Abe, of the Foreign Office, was murdered.

In order to explain the political situation in Japan as we found it, I am obliged to touch briefly on the political changes during the last fifty years,—that is, since the time of feudalism.

After Commodore Perry's visit, the Tokugawa government, whose shoguns had been the real rulers of the country for more than two centuries and a half, decided to open the ports to foreigners, while officials at the Imperial Court of the Mikado desired to continue the policy of exclusion. Finally the reigning Shogun was brought to see that it would be better for the country to have but one ruler, and resigned in favour of the Mikado. This inaugurated the wonderful Meiji Era—the era of the late Emperor.

Since they had always been men of action, it was the clever *samurai,* rather than the old nobles, who found a chance to show their ability under the new regime. They became prominent in both the Upper and Lower Councils, which were based somewhat on feudalism, and yet showed strongly the influence of Western ideas.

Political questions were freely discussed, political parties appeared, and the first conventions were held. The first cabinet was formed in 1885, with Prince Ito as Premier.

The Administration was divided into ten departments:—The Imperial Household, Foreign Affairs, Interior, Finance, Army and Navy, Justice, Education, Agriculture, Commerce, and Communications. A Minister of State was appointed head of each department. The Empire was divided into provinces, each ruled by a governor. In 1890 a national assembly was granted, and the first Diet was convened.

The government today is Conservative, and is controlled by the *Genro,* the elder statesmen. The Progressive party, the Seyukai, is led by Ozaki. The Socialists make a good deal of noise, but are still far from powerful; their opposition to the Russian war weakened their influence greatly. The Socialist party in Japan was largely responsible for the recent anti-American demonstrations.

For many years Prince Ito was considered the ablest man in the country. Okubo and Okuma were also noted leaders, while Prince Katsura, in recent times, held great power. Katsura was quite unpopular with the people while we were in Japan. It was felt that he had delayed a meeting of the Diet in order to form a party which would be stronger and at the same time more completely under his control. Each time when the assembly was postponed by a command from the Emperor, the blame was placed on Katsura. Finally Yamamoto was chosen to form a cabinet, which took a long time to do on account of the different parties. Ozaki, as head of the Progressives, wished to dictate to Yamamoto, but the latter would not comply, so things came to a standstill. People seemed to think that Ozaki was going too far, and that he had better take half a loaf instead of insisting upon a whole one. It appeared that the Japanese were not as yet advanced enough for his ideas, or else that he was too advanced for theirs. Later on, his party yielded somewhat, and Yamamoto made up his cabinet with Ozaki left out.

After the trouble had all blown over, people said that it had all been worked out by clever Katsura. If this is true, it was one of his last achievements, for the Prince, who is considered the greatest Premier Japan ever had, died in October, 1913. His career was an interesting one. His father belonged to the *samurai* class, and the boy, Katsura Taro, became a staff officer when only twenty-one. During the Franco-Prussian war he was in Germany studying military tactics. Later he was given charge of the reorganizing and modernizing of the Japanese army. The success of the Japanese in the Chinese and Russian wars is attributed to his genius and to his "silent and unrewarded toil." Only, after the battle of the Yalu, when he was made viscount, did his work begin to be appreciated. Later he was created prince. After the Chinese war he changed from soldier to statesman—was four times Prime Minister, and "almost a whole cabinet in himself."

Internal politics do not run any more smoothly in Japan than they do in our own country. On account of the frequent changes of cabinet there was often rioting in front of the Diet during the winter we were at the Embassy. Newspaper offices were attacked and burned, and the mob seemed to have an especial grudge against the police, who were hardly able to cope with the situation. Hearing that there was rioting near the Embassy one evening after dinner, several of us walked to a *matsuri* not far away, but the crowd was dispersing when we arrived, and only the policeman's sentry-box, which was overturned, remained to tell the tale.

Clubs are an important element in our modern civilization, and especially for foreigners in the Orient, where bachelors so greatly predominate—I believe the proportion is even more than that of forlorn damsels in Massachusetts. At Yokohama there are two organizations, the Yokohama United and a German club, besides the two American societies, the Asiatic and the Columbia.

The Tokyo Club has the reputation of being the most charming in the East. It is splendidly situated on a hill near the American Embassy.

V : Life in Tokyo

The charges are moderate, and the service is generally good. Japanese as well as Europeans belong to it. While we were in Tokyo my husband was invited to become the foreign vice-president, the president being an Imperial Prince. At first he begged off, but a committee of the club visited him and urged him to accept the office, saying that the Japanese were anxious to pay our country a compliment. The Tokyo Club is more than a register of social prominence in the city—it is also important as a political barometer, and this polite insistence upon L.'s accepting the place was, in its way, a tribute to America.

Many adventurers come to the East to seek their fortunes, and one hears strange stories, tragic or romantic as the case may be. A lover waits on the dock for his fiancée on the steamer, only to find that she has decided at the last moment to marry another whom she has met on the voyage; a wife returns from a long vacation at home to find her husband consoling himself with a *geisha;* a father who comes out to look for his son discovers him deep in debt and drinking himself to death. Such are a few of the many tales we heard.

Some differences in social customs may be noted here. It is polite, for instance, to remove your shoes at the door on entering a Japanese home. After you have entered it is only polite, as well as modest, to remain near the door! When you are offered tea or anything of the sort, it must be twice declined, but the third time it may be accepted.

In conversation one must exalt the person addressed, while everything belonging to the speaker must be held of no value at all. A father, on taking a bright boy to the teacher, would naturally say, "O honourable teacher, here is my idiot son!" And a mother, no matter how deeply she may feel the death of a child, must shed no tears but continue to smile and say, "Oh—child no good!"

What Hearn says about poetry is also true of the Japanese smile. When in danger, smile; when angry, smile; when sad, smile; in fact, it is etiquette always to smile! In so many ways the Japanese are an admirable race, and in none more so than in this. Their instincts are all for good taste and good manners.

Speaking of manners—of course, standards vary. It used to be a common thing in the country villages to see men and women bathing together in large tanks, but as Westerners disapproved of this custom, a few years ago an order went forth that men and women bathing together must put on suits. The result is that today they sit on the edge of the tank, or on the seashore, and dress and undress as they have always done, before one another, and wonder why they are obliged to put on bathing-suits when they go into the water! But an order is an order, they say, and must be obeyed.

In 1897, when we were in Japan, foreign clothes and top-hats were very popular, and today queer combinations of clothes are still noticeable. The foreign cap is much worn by the men, and a sort of loose-sleeved overcoat of English cloth, like an opera coat, is used in winter, worn over the kimono. But the *tabis,* or linen socks made like a mitten, and the clogs, are worn as before, while often an unmounted fur skin is wrapped about the neck. People well dressed in European clothes are called "high-collared"—in fact, this expression is applied to almost anything that is Western and modern. Many of the men who have been abroad are very correctly and smartly clad, but they usually put on a Japanese costume in the evening, for they call the European dress an "uncomfortable bag."

Some of the "high-collared" Japanese have at least one meal a day in European style, and part of the house is usually devoted to foreign furniture. They also believe that milk and meat should be eaten in order to make the race grow larger. Most of the men are anxious to learn Western ideas, and take great pride in showing inventions that have been introduced. They consider themselves quite up to date, and so they are in many ways.

When my husband was first in Japan, in 1889, a woman's highest desire was to wear European clothes, and if she could hire a costume and be photographed in it, she was perfectly happy. But I do not think they feel like that today. The novelty has worn off. Besides, Japanese dressmaking is a very simple matter; a kimono is made of straight breadths of cloth basted together. Compared with that, the plainest Western frock must offer many problems.

It is certainly better for us not to attempt to talk Japanese, for if one cannot speak it well it is safer not to try at all. One is very liable to address a nobleman in the language of a coolie, or to mystify a servant by speaking to him in the tongue of the higher classes—there are three ways of making a remark, according to the rank of the person addressed! No one can believe the difficulties of the language till he has tried it. To master it in any degree requires years of study.

V : Life in Tokyo

To illustrate this I will quote from Dr. Gordon, the missionary, who gives a bit of dialogue between teacher and pupil during a lesson. "The pupil says, 'The child likes *meshi.*' 'No,' says his mentor, 'in speaking of a child's rice it is better to use the word *mama*—the child likes *mama.*' Undiscouraged, the student tries again: 'Do you eat *meshi?*' But his teacher stops him and tells him that it is polite, in speaking to another of his having or eating rice, to call it *gozen*. Having taken this in, the student goes on with his sentence-building: 'The merchant sells *gozen.*' Again the teacher calls a halt, and tells him that *meshi* and *gozen* are used for cooked rice only, and that for unboiled rice *kome* is the proper word. Feeling that now he is getting into the secrets of the language, he says, '*Kome* grows in the fields,' but he is again stopped with the information that growing rice is called *ine.*"

More than one scholar in European tongues has declared Japanese to be the most difficult language in the world. One has said that a man "can learn to understand as much of Spanish in six months as he can of Japanese in six years." Chinese ideographs are said to outnumber the Japanese characters today, and in numerous instances have actually displaced them, even among the common people. Many characters have two meanings and only in combination can you know which is intended. There are no pronouns in the language, nor are there any "swear-words" or imperatives, the people are so polite.

Family names are also very confusing—to the Japanese themselves, I should think, as well as to us—because of the frequency of adoption. Each family feels that it must have an heir to take care of the aged members while they live and to pray for them when they die, so a child is adopted and given the patronymic. Blood doesn't seem to count at all, for even if a son is born later, it is the adopted child who inherits. Sometimes children brought up in foreign countries take foreign names. A naval officer told me of a charming Japanese girl whom he knew, named Bessie. One day she confided to him that she was going to marry Charlie. "Marry your brother!" exclaimed the astounded officer. "Yes," replied Bessie sweetly, "you not know—I not father's real child, and Charlie not father's real child. Charlie and I, we no relation—both adopted!"

Adoption is not always necessary, however, for if a man has no children he can easily divorce his wife, simply by telling her to return to her father's house, and he may then marry another woman. The modern law also gives this privilege of divorce to the wife, but custom is so strong that she never leaves her husband of her own accord.

Marriages are generally arranged by the parents, with the assistance of a mutual friend. The man and girl are allowed to see each other, but although they are not actually forced into marriage, few would dare to disobey their parents' wishes in the matter. They have a wedding feast, at which the bride and groom sit on the floor facing each other. The ceremony sometimes consists of their both drinking from a two-spouted tea-pot. The bride is clad in a white kimono and veil, which she keeps all her life, and wears once more when she is dead. Many presents are received, but the gifts of the groom, which are as costly as he can afford, are offered by the bride to her parents in gratitude for all that they have done for her in the past.

After the wedding the husband takes his bride to his home, no doubt to live with his father and mother. The wife must not only obey her husband, but is also much under the rule of her mother-in-law. A man sometimes brings his concubine into the house, and often her children as well, and these his wife is obliged to adopt. If husband and wife disagree, the go-between is usually consulted, and occasionally succeeds in arranging matters.

Japanese ladies, as a rule, do not go about very much, except those who have married foreigners or have lived abroad. A few ladies appear at foreign dinners with their husbands, but very often the men have dinners at which their wives do not appear. This may be partly owing to their inability to speak English.

But, as a whole, the women have little pleasure. When the man of the house entertains, he either takes his guests to a tea-house or calls in a *geisha* to help him do the honours, while his wife sits apart in a room by herself and is neither seen nor heard. The diversions, even of the well-to-do, are few, comprising the arrangement of flowers, the composition of poetry, and an occasional visit to the theatre.

Women are employed in manual work, in the fields, and in the loading of coal in the big ports, and more and more in the new industries. The kitchen-standard of wifehood is disappearing. Last winter a woman made a speech in public; this caused great excitement—in fact, it was said that she was the first Japanese woman to do such a thing. In spite of the many changes which are coming about, they are as far from being

"Little girls with littler girls on their backs"

suffragists as we were a hundred years ago. The sex as a whole are a long way from anything like economic freedom.

A woman has recently been made bank-president in Tokyo—a quite unheard-of innovation. She is Madame Seno, a sort of Japanese Hetty Green. In spite of the fact that she is over seventy, she goes to her office every morning punctually. Her tastes are very frugal. She wears plain cotton kimonos, and travels third-class. At the outbreak of the Russian war, however, she was the first to offer her subscription to the Government.

The children have a very good time, spinning tops, flying kites, and playing battledore and shuttlecock. In the life of Japan everything has its place and period, and the children's games succeed one another in such due order that it is almost impossible to buy the toys of one month when the season has passed into the next month. It is extraordinary how the little people combine their work and play, for you see a small boy carrying a baby on his back staggering around on stilts, and another small boy pulling a loaded cart and rolling a hoop at the same time, and little girls with littler girls on their backs tossing balls into the air or bouncing them in the streets. It is really an unusual thing to see a woman or young girl in the street without a baby attached to her. I think one of the reasons why the Japanese race has not grown larger is because the children from a very early age carry such weights on their backs.

Mr. Brownell tells a story of a Japanese girl which shows the filial duty and faithfulness that prevail. It seems she fell in love with a foreigner, and he with her. His intentions were good, and, although he was obliged to go away on a trip, he wrote her that he would soon be back to make her his wife. During his absence, however, her parents arranged another marriage for the girl, and on his return he found this letter from her:

"S<small>IR</small>:—

"I am married and is called Mrs. Sodesuka, and by our Japanese morality and my natural temperament I decline for ever your impoliteness letter.
"S<small>ODESUKA</small> O<small>TOKU</small>."

Chapter VI

THE GROWING EMPIRE

ALTHOUGH in many of her newer phases Japan is less fascinating to the casual tourist than where she is still "unspoiled," the efforts she is making to get into step with the rest of the world, and to solve the problems which are confronting her, are full of interest to the student and to the more sympathetic traveller.

To wide-awake Americans the growing Japan should be of especial interest, since however much we believe in and hope for continued peace between the two nations, there is bound to be more or less commercial competition.

Where the British Islands have stood in regard to shipping and commerce on the Atlantic, the islands of Nippon bid fair to stand on the Pacific. Even today the Pacific is by no means an empty ocean, but its development still lies largely in the future. It is the near future, however, and Japan knows it. The Panama Canal is almost completed; China is awakened and beginning to take active notice; Japanese colonies are being planted in South America and elsewhere.

While many countries of the Western world are facing a falling birth-rate, Japan's is rising rapidly. There is a tradition which accounts for this state of affairs. It seems that there was once a quarrel between the creators of the land, Izanami threatening his wife, Izanagi, that he would cause the population to die off at the rate of a thousand a day. The goddess, however, got the last word, and increased the birth-rate to fifteen hundred a day. Apparently she has been able to maintain the ratio to the present time—at any rate, there is an annual gain of half a million.

With a population already averaging three hundred to every habitable square mile, it is little wonder that the nation feels the need of extending her boundaries and to that end is trying to open up new territory to her emigrants.

Emigration began in 1885, when the King of Hawaii called for settlers in his island realm. Emigration societies were organized, under the control of the Minister of Foreign Affairs, and today the men of Nippon greatly outnumber the whites. The Foreign Minister still has entire charge of the societies: he grants all passports, and sees to the proper distribution of the thousands who every year leave their own country to settle more or less permanently in other parts of the world. Many emigrants go to Manchuria, Korea and Formosa, some to the Malay Peninsula and Australia, a few to the Philippines, and an increasing number to Central and South America. But they are a home-loving people, and eventually three-fourths of those who go out, return to Japan to settle down once more with their families.

Greatly to Japan's mortification, her people have been repulsed in California. Professor Peabody of Harvard returned recently from a trip to the Orient, and had this to say on the subject: "We accept as citizens the off-scourings of Eastern Europe, and shut our door on the thrifty Japanese, whose colour may be no darker and whose descent may be from the same original stock. What nags the Japanese in the matter is the indirect insinuation of bad blood, the intimation that a people whose education is compulsory and self-help is universal may not prove as serviceable elements in a commercial democracy as the average of Syrians or Copts; that, in short, the Far East is intrinsically inferior to the Near East." He points out that after twenty years the Japanese hold only about one per cent, of the agricultural land in the State of California, and that there are five thousand less of them there now than there were three years ago, owing to a "Gentlemen's Agreement," by which Japan limits her emigration to the United States.

This land question came up after we left Tokyo, but it naturally interested us intensely. The Californians seem to fear the Japanese because they live so cheaply and work so hard that it is thought they may come in time to own the whole state.

A recent competition, with a prize offered for the best essay on the California trouble, showed a world-wide ignorance of the real situation and its causes. Since this was true of both American and Japanese competitors, it seems to show that even the more educated among us need to think and study more deeply into the problem before making up our minds.

VI : The Growing Empire

An extract from the *Japan Magazine,* which is published in Tokyo, shows how men of the better class feel regarding the land question: "Japan is not angry, but she is earnestly anxious to know whether America will rest content to allow the California attitude to pass as national. No, Japan is not wrathful, but she is mortified to see any section of the country that calls itself her friend, somewhat abruptly suggest that her absence is preferred to her presence. . . . Happily, the California attitude does not represent the American people, so that Japan still has hopes of a reconsideration and a reinstatement. On the other hand, it is unfortunate that the majority of Japanese residents in the United States are not really representative of Japan. Certainly the average of emigrants going to America is not at all on an intellectual or social equality with the average citizen at home . . . they are the poorest and most unfortunate of their countrymen, and would never have left home if they could have succeeded as well in their own country. The same may be said of every immigrant from Europe. . . . When the lowest class can do so well, a better class would do even better. . . . The main hope lies at present in so instructing intending emigrants that they will be able to assimilate speedily and amicably with American society and abide by the customs and laws of the country."

It is interesting to note that in Japan they talk of the "white peril" and tell of the cruelty and oppression of Europeans to their "less civilized" yellow brethren. They have no difficulty in finding cases where might has made right, even in very recent times.

It is suggested by a Japanese newspaper that their diplomatists, in dealing with our country, have been imitating the attitude of the British toward the United States, apparently believing it to be in the end the one most likely to achieve results. The main features of this "attitude" are much patience and brotherly kindness, but unwavering firmness.

Before leaving the subject a few statistics are not out of place. The reason why the question centres about California is that sixty per cent of all the Japanese in the country are in that state, where most of them are engaged in agriculture. During the last five years the number of immigrants has steadily decreased. In 1911, the Japanese farmers produced more than twelve million dollars' worth of crops, which is nearly twenty percent, of the entire yield of the state. Reckoning their labour on land they do not control, however, they are responsible for at least ninety percent, of the agricultural products of California, whether vineyard, vegetable, or fruit. The most successful farmers are in the northern part of the state, where the low district along the river is tabooed by Americans, and but for the men from Japan would be idle and useless. The immense harvest of fruit and grain in the San Joaquin valley could hardly be gathered without them.

During the agitation against Asiatics, when the number of Japanese was reduced, and Indians, Greeks, Mexicans, and Italians took their places, the American managers admitted that one Japanese was equal to three or four of the other nationalities in agricultural work. The farmer from Nippon is a hard-working man, always eager to have his own little hut and a wife and family.

Dr. Sidney L. Gulick, in his recent book, "The American Japanese Problem," points out the one-sidedness of the attacks made upon the Japanese in California. He says, for instance, that "When Governor Johnson and Secretary Bryan came to Florin [a town used as an 'awful example' of Japanese occupation], Mr. Reese, already known for his anti-Japanese attitude, was chosen by Governor Johnson to be their guide and instructor, while Mr. Landsborough, known to Governor Johnson as pro-Japanese, was turned aside." The report of the State Labour Commission, which investigated the situation, was so favourable to the Japanese that the state government is said to have suppressed it—at any rate, it has never been published.

The *Los Angeles Times* says: "The Japanese have become an important factor in the agricultural and commercial life of the southwest. Their thrift is remarkable, their patience inexhaustible, and they are natural gardeners, seeming to read the secrets of the very soil and to know instinctively what will do well and what will do better. The result of this close study of soil conditions, close observation of crop and weather conditions, enables the Japanese to control to a great degree the vegetable-raising industry of Southern California."

Considering that there are more Italians in New York than there are in Rome, and that one person in every three in our metropolis is a Jew, while half the population of Norway is in this country—to mention a few cases—it doesn't seem as if we ought to object seriously to a handful of Japanese immigrants.

VI : The Growing Empire

Although California repulsed them, South America has proved very hospitable to the Japanese. The "Latin-American A-B-C" of Argentina, Brazil and Chile, receives their colonists eagerly. Guglielmo Ferrero, the Italian philosopher, finds traces of a possible racial likeness between the Japanese and the natives of South America. While he is by no means sure of this relationship himself, he says, "Japan will not shrink from relying upon the anthropologic theories above stated for the purpose of opening to its emigrants the ports of this immense and wealthy continent and establishing the strongest ties of close friendship where Europeans are gathering such harvests of wealth."

The friendship which exists between Japan and Argentina, however, is not based upon any real or fancied racial ties. It began at the time when the latter country sold the Island nation two new warships which she was having built in Europe, thus proving herself a friend in need. Emigration to Argentina has only just begun, but the future is very promising commercially, not alone on account of the cordial relations, but because the republic offers a good market for Japanese merchandise—with a population of but six million, she buys and sells more in a year than China with her three hundred million.

'There is a great demand for Japanese immigrants in Brazil, where there is no race prejudice to be encountered and much fertile land to be had for the asking. Brazil is a Portuguese country, which is especially appropriate, since Portugal was the first to send missionaries to Japan, nearly three centuries ago.

A company has been formed in Japan for the purpose of colonizing in Brazil, aiming to settle the surplus population in a country where it will be well treated. At least three thousand immigrants a year are promised by the company, but more will be welcomed, Brazil promising land, roads, and transportation from Japan. Farmers, who in their own country received perhaps fifteen cents a day, are able to save from one hundred to three hundred dollars a year to send home, while wages are steadily rising.

A writer in a recent issue of a Brazilian bulletin comments on the scene at the dock when the first shipload of Japanese immigrants arrived. "The spectacle was curious and very different to the disembarking of European immigrants," he says. "The men, many of whom had their chests adorned with the Manchurian medal, carried little flags in which the Brazilian and Japanese colours were mingled, green and gold, white and red. The extreme cleanliness of the Japanese was remarkable; while European emigrants, and particularly those from the south of Europe, leave the ship that has transported them in a filthy state, the cabins of the boat on which the Japanese travelled were on arrival as neat as at the time of departure. Each of them had in his baggage . . . numerous articles of toilet, tooth-paste, and tooth-brushes."

As yet there is little commerce between Brazil and Japan, but another year will probably see a change in this respect, for the opening of the Canal will make the route four thousand miles shorter, and the freightage, as a consequence, much lower.

The Panama Canal will make a considerable difference in Japanese trade with the United States. At present her exports to our country are nearly double her imports from us. There are now two routes to New York—the quicker one, to San Francisco and thence by rail, the slower one, all the way by sea, through the Suez Canal; the former is expensive, while the latter may require six months. It will be possible to make the trip by way of Panama in almost the time needed for the shorter route, but with the low freightage charge of the longer.

The Canal will also facilitate trade with the eastern coast of South America, giving direct intercourse, not only with Brazil, but also with Argentina. At present exports to these countries are sent via Europe and transshipped.

On account of her insular position Japan has always been a seagoing nation, but her shipping has increased enormously since the war with Russia. She now has over six thousand ships, manned for the most part by her own seamen. The question of building larger liners, such as are being put into commission for the Atlantic trade, has been discussed. At present the Japanese steamers which carry passengers are as good as the American ones, if not better. Instead of buying them abroad, Japan is beginning to build her own steamships—there are large shipyards at Nagasaki and Kobe.

In her efforts to cope with her rapidly growing population and multiplying industries, Japan is seeking trade-openings all over the world. Her business men are touring the globe in search of them. At present she is, perhaps, most interested in China, which has doubled the amount of her annual trade in the last ten years. The first months of 1913

VI : The Growing Empire

showed a gain of forty-six percent, over the corresponding months of 1912 in exports to China, while the United States exceeded her previous purchases by only three percent. Of the hundred thousand Japanese in the former country, nearly all are engaged in commercial pursuits, rather than in farming as they are in other parts of the world. Japan also has the advantage of being near this great market, and with labour so cheap she can easily compete with England, Germany, and the United States. She could make great profits if it were not necessary for her to buy most of her manufacturing machinery abroad.

America is by far Japan's best customer. She sold us and our colonies over a hundred million dollars' worth of goods last year—about a third of her total exports. Incidentally, she is an excellent customer of ours, for she bought over thirty million dollars' worth of cotton alone, in 1912, and much else besides.

Usually the Empire finds it necessary to import the raw materials and the machinery for their manufacture, while she exports the finished product. Much of her Oriental trade consists in yarn and cloth; the raw material is brought in from China and America and sold again to China and India.

In no way is the growth of Japan more striking than in her industries. Sixty years ago she had no foreign trade, for she had nothing to export. Today Great Britain finds her an interesting rival. Mills and factories have sprung tip like mushrooms, almost overnight. The conditions which accompanied this change and rapid development are worth noting.

In feudal times both the arts and the industries were carried on under the patronage of the nobility—the *daimyo* and the *samurai.* They were great lovers of beauty, these warlike lords; it is said that many a *samurai,* returning from the wars covered with glory, preferred the gift of an exquisite vase as a reward for his valour, rather than lands or decorations. They encouraged their subjects to make things; but, more than that, to make them beautiful.

Nevertheless, manufacturing conditions were very primitive. There was no division of labour, so that often a man would need to be skilled in several crafts in order to make a single article. Each man worked by himself. A boy inherited his father's trade, whether he liked it or not. Each trade had its guild, to which a worker must belong if he wished to be free to carry on his business. These guilds still exist today, but have far less power than labour unions in America or guilds in China.

The feudal system came to an end in 1868, and private ownership of property began. Organized industries appeared on a small scale: machinery was imported from Europe and America, railroads were built and factories started. Nine years later the first industrial exposition ever seen in Japan was held in Tokyo; soon afterward the Island Empire was sending exhibits to Europe and America to show the world what she could do. This, of course, resulted in stimulating the export trade and the manufacturing of such articles as were most in demand.

After the Chinese war, in 1895, there was a great boom. Old methods of private enterprise were no longer adequate to meet the increased demand. Stock companies began to be organized. The Government itself took over certain forms of industry for the purpose of raising revenues. Improved machinery was introduced from the Western world, and experts were engaged.

Since the Russo-Japanese war industries have multiplied so tremendously that the demand for labour has been very great. Wages have gone up, and the workers have become much more independent. As yet, there have been no labour strikes of any importance; fortunately, no Gompers or McNamaras have appeared.

For the first time in Japan women began to be employed. They are to be found in large numbers in the factories near Osaka (which is called the Chicago of Japan) and Kobe, as well as in the districts near Tokyo. Most of these women are peasants from the provincial sections who serve on three-year contracts. Children are still employed, although the Government does not allow them to go to work under twelve years of age.

Wages in all branches of industry are still very low, and the cost of living is rising. But living conditions, even at their worst, are much better than with us among corresponding classes. Weavers, dyers, and spinners receive from ten to twenty cents a day, while a streetcar conductor gets five or six dollars a month.

The factory owners keep their employees in compounds, where they provide some sort of shelter free and charge a nominal amount for meals. In the older type of factory there is often crowding and a low standard of living, but in the more modern and socialistic ones great attention is paid to the worker's needs, physical, mental and moral.

VI : The Growing Empire

There is a fine factory in Hyogo from which many of our mills might well take pattern. Besides having beautiful recreation and dormitory gardens, there are rows of pretty, two-storied houses with tiny gardens in front of each. The owners also furnish a theatre for the use of their employees, a cooperative shop, a spacious hospital, and schools and kindergartens for the children.

Japan has more than seventy cotton mills in operation, and can manufacture cloth as cheaply as any of its rivals. The home demand is large, since the lower classes wear only cotton the year round. Cotton towels, printed in blue and white, have become so popular in America during the last year or two that the export trade in them has increased enormously.

Four years ago a boy of eighteen, Torakichi Inouye, succeeded to the hereditary management of a large towel firm in Tokyo. He realized that foreigners seemed much attracted by the pretty designs, and were buying them in surprising quantities at the shops where they were for sale. So he began trying them on the American markets, with the success that we have seen. Today his factory is making two hundred thousand towels a day, and in ten months shipped over 175,000,000 pieces. He originated the idea of printing designs that could be combined into table-covers, bedspreads, etc. The patterns for the towels are cut in paper, like a stencil, and are folded in between many alternate layers of the cloth. The indigo-blue dye is then forced through by means of an air-pump.

Instead of importing all their machinery, as formerly, the Japanese are now beginning to manufacture it for themselves. They get the foreigners to come and teach them how to build steamships and locomotives, and as soon as they have learned whatever they wish to know they put their own countrymen in charge of the work. Although at one time there were many foreign engineers in different parts of the Empire, every year finds fewer of them filling important positions. This is true in every branch of industry.

Inventive genius is being cultivated, too, for clever people are not content simply to imitate. A system of wireless quite different from that generally in use is said to have been perfected for the navy. Wireless telephones are used over short distances, and are being rapidly improved and extended. Quite an advance has been made this last year in aviation also. Experts in both army and navy are making good records.

In spite of many difficulties several thousand miles of railway have been built during the last forty years. Engineers often find it necessary not only to tunnel through mountains, but under rivers the beds of which are shifting. To make matters even more interesting, there are typhoons, earthquakes, and torrents of rain which end in floods. Notwithstanding the cost of building and maintaining the roads under such conditions, railway travel is cheaper than with us or in Europe. First class costs less than third in an English train.

For the wherewithal to feed her people, Japan depends largely upon her native farmers. In spite of their poverty these are of a higher class socially than in most Western countries. The *samurai* and *daimyo* made much of agriculture, ranking it above trade. The Government today continues to do all that it can to aid and encourage farming. Experiment stations have been established, and various co-operative societies formed for the use of the farmers, who also have a special bank of their own. Prices are rising, and, on the whole, the prospects are good, although the nature of the land is against any great advance. The surface of the country is so mountainous that only about one-seventh can be cultivated, and that is not especially fertile. Sixty per cent, of the population is agricultural.

Each man owns his own little farm, which he tills in primitive fashion, growing rice, wheat, or beans, according to the soil or season. Almost no livestock is kept, and pastures are rarely seen. An average farm, supporting a family of six, has about three and a half acres.

The soya bean, which is much grown, really furnishes an industry in itself. It has many uses. *Soy,* the national sauce, is made from it, and also bean cheese. Recently an English chemist has discovered a method of producing artificial milk from it. Its oil is extracted and sold to foreign markets, rivalling the cotton-seed oil, which is better known. The pulp remaining is used as fodder and fertilizer.

Rice is the favourite crop and is of such good quality that much of it is exported to India, whence a cheaper grade is imported in return for the use of the poorer classes. Instead of forming the national diet, as we are inclined to suppose, rice is really such a luxury that many people never eat it except in sickness or on feast-days.

For all the Japanese farmer is so independent, he is often miserably poor. An acre of rice may in good years produce an annual profit of a dollar and a half, but there is quite likely to be a deficit instead. When one

A RICE FIELD.

considers that it takes the labour of seventeen men and nine women to cultivate two and a half acres of rice, this is not surprising. Vegetables do better than grain, and mulberry plantations for the raising of silkworms do best of all, but it has been figured that a hard-working man, with very likely a large family to support, does well if he clears a hundred and twenty dollars in the course of a year. As a result of this, most of the peasantry are in debt, and many of them are leaving their farms and going to the city, as they are doing in our own country.

Really more important than rice, of which we hear so much, is the sweet potato, of which we hear so little. The first one reached Japan some two hundred years ago as the gift of the King of the Loochoo Islands to the Lord of Satsuma. The latter prince was so pleased with the taste of it that he asked for seed-potatoes, and before long the Government commanded that the new vegetable should be grown throughout the country, since it could be raised even in famine years, when other crops failed. In Tokyo there are over a thousand sweet-potato shops, where one buys them halved or sliced or whole, all hot and nicely roasted, serving in cold weather to warm one's hands before delighting the inner man—or rather, child—for they are a delicacy much prized by children. There is no waste in their preparation, for not only are the peelings sold for horse-fodder, but the ashes in which they are roasted are used again around the charcoal in the *hibachi!*

The silkworm was introduced into Japan by a Chinese prince in 195 A.D., and a century later Chinese immigrants taught the people how to weave the new thread. Today sericulture is largely carried on by the women and children of the farm, and is twice as productive as the rest of the crops. As in poultry-raising, however, the gains are not in proportion to the size of the plant, the smaller ones being the more successful.

The mining industries have been much slower to develop than most of the others, although they are of ancient origin. A great deal of metal—gold, silver and copper—was exported during the Middle Ages. It has been suggested that Columbus had the gold of Japan in view when he set out upon the voyage which resulted in the discovery of America.

Japan has been described as the missionary to the Far East. Certainly, whatever her motives, her influence in Korea and Formosa has been most helpful. The latter island has been nearly freed from smallpox and other plagues, while its revenues have been increased six hundred per cent.

VI : The Growing Empire

Her influence in the liberalizing of China is marked, too, although it is less concentrated, of course, than in the smaller fields.

The Japanese have an undoubted advantage over other nationalities in China. Their agents know the language, but more than that, they are able to adapt themselves to native conditions of living and to "think Chinese." For ages past China has been the godmother of Japan, teaching her many valuable lessons in art and industry. It is now only fair that the pupil should do what she can to help her ancient teacher. Naturally the form which this expression of gratitude takes is by no means unprofitable commercially to the younger nation!

"With regard to that part of Manchuria which comes under Japanese influence," writes a British merchant, "the conveniences and facilities afforded by the Japanese to one and all in regard to banking institutions, railway communications, postal and telegraph service are far and away superior to those afforded by the Russian and Chinese institutions."

It has taken Europe six hundred years to do what Japan has done in sixty, and if the little Island Nation has left a few things undone, or has made mistakes and perhaps gone too far in some directions, it is not surprising. The marvel is that with the thrill and bustle of modern business life she has kept so much of the ancient charm and delight as to make us even today feel the witchery of her Spell.

Chapter VII

A YEAR OF FESTIVALS

MOST important and most generally observed of all Japanese festival is the New Year, the holiday season lasting for about two weeks. The most striking feature to us was the varied decorations of the gates, which were adorned with a collection of emblems of one kind and another producing an effect unique in the extreme, even if their significance was unknown. These decorations are put up before Christmas in the case of the foreigners, but those in front of the native houses are not completed until New Year, and remain in place throughout the holidays.

A large number of apparently incongruous articles are used in ornamenting Japanese homes for the New Year, and not until we learn the symbolic meaning of each one of these can we understand their use. They range from bamboo, ferns, oranges, pine-trees and branches of *yusuri*-tree to paper bags, straw ropes, bits of charcoal, seaweed and even lobsters, incomprehensible as it may seem to the Western mind that some of these objects should have any significance whatever.

As you enter a house you discover, stretched from post to post of the gateway above your head, a thick, twisted rope—the *nawa*—with the following emblems suspended from it: first, the *yebi*—lobster—whose bent back is the symbol of long life, suggesting the hope that he who passes beneath may not die until time has bowed his back in like manner. Surrounding the lobster, as a frame to its brilliant scarlet, are the *yusuri* branches, on which the young leaves are budding while the old have not as yet fallen, significant of the several generations of the family within. Almost hidden by the lobster and directly in the centre of the *nawa*, are perhaps the prettiest of all the emblems, two dainty fern-fronds, symbolical of the happiness and unity of wedded life, and carefully placed between the two, a budding leaflet emblematic of fruitfulness.

From Japanese mythology we learn the significance of the *nawa*—the rope of rice straw. Ama-terasu, the Sun-Goddess, in terror of her

VII : A Year of Festivals

brother, Susa-no-o, fled to a cave, from which she refused to come forth. Then the Eighty Myriads of Gods took counsel as to how they might induce her to bestow upon them the light of her face once more. They decided to give a wonderful entertainment, introduced by the songs of thousands of birds. Ama-terasu came out, curious to know the meaning of these sounds, daylight returned, and the gods stretched a barrier across the mouth of the cavern in order that she might never retreat to it again. The *nawa* represents this obstacle, and wherever it hangs, the sweetness of spring is supposed to enter.

But one may ask, what is the connection between the New Year and the coming of spring? According to the old Japanese calendar, the year began at any time between January sixteenth and February nineteenth, so it came, as a rule, at least a month later than with us, and the idea of spring was always associated with the New Year. Although spring arrives in Tokyo about the time it does in Washington, January first is far enough from any suggestion of buds and flowers: but the Japanese keep the old associations and call the first fortnight of the year "spring-advent" and the second fortnight "the rains."

The mention of spring suggests a charming stanza by an anonymous Japanese poet, which I give in Professor Chamberlain's translation:

"Spring, spring has come, while yet the landscape bears
Its fleecy burden of unmelted snow!
Now may the zephyr gently 'gin to blow,
To melt the nightingale's sweet frozen tears."

That the gods may not be forgotten, propitiatory offerings in the shape of twisted pieces of paper cut diagonally—*gohei*, meaning purification—are attached at intervals along the *nawa*, looking for all the world like the horns stuck in the hair in the children's game of "Horned Lady." Setting off the scarlet hue of the lobster, on either side is placed a *daidai*,—a kind of orange—expressing the hope that the family pedigree may flourish. The rather incongruous piece of charcoal—*sumi*, meaning homestead—comes next, and gently waving to and fro beneath the oranges may be seen strips of seaweed—*konbu*—signifying rejoicing.

On either side of the gateway stands the guardian pine-tree, indicative of long life, supporting the *nawa,* which is about six feet in

87

length—on the right the *me-matsu* (the red pine), and on the left the *O-matsu* (the honourable black pine). Behind, giving grace and dainty freshness to the whole, nod and sway the exquisite feathery branches of the bamboo, typical of health and strength. The full list of symbols is not always seen, as the task and the purse of the individual are both consulted before deciding upon his gateway decorations. But even among the poorest there is never a doorway wholly unadorned; the omission would be sure to bring harm to the householder and misfortune to his friends, and the gods unpropitiated would look frowningly down during the year. Although two diminutive pine-trees before a house may be all that can be afforded, the dweller within feels as securely guarded against harm in the coming year as if the whole panoply of emblems were waving over his humble doorway.

The pine-trees remind me of Bashô's epigram on New Year decorations, beautifully translated by E. W. Clement:

"At every door
The pine-trees stand:
One mile-post more
To the spirit-land;
And as there's gladness,
So there's sadness."

Much brighter colours are worn at the New Year than at other times, and presents are exchanged. The older people make gifts of dwarf trees, while the children give one another dolls and kites, and games of battledore and shuttlecock, which one sees both old and young playing in the streets. The small, stocky horses that drag the carts with their picturesque loads are adorned with streamers of mauve and lemon and rose in honour of the first drive of the year, and many of the carts carry flags and lanterns on bamboo poles, so that the streets are very gay. Tokyo is especially gay the last evening of the old year, because a *matsuri,* or fair, is held in the principal street, with little booths illuminated by lanterns, where anyone; who is in debt can sell his belongings in order to pay all he owes and begin the New Year fairly.

Small groups go from house to house, carrying the strange lion-dog's head, which they put through various antics, while they dance and sing

VII : A Year of Festivals

in order to drive away evil spirits. (The lion-dog is a mythical animal borrowed from the Chinese.) They are usually rewarded by the owner with a few pennies. People go about on New Year's Day, stopping at the doorways of their friends to say: "May you be as old as the pine and as strong as the bamboo, may the stork make nests in your chimney and the turtle crawl over your floor." The turtle and the stork symbolize long life.

Part of the preparation for the New Year festival consists in the annual house-cleaning. This custom is kept up today, and is carried out even in foreign houses. Under the old regime, we are told, officials of the Shogun's Court sent overseers carrying dusters on long poles to superintend the work and thrust their brooms into cracks and corners where dust might be left undisturbed by careless servants, at the same time making mystic passes with their poles to form the Chinese character for water. The merchants, too, have their "big cleaning," when all their wares are tossed out into the street. As one of the Japanese poets has said:

"Lo, house-cleaning is here;
Gods of Buddha and Shinto
Are jumbled together
All on the grass! "

One of the most attractive customs associated with the New Year is that of placing under the little wooden pillows of the children a picture of the *Takara-bune,* the Treasure Ship, with the Seven Gods of Good Fortune on board. This ship is said to come into port on New Year's Eve and to bring a wonderful cargo, among other rare things being the Lucky Rain-Coat, the Inexhaustible Purse, the Sacred Key and the Hat of Invisibility. This is the Japanese interpretation of our expression, "When my ship comes in."

At the Embassy the observance of New Year's Eve was a mixture of American and Japanese customs. We invited all the unmarried members of the Staff, and after visiting the *matsuri* we returned to the Embassy, and as the clock struck twelve we passed a loving bowl, and all joined hands and sang songs. Then, as the passing year was the year of the cock, and 1913 was the year of the bullock, someone crowed a good-bye to the rooster of 1912, and someone else mooed like a bullock as a welcome to the newcomer, and we had a very jolly time.

But New Year's Day itself is not without its religious and ceremonial observances. Every man is obliged to rise at the hour of the tiger—the early hour of four o'clock—and put on new clothes. Then he worships the gods, does homage to the spirits of his ancestors, and offers congratulations to his parents and the older members of the family. All this must be done before he can breakfast.

The first repast of the year is in every sense symbolic. The tea is made with water drawn from the well as the first ray of the sun touches it. The principal dish is a compound of six ingredients, which are always the same, although the proportions may be varied. A special kind of *saké* is drunk from a red lacquer cup in order to ensure good health for the coming year. In addition to these things, there is always an "elysian stand"—a red lacquer tray, covered with evergreen *yusuri* leaves and bearing a lobster, a rice dumpling, dried sardines, and herring roe, also oranges, persimmons and chestnuts, much as in a "lucky bag." All these articles of food are in some way emblematic of long life and happiness, and the stand itself represents the chief of the three islands of Chinese mythology, where all the birds and animals are white, where mountains and palaces are of gold, and where youth is eternal.

New Year calls are as much a part of the celebration in Japan as in the Western world. Originally, these were genuine visits, and the "elysian stand" was set before the guests for their refreshment, but among the higher classes the calls are now the most conventional of affairs, in which the visitor simply writes his name in a book or leaves a card in a basket, often without being received by the householder at all. The caller leaves also a little gift of some sort—such as a basket of oranges, a bunch of dried seaweed, or a box of sweetmeats—wrapped in a neat package and tied with a red and gold cord in a butterfly knot. A finishing touch is given to the parcel by a sprig of green in a quiver-shaped envelope tucked under the knot.

The seventh of January was the proper time to go out into the fields and gather seven common plants, among which were dandelion, chickweed and shepherd's purse. These were boiled with rice and eaten for health, strength and good luck.

Originally, the Japanese had no weekly day of rest and recreation, but in recent years the Sabbath has been made an official rest-day, to be observed by all in government employ. The mass of the people,

VII : A Year of Festivals

however, bring up their average of holidays by other occasions. There are during the year ten or twelve special feasts which are always observed—the Emperor's birthday, or when he eats first of the season's rice crop, or makes a pilgrimage to the shrines of his mythological ancestors, and other similar events, are all made the occasion of a national holiday and popular rejoicing. Besides, every section of a city or district in the country has a little *matsuri* every day or two, and these, of course, are held holiday, but it must be remembered that many of the festivals mentioned in this chapter belonged to Old Japan, and are dying out today.

Some festivals take the names of animals, such as the Horse Day, and the years are also named after animals, 1914 being the year of the tiger. The Fox Temple Festival is well known, when the people pray for good crops. Among other holidays are the Lucky Day, the seventh day of the seventh month, when two planets are in conjunction, and the first day of the eighth month. Certain prescribed flowers and plants are used on each of these occasions. Any important date, such as that on which a young man comes of age, or an official is promoted in rank, is also made a festal day.

The twenty-eighth day of every month is observed by the Japanese, but more generally in the first month than in any other, in order to begin the New Year properly. We went to a Buddhist temple in Uyeno Park, where they beg the god of luck to protect them and keep them from misfortune throughout the year. Before entering the temple, as is always done, they purify themselves by washing their hands and scattering little offerings of money done up in paper. On account of some ancient custom, money is much more valued in Japan if wrapped in paper. Candles are lighted, and priests sitting cross-legged with their backs to the audience read from sacred books. A holy fire is kindled, and each worshipper buys a hundred tapers and walks from the fire to the shrine, praying, I suppose, for they seem to be saying something. As they reach the fire again, they throw a taper into it, and repeat the ceremony till all are gone. Surrounding the temple are little booths, where toys are for sale and gay lanterns and good things to eat and drink are displayed, so that when the prayers have been offered, the people can enjoy themselves in feasting, watching the jugglers at their tricks, or making small purchases at the booths.

Display of dolls, dolls' festival.

VII : A Year of Festivals

On the night of February third, distant shouts were heard at the Embassy. Upon inquiring what the noise was about, I was told that this was called "Bean Night," when the servants in most houses throw beans out into the garden, crying, "Demons go out, luck come in." As I passed a temple that evening, I saw crowds of people, and noticed some Shinto or Buddhist priests doing a religious dance.

The third of March is the Dolls' Festival, the great day of the year for little girls. At all times of the year the Japanese have miniature belongings for children which are very attractive, but just before this festival the shops are even prettier than at Christmas in America, and the windows are always arranged either to show the *No* dance—two figures in curious dress in front of a gold screen with pine-tree decorations—or the Emperor and Empress. These dolls are placed on the top shelf with a screen behind and a canopy overhead to suggest a palace. Although for twenty years or more the Emperor has generally appeared in uniform on State occasions, and the Empress has been gowned in the latest Parisian style, these Imperial dolls wear flowing robes and have strange crowns upon their heads, the Emperor, too, having his hair curiously arranged; and they sit in Japanese fashion on a raised platform. On the shelf below are ladies-in-waiting, then follow musicians, lanterns and articles of food down the steps in order, all very tiny and perfectly made.

For a picture of this festival as it is kept even today I borrow from Miss Alice M. Bacon's "Japanese Girls and Women," only adding that I was so delighted with the toys myself that I bought many of them, and with the aid of Watanabe set them up in proper order at the Embassy:

"It was my privilege," says Miss Bacon, "to be present at the Feast of Dolls in the house of one of the Tokugawa *daimyos,* a house in which the old forms and ceremonies were strictly observed, and over which the wave of foreign innovation had passed so slightly that even the calendar still remained unchanged, and the feast took place upon the third day of the third month of the old Japanese year, instead of on the third day of March, which is the usual time for it now. At this house, where the dolls had been accumulating for hundreds of years, five or six broad, red-covered shelves, perhaps twenty feet long or more, were completely filled with them and with their belongings. The Emperor and Empress appeared again and again, as well as the five Court musicians, and the tiny furnishings and utensils were wonderfully costly and beautiful. Before each Emperor and Empress was set an elegant lacquered table service—tray, bowls, cups, *saké* pots, rice baskets, etc., all complete—and in each utensil was placed the appropriate variety of food. The *saké* used on this occasion is a sweet, white liquor, brewed especially for this feast, as different from the ordinary *saké* as sweet cider is from the hard cider upon which a man may drink himself into a state of intoxication. Besides sides the table service, everything that an Imperial doll can be expected to need or desire is placed upon the shelves. Lacquered *norimono,* or palanquins; lacquered bullock carts, drawn by bow-legged black bulls—these were the conveyances of the great in Old Japan, and these, in minute reproductions, are placed upon the red-covered shelves. Tiny silver and brass *hibachi,* or fire-boxes, are there, with their accompanying tongs and charcoal baskets—whole kitchens, with everything required for cooking the finest of Japanese feasts, as finely made as if for actual use; all the necessary toilet apparatus—combs, mirrors, utensils for blackening the teeth, for shaving the eyebrows, for reddening the lips and whitening the face—all these things are there to delight the souls of all the little girls who may have the opportunity to behold them. For three days the Imperial effigies are served sumptuously at each meal, and the little girls of the family take pleasure in serving the Imperial Majesties; but when the feast ends, the dolls and their belongings are packed away in their boxes, and lodged in the fireproof warehouse for another year."

  As we may well believe from the tenderness with which it is treated, the Japanese doll is not simply a plaything but a means of teaching a girl to be a good wife and mother. It is never abused, but is so well cared for that it may be in use for a hundred years. Certain large dolls, representing children two or three years old, were formerly believed to contain human souls, and it was thought that if they were not well treated they would bring ill luck upon their owners.

  A story is told of a maid who was much disturbed by dreams of a one-armed figure—the ghost of a girl or woman—which haunted her bed at night. These visitations were repeated so many times that she decided to leave the place, but her master prevailed upon her to stay until he had made a thorough search of her room. Sure enough, in the corner of a cupboard shelf, he came upon an old one-armed doll, left there by

VII : A Year of Festivals

a former servant. The doll's arms were repaired, it was honourably put away, and the restless little ghost was laid.

Lafcadio Hearn says, "I asked a charming Japanese girl: 'How can a doll live?' 'Why,' she answered, '*if you love it enough,* it will live.'"

But as all things earthly must have an end, so even a Japanese doll at last comes to the close of its life. It is lovingly cared for even then, is not thrown away, is not buried, but is consecrated to Kojin, a god with many arms. A little shrine and a *torii* are erected in front of the *enoki*-tree, in which Kojin is supposed to live, and here the doll finds its last resting-place.

On the eighth of April is celebrated the religious festival known as the Baptism of Buddha, when crowds assemble at all the temples, and pour *amacha,* or sweet tea, over the statue of Buddha. In the centre of a small shrine set up for the occasion is the image, adorned with flowers and surrounded by small ladles to be used by the worshippers. The right hand of the image is uplifted toward heaven and the left pointed downward toward the earth, "in interpretation of the famous utterance attributed to Buddha at birth: 'Through all the heights of heaven and all the depths of earth, I alone am worthy of veneration.'"

The ceremony is said to have originated in the effort to interpret the meaning of the *sutra*—a Buddhist text—called Wash-Buddha-Virtuous-Action *sutra.* In this we are told that "a disciple once asked Buddha how best to enjoy the virtue ascribed to the Master both in heaven and on earth." The answer was in substance that the worshipper would find peace by pouring a perfumed liquid over Buddha's statue, and then sprinkling it upon his own head. While performing the ceremony, the devotee must repeat the golden text, "Now that we have washed our sacred Lord Buddha clean, we pray that our own sins, both physical and spiritual, may be cleansed away, and the same we pray for all men." This festival is an especial favourite with children, who throng the temples, each one throwing a small copper coin into the shrine and deluging the god with sweet tea, which is usually a decoction of liquorice and sugar in water.

At the Boys' Festival, on the fifth of May, over every house where a boy has been born during the year a bamboo pole is set up, from which flies a paper carp, the fish moving in the breeze as if ascending a stream. The carp is the boldest of fish in braving the rapids, so to Japanese boys

DISPLAY OF ARMOUR AND TOYS, BOYS' FESTIVAL.

VII : A Year of Festivals

he symbolizes ambitious striving. In every household where there are sons the favourite heroes of olden time are set out in the alcove of honour of the guest-room. Among them will be seen the figure of an archer clothed from head to foot in gay armour, with a huge bow in his hand and a quiver full of arrows on his back. This is Yorimasa, the famous knight, who was the greatest archer of his time. On this day, too, pride of family and veneration for ancestors are inculcated by bringing out the antique dishes, the old armour and the other heirlooms that during the rest of the year are stored in the *godown*.

The Gion Festival, on the seventh of June, in honour of the mythical Prince Susa-no-o-no-mikoto and his consort, Princess Inada," and their son, Prince Yahashira, is famed for its magnificent procession, in which the car of the god is drawn. In the centre of the car is a figure attired in rich brocades; in front is a beautiful youth, who is accompanied by other boys, all wearing crowns; at the back is the orchestra that furnishes music for the procession. This display is witnessed by crowds of people, who throng the Shijo Road, in Kyoto, where it occurs.

In ancient times it was customary to atone for a crime by shaving the head and cutting the nails of the fingers and toes. This custom has now been modified to a sort of vicarious atonement, called *harai*. *Gohei*, which in this case is cut in the shape of a human figure, is rubbed on the body of the evil-doer in order that it may take his sins, and is then thrown into the stream and carried away. Repentant sinners obtain *harai* from the priests of Shinto temples.

This ceremony, which occurs in June and is called the Festival of the Misogi, is referred to in the following old song:

"Up Nara's stream
    The evening wind is blowing;
Down Nara's stream
    The Misogi is going:
So Summer has come, I know!"

A festival of fairy-land is the *Itsukushima*, celebrated at Miyajima, on the Inland Sea, from the fifteenth to the seventeenth of June. Brilliant decorations are everywhere—on the long avenue by which the shrine is approached, and over the water, where bamboo-trees have been set up, and flags and lanterns are hung from them. Musicians in three boats furnish music for the assembled crowds. The place is thronged by thousands on the last day of the festival, when the boats with the musicians are stationed under the great *torii,* and the sweet sounds floating over the water and the myriad lights reflected in the sea make the scene one of indescribable enchantment.

On the seventh of July occurs the *Tamabata Matsuri,* or Festival of the Stars, which, like so many other Japanese customs, was introduced from China. A charming nature myth tells us that beside the East River of Heaven, the Milky Way, lived the fair Princess Tanabata, who was known to the human race as the star Vega. She was a weaver by profession. As she was obliged to marry in order to fulfill her destiny, Heaven chose for her the great male star, Kengyu (Aquila), whose abode was on the West River. In her happiness the Princess forgot her weaving; whereat Heaven was so displeased that she was sent back in disgrace to the East River, and ever after was allowed to see her husband only once a year. All devout Japanese pray for fine weather on July seventh, as that is the date on which the unfortunate lovers meet; for, if even a few drops of rain fall, the East River will rise above its banks and prevent the Princess from crossing to her waiting spouse.

On the evening of this day, the young maidens of the family lay a straw matting in the garden, and place on it a table with fruits and cakes as offerings to the two stars. Then they present their petitions for themselves and their true loves. Some pray for long life and a large family; others set up a bamboo pole, on which they hang a piece of embroidery as an emblem of their desire for skill in needlework; still others attach to the pole pieces of paper, on which are written the poems they bring in praise of the heavenly couple. This festival has scant observance in large cities.

Touched with a peculiar tenderness and pathos is the Festival of the Dead, observed from the thirteenth to the fifteenth of July. In every house new mats of rice straw are laid before the little shrines, and a tiny meal is set out for the spirits of the departed. "When evening comes, the streets are brilliant with flaming torches, and lanterns are hung in every doorway. Those whose friends have only lately left them make this night a true memorial to their dead, going out to the cemeteries, where they offer prayers, burn incense, light lanterns and fill bamboo vases with the flowers they have brought. On the evening of the third day the Ghosts

VII : A Year of Festivals

of the Circle of Penance are fed, and those who have no friends living to remember them. Then on every streamlet, every river, lake and bay of Japan—except in the largest seaports, where it is now forbidden—appear fleets of tiny boats, bearing gifts of food and loving farewells. The light of a miniature lantern at its bow and blue wreaths of smoke from burning incense mark the course of each little vessel. In these fairy craft the spirits take their departure for the land of the hereafter.

In September occurs the Moon Festival, which appears to have no religious significance whatever, but to be simply an occasion for enjoying the beauty of the moon. It was doubtless borrowed from the Chinese in the eighth century, and is still celebrated in some places. The ancient Chinese, however, observed it in solemn fashion, going to the top of some pagoda and writing poems about the Queen of the Night, but the Japanese of olden times combined with pure aesthetic enjoyment the pleasures of actual feasting. They used to gather in the garden of some restaurant by a lake or river, where a banquet of rice dumplings, boiled potatoes and beans was set out, and enjoyed at the same time the good food and the scene before them.

Also in September is the Ayaha Festival, in honour of the two Chinese women who first taught weaving to the Japanese, many centuries ago. These teachers died in September, and on the seventeenth of that month cotton and hempen fabrics are offered to their spirits at the shrines built in their honour.

At the temple of the goddess Amaterasu-Omikami, near Shiba Park, Tokyo, the Shinmei Feast is observed from the eleventh to the twenty-first of September. This is especially the time to offer the petition, "O God, make clean our hearts within us," hence much ginger is sold, the plant being supposed to prevent impurity. A sweetmeat called *ame* is sold in cypress-wood baskets, curved like the roofs of ancient shrines. Cypress is held sacred because the roof-trees of old shrines were made of it, and is supposed to have the power of warding off diseases.

One of the most curious of all Japanese festivals is the Laughing Festival of Wasa, celebrated in October. A procession is formed of old men carrying boxes full of oranges and persimmons impaled on sharpened sticks, followed by children with the same kinds of fruits on bamboo rods. On reaching the shrine, the leader turns round and makes up a comical face, which is greeted with shouts of laughter.

According to the legend, the gods, once upon a time, met in the great temple at Izumo to consider the love affairs of the kingdom. When all were seated, one alone, Miwa-Daimyo-jin, was missing, and although search was made, he could not be found. Now, this god was so deaf that he had misunderstood the day appointed for the assembly, and he appeared at Izumo only after all was over. The Laughing Festival commemorates the laughter of the gods when they heard of poor Miwa-Daimyo-jin's mistake.

Another October celebration is held in memory of Nichiren, called the Luther of Japan, who endeavoured to purify Buddhism from the superstitions that had crept into it. He was the founder of the sect named for him. On October thirteenth great numbers of his disciples assemble at Ikegami, the place of his death, near Tokyo, carrying lanterns and banners, and reciting a *sutra* in concert.

A curious feast is observed by merchants on the twentieth of October in honour of Ebisu, one of the seven gods of good luck, who is especially the guardian genius of tradesmen. They invite their friends and relatives to a banquet, upon which a large picture of the god looks down from the wall. Fishes, called *tai,* are laid before this picture as offerings, and are also eaten by the guests. After the feast has proceeded a little way, sport begins. Perhaps one of the guests starts an auction of the dishes before him, his companions bidding up to thousands of *yen*[5] the joke continuing until it runs itself out. This little buying and selling episode is to emphasize the fact that it is a merchants' festival that is being celebrated.

The present Emperor's birthday is the thirty-first of August, but henceforth it is to be celebrated on the thirty-first of October, which brings it very near to the third of November, the late Emperor's birthday, so long a holiday all over Japan. Although this is one of the annual festivities, the celebration is so largely official and diplomatic that I have described it among Court Functions.

The fall *matsuri* in Tokyo is held early in November at the Shokonsha, a temple sacred to the memory of the patriots who have given their lives for their country. It is especially a soldiers' festival, and is the occasion when the garrison comes in a body to worship at this shrine. The troops form by divisions in front of the temple and salute, presenting arms while

---

[5] The yen is fifty cents.

the bugles sound a sacred call. Afterward the soldiers have a race-meeting on a half-mile track, which is made very amusing by the rivalry between the different divisions and the mad careerings of the little horses. This is a large *matsuri,* and the booths of peddlers and mountebanks line the streets for blocks.

November eighth is the day of the *Fuigo Matsuri,* when thanks are returned to the god of fire, who invented the bellows—*Fuigo* meaning bellows. As the centre of the worship of this god is in Kyoto, it is observed to a greater extent there than elsewhere, beginning in a curious way, by opening the windows before sunrise and throwing out quantities of oranges to the children who are always waiting outside.

The Japanese counterpart of our New England Thanksgiving occurs the twenty-third of November, when the Emperor is the chief celebrant, making an offering of the new rice of the year before the shrine of his ancestors, and in behalf of the nation uttering a prayer of thanksgiving and a plea for protection. After presenting this offering His Majesty partakes of a sacred feast, consisting of the first fruits of the year, and the next day he invites the highest officials of the State to a grand banquet at the palace.

Near the end of December comes the *Kamado-harai,* Feast of the Oven. The *kamado* is the fire-box on which the food is cooked, and it has a god of its own. As the year draws to a close, the god of the *kamado* carries to heaven a report of the conduct of the household during the twelve months. So the priests are called in to pray the oven-god that he will give as favourable an account as possible. As modern stoves are now taking the place of the old *kamado* to some extent, this feast is less observed in the larger cities than in the country districts.

At a shrine in Shimonoseki the festival of *Wakamegari-no Shinji* is observed on the thirty-first of December. A flight of stone steps leads through a stone *torii* down into the sea far below the lowest tide-mark. The Shinto priests, in full robes, are obliged to descend these steps on the feast-day until they reach and cut some of the seaweed (*wakame*), which they offer at the temple the next day. Japanese legend relates that the Empress Jingo sailed from this spot to the conquest of Korea, bearing two jewels that were given her by the god of this shrine. When off the Korean coast, she threw one jewel into the water, and a flood tide at once bore her ships high up on the shore; then she tossed the other gem into the waves, and the swift ebbing of the tide left the fleet safely stranded.

Chapter VIII

CULTS AND SHRINES

"He that practiseth righteousness receiveth a blessing; it cometh as surely as the shadow followeth the man."

THE quotation at the head of this chapter is of special interest, because it reminds one so much of a precept from the Bible. It is taken from a little Japanese text-book of ethics, which is ascribed to a Buddhist abbot of the ninth century.

There are two distinct but perfectly harmonious forms of non-Christian belief in Japan today—Shinto and Buddhism—which dovetail so well that each one contributes something of value to the Japanese character. The Confucian philosophy, also, had its share in developing *Bushido,* the "Soul of the People."

Shinto is the native religion of Japan, and both because it is so little known outside of that country and because a study of it goes so far to explain many national characteristics, it seems worthwhile to consider it at some length. The word Shinto may be translated as the Way of the Gods, and defined in brief as a worship of ancestors, especially of the Emperor and his forebears. Human beings are believed to be the children of the sunshine, and sin is hardly recognized.

Shinto is a combination of primitive instincts. It is based on hero worship, and it has myriads of deities, who live in every conceivable object, from the spirit of the sewing-needle to the gods of thunder and lightning, or of the sun, moon and stars. "The weakness of Shinto," says Dr. Nitobe, the eloquent exponent of Japanese beliefs, "lies in the non-recognition of human frailty, of sin." The sum total of its moral teaching is this, "Be pure in heart and body."

The Shinto idea seems to be that it is only necessary to act out the natural impulses of the heart in order to be pure. But where there is no sense of sin, there can be no consciousness of need, no incentive to higher things. Shinto lacks ideals. It allies itself with the practical affairs

VIII : Cults and Shrines

of every-day life, inculcating industry and personal cleanliness, some of its sects even prescribing mountain-climbing and abdominal respiration as religious duties. But, as it has no theology, it offers no explanation of the great problems of the universe; and, having no sacred writings, it has no authority on which to base a system of ethics. Theology and the spiritual element in religion came to Japan with Buddhism; while ethics was the gift of Confucianism.

The first sign of a Shinto temple is the *torii*. This peculiar gateway, though originally erected only by the Shintoists, has been adopted by the Buddhists, who have changed it by turning up the corners of the top beam and adding inscriptions and ornament. Passing under the *torii* you stand before the huge gate, generally painted red, guarded by wooden figures, or keepers. These are supposed to be Ni-o—two gigantic and fierce kings—and they occupy a sort of cage with wire in front, that stands on either side of the entrance. Every worshipper makes a wish as he enters the temple, and throws at the kings little wads of paper precisely like the spitballs of school children. If the wads go through the wire, the wishes are supposed to come true.

The temple itself stands in a courtyard inside the gate, and is rather plain and undecorated, much like Japanese houses. A flight of steps leads up to a balcony on the front, there is matting upon the floor inside, and an altar in the centre supports a big bronze vase, which usually contains pieces of gold paper, called *gohei*. A mirror is the most important article in a Shinto shrine, the idea being that it is a symbol of the human heart, which should reflect the image of Deity as the glass reflects the face of the worshipper. The mirror is not found in the temples of merely local divinities, but only in those sacred to the Sun-Goddess herself, and even there is not exposed to view. Wrapped in a series of brocade bags—another being added as each in turn wears out—and kept in a box of cypress wood, which is enclosed in a wooden cage under silken coverings, the mirror itself is never visible to the eyes of the curious.

Two famous Shinto shrines—at Ise and Kitzuki—are especially revered on account of their great age. Kitzuki is so ancient that no one knows when it was founded. According to tradition, the first temple was built by direct command of the Sun-Goddess herself, in the days when none but gods existed. The approach to the sacred enclosure is most imposing. A beautiful avenue, shaded by huge trees and spanned

GRAND SHRINE OF ISE.

VIII : Cults and Shrines

by a series of gigantic *torii,* leads from a magnificent bronze *torii* at the entrance to the massive wall that surrounds the temple courts. Within are groves and courts and immense buildings. The people are not admitted to the great shrine itself, but offer their petitions before the Haiden, or Hall of Prayer. Each pilgrim throws money into the box before the door, claps his hands four times, bows his head, and remains for a few minutes, then passes out. So many thousands throng this court that—to borrow Hearn's figure—the sound of their clapping is like the surf breaking on the shore.

Although the shrine at Kitzuki is the oldest, the temples at Ise are more venerated. The inner shrine itself is a plain wooden building set within successive courts, but stately cryptomerias and the most magnificent camphor groves in all Japan give the place an unusual air of grandeur and sanctity.

Wedding and funeral customs are extremely interesting. They have both the religious and the civil marriage in Japan. To make it legal, the parents must sign in the register. Marriages in Shinto temples have been unusual until recently, as they have generally taken place in the home. The custom is changing now, and temple weddings are becoming more frequent. Funeral customs are changing also. Formerly it was always the Buddhist priest who conducted the burial service, now the aristocrats are interred according to Shinto rites.

At a wedding that we witnessed in a Shinto temple the couple first listened to a sermon by the priest, then they were given tapers at the altar. The bride lighted her candle first, and the bridegroom lighted his from hers. After this the two tapers were put together in such a way that they burned as one, symbolizing the perfect unity of wedded life. The bride was handsomely dressed—the *obis* for these occasions sometimes cost over one hundred dollars—and wore the headdress with horns, half hidden by a veil called the "horn-hider." This name would seem to refer to the Buddhist text, "A woman's exterior is that of a saint, but her heart is that of a demon." After the marriage ceremony, the bridal party was photographed in the temple courtyard in a decidedly up-to-date fashion. At the house the bridal couple drank the nuptial *saké,* which had been prepared by two girl friends of the bride. This was poured from a gold lacquer vessel into one of silver lacquer—the two representing husband and wife—then into a cup, which the master of ceremonies handed to the bride and afterward to the groom, and from which they both drank.

105

As Shinto is the faith of the reigning family, the funeral ceremony of a prince throws a good deal of light upon the cult itself. I did not witness such a ceremony myself, so I condense the vivid description given by the Baroness d'Anethan, who, as wife of the Belgian Minister, resided in Tokyo for many years.

The funeral procession was headed by over eighty bearers dressed in white, the Japanese sign of mourning, each carrying a huge tower of flowers. Following these were officers in uniform holding cushions, on which rested the Prince's numerous grand crosses and orders. Next came various persons surrounding a casket, which contained the favourite food, the shoes for the journey (large wooden *geta*), the sword to guard against evil spirits during the soul's fifty days' wanderings, and the money to pay for the ferry-boat that crosses the river to Eternity. Finally appeared a beautifully fabricated casket of pure white wood (the Shinto sign of purity), embossed with the family arms in gold, in which the body was arranged in a sitting position. The chief mourner, a young prince, was dressed in the old-fashioned Court mourning, consisting of a wide, full, black silk petticoat, covered partially by a short white kimono, crowned by an unusual form of headdress, made of what looked like stiff black muslin. The two princesses of the family also wore ancient Court mourning—a greyish-brown *hakama* (a kind of divided skirt)—and had their black hair puffed out at the sides like great wings and hanging down the back.

Arriving at the cemetery, the Corps Diplomatique walked up a path paved in wood and bordered on each side by covered seats, at the end of which were high trestles supporting the coffin. The service now began, accompanied by weird funeral music. Low white wooden tables were placed before the coffin, all sorts of objects being offered to the departed by the priests. First was a long box, containing the name which His Imperial Highness was to bear in the next world. After this followed a repast of various kinds of fish, game, sweetmeats and fruit—the favourite foods of the deceased. These articles were handed with great ceremony from one priest to another. There were ten priests, and as each one took the dish, which was placed on a stool of white wood, he clapped his hands twice to call the gods, and the last priest, bowing very low, finally set it on the table. After all the food had been deposited, prayers were intoned from an immense scroll, the final ceremony being

VIII : Cults and Shrines

that each member of the family, and after them, the Corps Diplomatique, approached the coffin, carrying branches of some particular tree, from which floated long papers inscribed with prayers. The actual interment took place some hours later, and with the remains of the Prince were buried the various articles of food and clothing.

Our visits to the cemeteries showed us the veneration of the Japanese for their noble dead, and impressed us with the significance of ancestor worship in the Shinto cult. The big graveyard in Tokyo, where Nogi and his wife were buried, was most interesting. Modern cemeteries in Japan are much like ours, each owner having an enclosed lot and misshapen stones or stone lanterns to mark the graves, but they are not so well kept up as in America. Attached to the fence surrounding the lot is a wooden box, in which visitors leave their cards when calling at the abode of the dead. The mourners sometimes burn incense and leave branches of laurel, too. As we approached the resting-place of Nogi and his wife, we saw crowds of people standing near, for although months had passed since their dramatic death, the Japanese were still visiting their graves in great numbers.

In many cemeteries are the statues of "The Six Jizo"—smiling, childish figures about three feet high—bearing various Buddhist emblems. A bag of pebbles hangs about the neck of each one, and little heaps of stones are piled up at their feet and even laid upon their shoulders and their knees. Jizo is the children's god. He is the protector of the little souls who have gone from this world to the Sai-no-Kawara, the abode of children after death, where they must pile up stones in penance for their sins! When this task is done, the demons abuse them and throw down their little towers; then the babies run to Jizo, who hides them in his great sleeves, and drives the evil spirits away. Every stone that is laid at the feet of Jizo is a help to some little one in working out its long task.

Hearn gives an interesting account of a wonderful cave at Kaka, on the wild western coast of Japan, which can be visited only when there is not wind enough "to move three hairs," for the strongest boat could not live in the surf that beats against the high cliffs and dashes into the fissures in their sides. But let one make the journey safely, and he shall find in this grotto an image of Jizo, and before it the tiny stone heaps. Every night, it is said, baby souls make their way to the cavern, and pile

Cloisonné Work

VIII : Cults and Shrines

up the pebbles around their friend, and every morning the prints of little bare feet—the feet of the baby ghosts—are seen in the moist sand.

Buddhism has become so complicated and changed in the different countries through which it has travelled since it originated in Southern India, and there are today so many sects, that it is difficult to define.

The Ikko sect undoubtedly holds the purest and loftiest form of this faith. Its chief teaching is, that "man is to be saved by faith in the merciful power of Amida, and not by works or vain repetition of prayers. For this reason, and also because its priests are permitted to marry, this body has sometimes been called the Protestantism of Japan."

All the followers of Buddha believe in reincarnation; they feel that life is a struggle, which human beings must get through with as well as they can, and that as they are frail, they return to this earth in various forms in punishment for their sins, always toiling on, until at last their purified souls merge in the Divine and realize calm. As an old Japanese writer puts it, "Though growing in the foulest slime, the flower remains pure and undefiled. And the soul of him who remains pure in the midst of temptation is likened unto the lotus."

There have been many Buddhas, who have returned at different times to this world, Yamisaki being the latest. Buddhism has degenerated in Japan, having absorbed the Shinto gods, and as it is based on a pessimistic view of life, it appears to be rather a depressing religion.

Buddhist temples are adorned with wonderful carving and lacquer work, and contain bronzes and golden Buddhas. One of the largest and most magnificent in Japan, surrounded by gardens of great extent and beauty, is the Eastern Hongwanji temple in Kyoto. The shrines of the Ikko sect are called Hongwanji, meaning "Monastery of the Real Vow," from the vow made by Amida that he would not become Buddha unless salvation was granted to all who sincerely desired it and testified their wish by calling upon his name ten times. There is no government fund for this shrine, and it has no regular source of income, yet it has been the recipient of munificent gifts from royal personages and men of wealth, and has all the prestige that could come from temporal support and the sanction of government.

When we visited this temple, we were ceremoniously received by the priest in charge and a number of his confrères. The head priest, short, fat and clean-shaven, who met us at the gate, grunted and drew

EASTERN HONGWANJI TEMPLE, KYOTO.

VIII : Cults and Shrines

the air through his teeth in greeting us, as a symbol of great politeness and respect. His costume was a black silk robe over a soft white undergarment, and a gold brocade band about his neck.

As we passed into the building, we were told that the present structure, which is said to have cost seven million *yen* and was sixteen years in building, was erected on the site of an ancient temple that had been destroyed by fire. It is noteworthy that the new temple contains a system of tile pipes in the roof and ceiling, from which, in case of fire, water may be dropped over the entire area.

Before the altar is a broad sweep of stone flooring, and in front of that a railing, outside which the people come to worship. Several were kneeling there as we passed, their palms together in the traditional attitude of Christian prayer. Others were prone on the floor. The ragged, the lame and the desolate, blind and deaf to the passing crowd, knelt upon this bare stone pavement—separated from the altar by a railing beyond which they might not pass—their hands lifted in supplication or adoration, their heads bowed in humility. The scene called to mind the legend of Sandalphon, the Angel of Prayer, whose mission Longfellow has so beautifully described. We looked at the silent god standing within the lotus—sacred emblem of humanity—veiled by the pervading incense, and we wondered how many of those unspoken prayers penetrated to the mysterious depths where Buddha dwells.

To the left of the altar is a space reserved for the priesthood, where Buddhist monks come daily to their morning devotions and religious exercises. Although the priests do not live in the temple, they sometimes pass the night here in meditation, seated on the long rows of mats that we saw arranged in orderly fashion. About forty priests are usually in attendance at the morning services, but on occasions of State ceremony larger numbers gather from all parts of the Empire. On the twenty-fifth and twenty-sixth of each month services are held in memory of the founders of the temple.

The priests conducted us between the railing and the altar, bowing their heads as they passed. A number of small coins were scattered on the matting—these were offerings left by worshippers. Our hosts, who treated us with unfailing courtesy, pointed out further details of the building, and afterward took us to a room where we were served with tea and small cakes. We were told that this apartment had been donated by the present Emperor.

We followed one of the priests into the walled garden and through its narrow paths. We crossed brooks on bamboo bridges, and looked into the calm waters. Among the trees were small temples and tea-houses overhanging the water, and curiously shaped stones and crooked pines. Hongwanji garden has all the fascination of a true Japanese garden, and has, besides, the additional charm of age, for it is over three hundred years old. We sat in this ideal spot, in one of the pretty tea-houses with its soft mats and lacquer and polished wood, and again drank tea from wee porcelain cups and ate sugared cakes.

The memory of this temple garden clings to me still. I imagine the priests sitting on the little covered wooden bridge gazing into the calm water with the lotus flowers, while the crickets sing in the silence—crickets who were perhaps once human, now doing penance for their sins. I hear the priests murmur over and over *Namu Amida Butsu*, the Japanese rendering of the Sanskrit invocation meaning "Hail to the Eternal Splendour of Buddha!" I see them meditating on the unending life that they believe to be in store for them, until evil shall have left them, and they shall be absorbed into Nirvana, "as a dewdrop sinks into the shining sea."

As we left the temple we were shown the great coil of ropes made of human hair. There were originally twenty-nine of these cables, the longest of which measured two hundred feet. It seems that at the time when the old shrine was burned, and they wished to rebuild it, the church had no funds. People came together from all over the Empire, and set to work like beavers. The men gave what they could, in work and money; the women had nothing, yet they, too, wished to help. In a frenzy of religious zeal they cut off their hair—their most treasured possession—and cast it at the foot of the shrine of Buddha. From their offerings were woven the cables that hoisted the tiles to the roof and lifted into place the great wooden pillars of the temple.

The temple of Buddha, with its unpainted exterior, its bare pillars in their naked simplicity, its glint of gold, its magnificent carvings, the delicate fragrance of burning incense, its candles, its wealth of symbolism—all this is a fading memory; yet its fascination lingers. We wonder how much of the temple of Buddha we really saw, how much we felt the presence of that power which is so intimately linked with the spirit of the East and with the genius of the Oriental peoples. We felt the

VIII : Cults and Shrines

reverence—unexpressed in word or outward act—with which our hosts, the priests, drew our attention to the inscription above the altar, painted in golden Japanese characters by the hand of the late Emperor, which, being interpreted, means, "See Truth."

The temples at Nikko, the finest in Japan, are part Shinto, part Buddhist. A ceremony which we once witnessed there, in the mausoleum of Iyeyasu, the great Shogun, was full of interest. After taking off our shoes at the entrance, we wandered over the mats, looking at the gloriously carved panels, till we were informed that all was ready and were invited to enter an inner room. I was given a peach-coloured brocade robe, which I threw over my shoulders, but was told that it was not necessary to don the skirt, which forms the rest of the ceremonial costume. They gave us two camp-chairs, as we preferred to sit on them rather than on our heels, in Japanese fashion. On either side of us squatted three priests in white and green robes with curious black open-work hats on their heads. We faced the inner shrine, in which stood, on a table, a vase containing the gold paper for purification, such as is seen in Shinto shrines.

Then began the most unearthly music that I have ever heard, made by the three priests on L.'s side, who were musicians. One had a strange instrument made of flutes put together, resembling a small organ, which gave out a sound somewhat like a bagpipe. While this man played a weird tune on his pipes, another with a different instrument made a most unpleasant whistle, like that of a train, which continued throughout the entire ceremony.

Besides the green-robed musicians there were on my side white-robed priests with even quainter head-gear, who moved about on their knees and presented food and drink before the altar with many bows and much clapping of their hands. This service led to the opening of the door of the inner shrine, into which we were afterward taken and served with *saké*. Then we were conducted behind one beautiful set of painted screens after another till we came into the innermost place, gloriously decorated in lacquer and painting but in absolute darkness, except for the glow of the lanterns which we took with us. On emerging from these hidden recesses, we left the temple, with polite bows to the priests and thanks for their courtesy. As we walked away from the building, we could hear the screeching instruments, the priests going on with the service as the offerings were brought out of the sacred place.

THE HONDEN, IYEYASU, NIKKO.

VIII : Cults and Shrines

Just as we were departing, I was given this translation of the Precepts of Iyeyasu, which I have been glad to preserve as a souvenir of beautiful Nikko:

PRECEPTS OF IYEYASU

Life is like unto a long journey with a heavy load. Let thy steps be slow and steady, that thou stumble not. Persuade thyself that imperfection and inconvenience is the natural lot of mortals, and there will be no room for discontent, neither for despair. When ambitious desires arise in thy heart, recall the days of extremity thou hast passed through. Forbearance is the root of quietness and assurance forever. Look upon wrath as thy enemy. If thou knowest only what it is to conquer, and knowest not what it is to be defeated, woe unto thee! it will fare ill with thee. Find fault with thyself rather than with others. Better the less than the more.

Translated by Prof. K. Wadagaki,
of the Imperial University.

The Japanese, like Arabs and Hindoos, not content with worshipping at near-by shrines, often make pilgrimages to holy places at a distance. There are several of these resorts in the Empire, some of the most famous being the temple of the Sun-Goddess at Ise, the holy mountain Fuji, the monastery of Koya-san, and the lovely island of Miyajima, in the Inland Sea. As most of the pilgrims belong to the artisan and peasant classes, and have scarcely more than enough for their daily needs, they have evolved a scheme for defraying the expenses of these trips by forming a great number of associations, or brotherhoods, the members of which contribute each a cent a month. At the proper season for the pilgrimage certain members are chosen by lot to represent the brotherhood at some shrine, and their expenses are paid out of the common fund. No distinctive dress is worn by most of them, but those on their way to Fuji and other mountains are attired in white garments and broad straw hats.

These Japanese pilgrims are not only performing a pious duty, they are also taking their summer vacation. After their prayers are said, as at the various festivals I have described, they do not hesitate to join in all the amusements that are provided. It makes little difference to the mass of the common people whether they worship at a Shinto or a Buddhist shrine,

OFF MIYAJIMA.

and the Government actually changed Kompira from Buddhist to Shinto without in the least detracting from its popularity. The relics guarded in these temples of Buddha remind us very much of the sacred memorials cherished by the Roman Church—holy garments, holy swords, pictures by famous saints, and bits of the cremated body of a Buddha.

It was from her religions that Japan drew her Knightly Code, *Bushido,* obedience to which raised the *samurai* from the mere brutal wielder of swords to the chivalrous warrior. From Shinto he imbibed veneration for his ancestors, the strongest possible sense of duty to his parents, and the most self-sacrificing loyalty to the sovereign. Buddhism gave him a stoical composure in the presence of danger, a contempt for life, and "friendliness with death." It made him calm and self-contained. Finally, the *samurai* obtained from the teachings of Confucius his principles of action toward his fellow men.

Bushido is spoken of as "the Soul of the People." The Greeks of old located the soul in the kidneys, the Romans in the heart, and it is only in recent years that it has been described as in the head; even then the soul at best is indefinable, so I am at a loss to tell exactly what *Bushido* means.

When I asked a Japanese to define *Bushido,* he answered, "Loyalty—the loyalty of the servant to his master, of the son to his father. The servant is willing to make any sacrifice for the master. The Forty-Seven Ronins are an example of this. General Nogi is another instance of the same thing. Nogi felt that his death would remind the younger generation of the Spartan virtues of the older days, which they were forgetting, and would be a good thing for the country. He also wished to die in order that his master, the Emperor, might not be lonely."

The Japanese national hymn, as translated by Professor Chamberlain, fitly embodies this sentiment of loyalty to the Emperor:

"A thousand years of happy reign be thine;
Rule on, my lord, till what are pebbles now
By age united, to mighty rocks shall grow,
Whose venerable sides the moss doth line."

"Among the rare jewels of race and civilization which have slowly grown to perfection is the Japanese virtue of loyalty," writes Dr. W. E. Griffis; "In supreme devotion, in utter consecration to his master, in service, through life and death, a *samurai's* loyalty to his lord knew no equal. . . . Wife, children, fortune, health, friends, were as naught—but rather to be trampled underfoot, if necessary, in order to reach that 'last supreme measure of devotion' which the *samurai* owed to his lord. The matchless sphere of rock crystal, flawless and perfect, is the emblem of Japanese loyalty."

The material side of *Bushido* is the fighting spirit, and the germ of the spiritual side is the idea of fair play in fight—a germ which developed into a lofty code of honour. In feudal times Japanese warriors endured severe discipline. They were obliged to be expert with the fencing-stick, skilled in *jiu-jutsu,* the aristocratic form of wrestling, in archery, and in the use of the spear and the iron fan, as well as the double sword. They felt that mastery of the art of battle gave self-control and mental calm.

Mental exercises were practised more generally in olden times than they are today. There are several cults for the training of the mind, such as *Kiai* and *Zen,* both Buddhist practices. The secret of *Kiai* condensed is: "I make personality my magic power. I make promptitude my limbs. I make self-protection my laws."

Zen teaches: "Commit no evil, do only good, and preserve the purity of your heart and will. If you keep aloof from mundane fame and the lusts of the flesh, and are inspired by a firm resolve to attain the Great Truth, the gates of Stoicism will be opened to you."

Bushido is the foundation of the nation, built of rock. It is strong and true, and whatever is built upon it in the future, even if it topple and fall, can always be rebuilt again, for the rock is there forever. May they build something worthy to rise on such a firm foundation!

CHAPTER IX

NEW LIGHT FOR OLD

THE Old and the New Japan jostle each other at every turn. One day we visited the tomb of the heroic Nogi, who sacrificed his life on the altar of *Bushido,* and the next we received at the Embassy the pupils of the Tokyo Normal School, who will have so large a share in the continued remodelling of the nation. The Land of the Rising Sun has undergone decided changes within the last fifty years in her desire to make herself the equal of the Great Powers of Christendom; she has been willing to cast aside tradition, to modify her form of government, to adopt Western customs. But none of these things appears to me so vital as the reconstruction of her educational system and the free admission of a new religious belief.

The old system of Japanese education was derived from Chinese models as early as the eighth century, but for many hundred years it was barely kept alive in Buddhist monasteries, and was never fully carried out until the Tokugawa period. The higher institutions were devoted entirely to the study of Chinese history and literature, and their object was chiefly to train efficient servants of the State. Buddhist priests were the usual teachers of the lower classes, but retired *samurai* often opened elementary schools, such as that pictured so vividly by one of their pupils:[6]

"This primitive school," he says, "consisted of a couple of rooms, where some twenty or thirty boys (and a very few girls), ranging in age from seven to fourteen, spent the forenoon, each reading in turn with the teacher for half an hour some paragraphs from Confucius and Mencius, and devoting the rest of the time to calligraphy. Of the three R's, 'riting demanded the most time and reading but little, 'rithmetic scarcely any, except in a school attended by children of the common people as distinct

---

[6] Dr. Nitobe, in "The Japanese Nation."

from those of the *samurai*. Sons of the *samurai* class had other curricula than the three R's. They began fencing, *jiu-jutsu*, spear-practice and horsemanship, when quite young, and usually took these lessons in the early morning. As a child of seven, I remember being roused by my mother before dawn in the winter, and reluctantly, often in positively bad humour, picking my way barefooted through the snow. The idea was to accustom children to hardihood and endurance. There was little fun in the schoolroom, except such as our ingenious minds devised behind our teacher's back."

Yet this primitive system of education trained leaders of sufficient wisdom, unselfishness and breadth of view to guide Japan safely from the old to the new. Okubo and Kido, two members of the embassy that was sent to the treaty powers in 1871, discovered, upon landing in San Francisco, that the very bell-boys and waiters in the hotel understood the issues at stake in the election then going on. This convinced them that nothing but education could enable Japan to hold her own beside the Western world. Okubo said, "We must first educate leaders, and the rest will follow." Kido said, "We must educate the masses; for unless the people are trained, they cannot follow their leaders." Between the two, they got something of both.

The younger generation lost no time in availing themselves of their new privileges, and indeed they are today so eager for learning that, after their daily work, many of them sit up the greater part of the night to study. In consequence, they often grow anaemic, nervous and melancholy.

While the Japanese seem now to have adapted their elementary schools to the needs of their people, they have not been so successful with their secondary schools, called "middle" for boys and "high" for girls. The course of study for boys is much the same as in this country, except that instead of Greek and Latin they have Chinese and Yamato—old Japanese. English occupies six hours a week through the whole five-year course, but is taught only for reading, so that while most educated Japanese can understand some English and have read the classics of our literature, they may not be able to carry on a conversation in our language. In girls' high schools there is a room that might be styled "a laboratory of manners," where pupils have a "course in etiquette, including ceremonial tea and flower arrangement." The certificate of the middle school legally admits a student to the government colleges,

IX : New Light for Old

but as there are only eight of these institutions in the country, they cannot receive all who apply. Consequently, students must pass a rigid entrance examination. There are four Imperial universities, of which that in Tokyo is the oldest and has about six thousand students, and several private universities, one of which, Waseda, has an enrollment of more than seven thousand.

It did not escape the notice of the wisest leaders that perhaps the weakest point in this new educational system was its lack of moral training, all religious teaching being forbidden in government schools. Accordingly, in 1890, the late Emperor issued the Imperial Rescript on Education, a printed copy of which with the Emperor's autograph is sacredly cherished in every school, and upon which nearly all modern Japanese text-books of ethics are based. The most important part of this document reads as follows:

"Ye, Our subjects, be filial to your parents, affectionate to your brothers and sisters; as husbands and wives be harmonious, as friends true; bear yourselves in modesty and moderation; extend your benevolence to all; pursue learning and cultivate the arts, and thereby develop intellectual faculties and perfect moral powers; furthermore, advance public good and promote common interests; always respect the Constitution and observe the laws; should emergency arise, offer yourselves courageously to the State; and thus guard and maintain the prosperity of Our Imperial Throne, coeval with heaven and earth."

I was much interested in two secondary schools in Tokyo. We had the pleasure of entertaining the graduating class of young men from the Normal School. Professor Swift, who accompanied them, had been teaching in Japan for twenty-five years, having had the present Emperor at one time in his school. He said his students had never been received at the Embassy before, and in fact, he thought none of them had ever been in a European house. There were about forty of the Japanese and one young Chinaman. I think most of them were perhaps about twenty years old. They wore European dress, but the Japanese master came in his native costume. According to their rules of politeness, they gathered about the door, and could scarcely be induced to come in to shake hands with us. When they finally did come, they backed into a corner, and in true Japanese fashion had to be invited three times before they would enter the tea-room.

These students go out through Japan to teach English after they graduate. They did not speak English, however, quite so well as I had expected, but no doubt they were a little frightened, and probably they were more used to such questions as I heard at one school when the teacher read to the class, "Where was Phineas when the mob gathered about the portal?" Our guests enjoyed the mechanical bear and tiger, for, like most people of the East, the Japanese are especially fond of such toys. The students seemed to take interest in the photographs also, and when one asked for music, we started the Victor and allowed them to choose their own records.

Male and female teachers are trained in separate normal schools, which are government institutions. All their expenses—for board, clothing, tuition and books—are met by the State. After a preparatory course of one year, they take the regular course of four years, which covers a very full curriculum. Music, gymnastics, manual training, law and economics form part of this very modern course of study, and commerce and agriculture may be added. English is also included, but made optional. The necessary training in teaching is given in a practice school attached to each normal school. A shorter course of one year is devoted chiefly to the study of methods and practical work. A severe military training is given in the schools for males. Graduates from the regular course are obliged to serve the State as teachers for seven years, and those from the shorter course for two years.

The second school which particularly interested me was Miss Tsuda's. Miss Tsuda herself was one of several Japanese children from good families who, when they were very young, were sent to America to be educated. Three of the girls, it is said, decided at school how they wished to live their lives. One said that above all things she should marry for love and in the Western fashion, and so it was—she met a young Japanese studying in America, and they were married and returned to Japan. The second one said she wished to be a power, and she returned home and in Japanese fashion was married by her parents to a very prominent leader in political life. Miss Tsuda felt that she wished to help her countrywomen, and that she would remain unmarried and devote her life to education. So, curiously enough, these three women have carried out the ideals of their girlhood.

The school for the higher education of Japanese girls which Miss Tsuda has established is practically a post-graduate course, to fit

MISS TSUDA'S SCHOOL, TOKYO.

them for teachers. One class that I visited was reading really difficult English—something of George Eliot's. Miss Tsuda herself is a graduate of Bryn Mawr, and speaks most beautiful English—perhaps the most perfect I have heard from any Japanese. The school is supported chiefly, I understand, by people in Philadelphia. I was told that the Bible was taught, but that the study of it was not compulsory, and that many of the girls were Buddhists. These students are from all stations in life.

The outside of the buildings was in Japanese style, but the schoolrooms were like those in America; the pupils sat in chairs and had desks. I inquired why they did not sit on the mats, and Miss Tsuda said they had adopted chairs and desks because the girls felt that on the whole the chairs were more comfortable, and that they could move more quickly. It is thought the race will grow taller if they all learn to use chairs, instead of sitting on their legs as they have always done. The majority of the girls had writing-boxes and books upon the floors of their own rooms, and kept their bedding in a cupboard after the custom of their people, but they were allowed to have chairs if they asked for them. Hanging upon the *shoji* were Christian mottoes, photographs of their relatives, and in one case a picture of Nogi. European food is given here, as well as Japanese, and our methods of cooking are taught.

These students have modern gymnastic training every day, and they also play baseball, which the old-fashioned Japanese think very unladylike. Every Saturday evening they play games, have charades, and act little plays, both in English and Japanese.

On a previous visit, some years ago, L. had gone over the Imperial University with Professor Yoshida. At that time Tokyo University and the Engineering College had lately been amalgamated. He said it seemed strange, coming from an American university, to see the complete neglect of what we call classics, Latin and Greek. All the modern sciences, medicine, the 'ologies and law were studied in English, German and French.

One department, the seismic, established especially for the separate study of volcanic disturbances and earthquakes, was then peculiar to this university. It is particularly interesting to the Japanese, for they are constantly experiencing such disturbances—the late eruption in the province of Satsuma is a hint that results might be still more serious.

In the art schools in Tokyo, which we visited, we saw the students painting and carving in their peculiar, painstaking way.

IX : New Light for Old

An American teacher, who is not herself a missionary but has lived with missionaries in Japan for some time, and whom I consider an impartial judge, has given me her opinions on educational matters, including the work of the mission schools. The Japanese need, she feels, both moral and commercial instruction of the kind that only Western teachers can give. This teaching should be well given by the mission schools. At first, as in Korea, these schools were the only sources of Western thought, so they were frequented by all the Japanese who wished for any sort of progress. Everything was gobbled down hungrily. Even if they were not religiously inclined, they pretended to be, for this was their only means of learning English.

At the present time, the government schools teach Western branches, but they are hampered by a narrow-minded educational board with antiquated methods, and tied up by miles of red tape, so that their teaching of Western studies is away behind the times. We might consider the English heard all over Japan a fair sample of the superficiality that prevails, but, to be impartial, we must take into account the difficulties that have to be overcome by students and teachers. Because of the ideographs and other peculiarities of their own tongue, it is far more difficult for the Japanese to learn English than for us to learn French or German.

Government schools are superior in Japanese branches—they teach Japanese and Chinese classics and ethics, Japanese law and ideals better than the mission schools—and certificates from them give better positions, so ambitious Japanese go to them, but in Western subjects they try to do too many things. The students work only for examinations, not for really substantial progress. This is noticeable, except in rare individuals, who would probably progress under any conditions. The best Japanese educators realize this as well as the foreigners and greatly deplore it.

The reason that some of the mission schools are not so good as they might be is that they are too much occupied with proselyting, and hardly give more than superficial training to students. It would be better for the Japanese in the end if more real educators were sent out rather than so many preachers. If the mission schools would combine in having Japanese teachers for Japanese subjects, there could be concentration of effort and expense.

There is also a crying need, my friend says, of schools for foreign children, because there are no good ones in Japan, and it is expensive to send the boys and girls to America or Europe. An international foreign language school, too, is much needed. *The ignorance of foreign tongues is one of the greatest barriers to amicable relations with other countries.* The inscrutability of the Japanese, which we hear so much about, is due principally to their lack of familiarity with languages.

To understand the religious situation in Japan at all, it is necessary to take another backward glance over her history. Except during the two hundred and fifty years of the Tokugawa Period, the country has always been open to foreigners and foreign ideas. Chinese and Koreans, who brought new religions, a new civilization and a new philosophy, were gladly received. Young men from Japan sought learning in other countries, even in distant India. So, when Francis Xavier and his intrepid Jesuits made their way thither in the sixteenth century, they found a cordial welcome awaiting them.

For fifty years Christian work went on; hundreds of thousands of Japanese accepted the Roman Catholic faith. But the Roman Church claims to be superior to the State, and the rulers of Japan saw reason to believe that the priests were aiming at political power. At once they reversed their former policy, branded Christianity as "*Ja-kyo,*" the "Evil Way," and set about its extermination. Thousands of converts laid down their lives for the new faith in the terrible persecution that followed; foreigners were driven out of Japan, and her own people were forbidden to leave her shores.

After the "Long Sleep" of the Tokugawa Period, the Meiji Era, known as the "Awakening," began in 1867. Once more Christianity was brought in, but this time in the guise of Protestantism, and again it made rapid progress. By the middle of the eighties some Japanese leaders of opinion were even advising that it should be declared the national religion, although this was largely for political reasons. However, full religious liberty was granted in 1889.

In the early nineties came the reaction. The conservative element in the nation began to make itself heard against the mad rush for new things. Japanese students returning from abroad brought stories of vice and crime in Christian lands. The Japanese began to discover, too, that the standard of Christian ethics was a higher one than they had ever known, and demanded a change of life as well as of belief, and that the diplomacy of so-called Christian countries was often anything but Christian. So those who had simply "gone with the crowd" into the Christian ranks fell away. The churches were sifted.

This revulsion of feeling was not lasting. Gradually the Japanese came to modify their conclusions. Those who remained in the churches did so from conviction, and a stronger church was the result. In this period of reaction Japan simply stopped to take breath, to adjust itself to the new life upon which it had entered. Progress now may be slower, but it is more substantial.

The missionary question is absorbing, if one has time to see what has been done and what is being done now in the schools and kindergartens and hospitals, although today these Christian teachers are not playing so important a role as they did a few years ago. At first the Japanese went to the foreigners as their advisers and teachers, but now that they have travelled more and know more of Western ideas they do not need them so much. Six hundred thousand dollars goes yearly from America to Japan for missions. Japan is a poor country, but some people feel it is time for the rich men there to come forward and contribute to their own charities, rather than to let foreigners do so large a share. I feel that there is more need of missionaries in China today, especially medical missionaries.

Fifty years ago there was desperate need of medical missionaries in Japan. "When Dr. Hepburn opened his dispensary in a Buddhist temple at Kanagawa, diseased beggars were very common on the streets, for hospitals were unknown. Now there are over one thousand public hospitals managed by Japanese doctors, who are well fitted for their profession—some have been educated in Germany and are very skilful.

As there are natural hot springs in Japan, lepers in the early stages of the disease go there in the hope of being cured, but as a cure is not possible, they gradually become worse and cannot leave the country, so one often sees them begging in the streets. The only beggars I have ever seen in Japan have been victims of leprosy.

Up to 1907 there were no hospitals for lepers except those founded by foreign- missionaries. In that year the Government established five of these institutions, but as they are always crowded, the poor sufferers cannot be received unless they are very ill. Father Testevinde, a French Catholic priest, founded the first private hospital for lepers—which is still the largest—in 1889. Miss Riddell, an English-woman, has established another, which she is now trying to enlarge.

Eye troubles are especially prevalent in Japan, but the blind earn their living by massage, and the note of their flute is often heard in the street. There is a great deal of tuberculosis, but there are no sanatoriums for consumptives, who are taken into the regular hospitals. As the sufferers are kept in their homes until the last stages, the disease is spreading rapidly.

It is very common to see children afflicted with skin-diseases. Japanese mothers believe that inborn wickedness comes out in this form. Since they no longer shave the children's heads as in the old days, however, the skin trouble is disappearing somewhat. Well-organized dispensaries and district nurses are certainly much needed in out-of-the-way villages, but no provision has as yet been made for such work. Midwives, however, are to be found.

The Episcopal hospital in Tokyo, where Japanese women are taught nursing, is supposed to be the best in the country. Dr. Teusler is doing excellent work there. The Japanese hospitals are not so well managed as the best foreign ones, and the training for women nurses is not so long or so thorough as in America. It is difficult for foreigners to judge their hospitals, because they are intended for Japanese patients and their whole manner of living is so different from ours. At first, on account of native customs, only the poorer class of women could be induced to take up nursing as a profession, but today the better class are engaging in it.

In no branch of medical work has Japan made greater progress or achieved finer results than in the Red Cross. In 1877 the *Hakuaisha* was formed—the Society of Universal Love—which cared for the wounded in the great civil war. Japan joined the European Red Cross League in 1887.

The Japanese Red Cross was finely organized for service during the war with Russia. The first work was the care of the Russian sailors at Chemulpo, who were even presented with artificial limbs by the Empress of Japan. During the war six thousand sick and wounded Russian prisoners were cared for by the Japanese. In return the Russians subscribed to the Japanese Red Cross. The women nurses remained at home stations, all relief detachments at the front consisting of men only, but on the relief ships there were both sexes. An American nurse who was in Japan during

RED CROSS HOSPITAL BUILDINGS.

the war said we had many things to learn from the Japanese and few to teach, in the way of handling the wounded.

The pamphlet called, "The Red Cross in the Far East," states that if a member dies, his *hair* or his *ashes* with the death certificate and his personal belongings shall be forwarded to his former quarters.

The Red Cross in Japan numbers now more than one million five hundred thousand members, has twelve hospitals and two hospital ships, and nearly four thousand doctors, apothecaries and nurses ready for service. On her first voyage, the hospital ship *Kosai Maru,* was out from March, 1904, until December, 1905, and transported more than thirteen thousand patients. There are Red Cross stations also in Formosa and Port Arthur. The Empress Dowager often attended the meetings of the society, and assisted with large contributions. The Japanese Red Cross is said to be the largest, the best and the richest in the world.

To return to distinctively religious work, the time that I could myself give to the observation of missions was limited, but I saw something of the Episcopal work in Tokyo. Bishop McKim was absent most of the winter in the Philippines, but the Rev. Dr. Wallace, whom we had known in Honolulu years before, conducted the services. Japanese services were also held at the cathedral, and a school for native children was carried on by the mission. The bishop's house and that of Dr. Wallace, which were in the cathedral compound, were of brick and looked fairly comfortable.

As the lower classes are decidedly emotional and are easily influenced by revival meetings, while the better class naturally tend toward philosophy and other intellectual studies, there is room for Christian workers of different denominations. In actual numbers there are more of the Episcopalians than of any other Protestant denomination, as they include the English, Canadians, Australians and Americans. Next to these in number are the Presbyterians. There is a Unitarian mission conducted by the Bev. Dr. MacCauley, who has been there many years and whom we knew well. The Baptists are prominent in Yokohama. The American Board missionaries—the Congregationalists—I have been told, do the best work.

A very kindly spirit exists among them all, but they could economize greatly if they worked even more in union. Each mission, for instance, has its Japanese secretary, because of the difficulty of the language, but if they combined, they could do with fewer secretaries, and could also have Japanese teachers for Japanese subjects. A few big, broad-minded men—like Dr. Greene, who was looked up to by every one—who were men of affairs as well as clergymen, could do much good by acting as the heads of the missions and directing the Japanese Christians, somewhat as is done in the stations of the American Board.

Right here I wish to pay my tribute to the beautiful life and the great work of the Rev. Dr. Greene, whose death last September left the American Board mission poorer for his loss. Dr. Greene and his wife went to Japan in 1869, when the government edict banning Christianity was still in force. They lived to see the country under a constitutional government, with a modern system of education and full religious liberty. Dr. Greene was a missionary statesman; he was the intimate friend of Count Okuma and other Japanese leaders. As teacher, author, translator of the New Testament, and president of the Asiatic Society, he did a varied work. A few months before his death 'the Emperor conferred upon Dr. Greene the Third Class of the Order of the Rising Sun, the highest decoration awarded to civilians residing in Japan.

A work frequently overlooked is the service rendered in translation and the compilation of dictionaries. When Dr. Hepburn, to whom I have already referred, reached Japan in 1859, immediately after establishing his dispensary, he began the preparation of a Japanese-English dictionary, and as he had previously lived for several years in China, he was able to make rapid progress. In 1867 he brought out his great lexicon, which was published in Shanghai, because printing from metal type was not then done in Japan. When an invoice of it arrived in Yokohama, "Two worlds, as by an isthmus, seemed to have been united. . . . As a rapid feat of intellect and industry, it seemed a *tour de force,* a Marathon run." Later, Dr. Hepburn assisted in translating the Bible into Japanese. For all his work—as physician, lexicographer, translator of the Bible—and especially for his noble character, he was known in Japan as *"Kunshi,"* the superior man. Engraved on his tombstone are the words, "God bless the Japanese."

The following statistics, given out recently by the Japanese Bureau of Religion, are interesting as showing the number of adherents to each of the great faiths:

Christians,	140,000
Buddhists,	29,420,000

Believing Buddhists,	18,910,000
Shintoists,	19,390,000
Believing Shintoists,	710,000
Temples with priests,	72,128
Temples without priests,	37,417

The discrepancy between the number of "believing Shintoists" and Shintoists is explained when we remember that all persons in government employ—military and naval officers, officials in the civil service, and teachers in government schools—must be nominal Shintoists, even though they are Buddhists at heart.

I cannot better close this chapter than by giving the opinions of a few representative people of different faiths and nationalities upon the subject of missions in Japan.

Professor 'Masumi Hino of Doshisha University, *a Christian Japanese,* gives reasons why none of the old faiths will meet the needs of Japan today. He says, "Shinto stands for polytheism, which in Japan stands side by side with skepticism and religious indifference." He credits Confucianism with teaching "fair and square dealings with every man," but adds, "It nevertheless fails to meet the people's yearning after the eternal values." Buddhism will also, he believes, "fail to be the supreme spiritual force in Japan," because it does not attach sufficient importance to ethical teaching; because it sinks the individual in "the absolute and the whole;" and because its belief in immortality is "based on the pessimistic view of life."

Professor Hino acknowledges his own debt and that of the Japanese people to all three religions, but questions whether any of these can meet the pressure of twentieth-century life and problems. For himself he believes Christianity alone "is able to meet the demands of the coming generation in Japan."

Mr. E. J. Harrison, *a resident of Japan for fourteen years,* says in his book, "The Fighting Spirit of Japan":

"I venture the opinion merely for what it may be worth, but that opinion is, that those who flatter themselves that the day will ever dawn when the Japanese as a people will profess Christianity imagine a vain thing, and are pursuing a will-o'-the-wisp. They will dabble in Christianity as they have dabbled and are dabbling in numerous other 'anities,' 'isms,' and 'ologies'; but the sort of Christianity which will ultimately be evolved in Japan will have very little in common with its various prototypes of the Occident." Most people residing in Japan for any length of time agree with Mr. Harrison.

Then there is the *missionary opinion.* As recently as August 22, 1913, Rev. Dr. Greene wrote from Tokyo:

"Everything points to an increased appreciation of the place of religion in human life. The rapid headway which the more spiritual philosophy of the West, as represented by Bergson and Eucken, is making among the thoughtful men of Japan, including the young men of the universities, suggests much promise. Professor Anezaki, head of the department of Comparative Religion in the Imperial University of Tokyo, said not long ago that the students were weary of the materialism still propagated by certain of the older Japanese thinkers, and were seeking guidance of younger men imbued with the more recent philosophical thought.

"If the Christian leaders will but put themselves in harmony with this deep-flowing stream, they may well indulge the brightest hopes."

At a special gathering of public men in Tokyo in 1913, when evangelistic preachers from America were present, Baron Sakatani, the Mayor, although *not a Christian himself,* said:

"You men of the West owe us a lot. Your civilization has come in and broken down very largely the old faiths of Japan. We are looking for a new and better one. You owe it to us to help us find something to take the place of that which we have lost."

A year or two ago, the Minister of Education, who is *not a Christian,* called a conference of Buddhists, Shintoists and Christians, at which he said, "What Japan needs is more vital religion, and I ask each of you to become more in earnest in bringing your faith to bear upon the lives of our people."

Chapter X

PROSE, POETRY AND PLAYS

THE Japanese are true story-tellers, and for centuries their folklore has been passed down by word of mouth. The stories which Madame Ozaki, Pasteur and others have so cleverly translated into English are a great delight to me, many of them are so full of humour, pathos and charm. They fall into three characteristic types:—stories of the unreal world, legends of the great warriors of feudal days, and tales of love. Instead of trying to describe them I will give an example of each in condensed form.

Fairy tales play an important part in the literature of the people, and, except possibly the Norwegian, I think none compare with those of Japan. They have a strange and fascinating quality which specially distinguishes them from ours—they deal with imps and goblins, with devils, foxes and badgers, with the grotesque and supernatural, instead of the pretty dancing fairies, the good fairies that our children know.

"The Travels of the Two Frogs," from the charming version in Mr. William Elliot Griffis' "Fairy Tales of Old Japan," is given here in condensed form.

THE TRAVELS OF TWO FROGS

Once upon a time there lived two frogs—one in a well in Kyoto, the other in a lotus pond in Osaka, forty miles away. Now in the Land of the Gods they have a proverb, "The frog in the well knows not the great ocean," and the Kyoto frog had so often heard this sneer from the maids who came to draw water with their long bamboo-handled buckets that he resolved to travel and see the "great ocean."

Mr. Frog informed the family of his intentions. Mrs. Frog wept a great deal, but finally drying her eyes with her paper handkerchief she declared that she would count the hours on her fingers until he came back. She tied up a little lacquered box full of boiled rice and snails for his journey, wrapped it round with a silk napkin, and putting his extra clothes in a bundle, swung it on his back. Tying it over his neck, he seized his staff and was ready to go.

"*Sayonara!*" cried he, as with a tear in his eye he walked away—for that is the Japanese for "good-bye."

"*Sayonara!*" croaked Mrs. Frog and the whole family of young frogs in a chorus.

Mr. Frog, being now on land and out of his well, noticed that men did not leap, but walked upright on their hind legs, and not wishing to be eccentric he began walking the same way.

Now about the same time, an old Osaka frog had become restless and dissatisfied with life on the edge of a lotus pond. Close by the side of his pond was a monastery full of Buddhist monks who every day studied their sacred rolls and droned over the books of the sage, to learn them by heart. Now the monks often came down to the edge of the pond to look at the pink and white lotus flowers. One summer day, as a little frog, hardly out of his tadpole state, with a fragment of tail still left, sat basking on a huge round leaf, one monk said to another, "Of what does that remind you?" "That the babies of frogs will become but frogs!" answered one shaven-pate, laughing; "What think you?" "The white lotus springs out of the black mud," said the other solemnly, and they both walked away.

The old frog, sitting near-by, overheard them and began to philosophize: "Humph! The babies of frogs will become but frogs, hey? If the lotus springs from mud, why shouldn't a frog become a man? If my pet son should travel abroad and see the world—go to Kyoto, for instance—why shouldn't he be as wise as those shining-headed men, I wonder? I shall try it, anyhow. I'll send my son on a journey to Kyoto—I'll cast the lion's cub into the valley!"

Now it so happened that the old frog from Kyoto and the "lion's cub" from Osaka started each from his home at the same time. Nothing of importance occurred to either of them until they met on a hill near Hashimoto, which is half-way between the two cities. Both were footsore and websore, and very, very tired.

"*Ohio!*" said the lion's cub to the old frog, by way of good morning, as he fell on all fours and bowed his head to the ground three times.

"*Ohio!*" replied the Kyoto frog.

"It is rather fine weather today," said the youngster.

"Yes, it is very fine," replied the old fellow.

"I am Gamataro, the oldest son of Lord Bullfrog, Prince of the Lotus Ditch."

"Your lordship must be weary with your journey. I am Sir Frog of the Well in Kyoto. I started out to see the great ocean from Osaka, but I declare my hips are so dreadfully tired that I believe I'll give up my plan and content myself with a look from this hill, which I have been told is half-way between the two cities. While I see Osaka and the sea, you can get a good look at Kyoto."

"Happy thought!" cried the Osaka frog. Then both reared themselves up on their hind legs, and stretching up on their toes, body to body, and neck to neck, propped each other up, rolled their goggles, and looked steadily, as they supposed, on the places they each wished to see.

Now every one knows that a frog has eyes mounted in that part of his head which is front when he is down, and back when he stands up. Long and steadily they gazed, until at last, their toes being tired, they fell down on all fours.

"I declare!" said the older frog, "Osaka looks just like Kyoto! As for that great ocean those stupid maids talked about, I don't see any at all, unless they mean that strip of river which looks for all the world like Yedo. I don't believe there is any great ocean!"

"For my part," said the other, "I am satisfied that it's all folly to go further, for Kyoto is as like Osaka as one grain of rice is like another."

Thereupon both congratulated themselves upon the happy, labour-saving expedient by which they had spared themselves a long journey. Then they departed, after exchanging many compliments, and, dropping once more into a frog-hop, leaped back in half the time . . . the one to his well, the other to his pond. And so to this day the frog in the well knows not and believes not in the "great ocean!"

Excellent collections of fairy tales have been made by F. Hadland Davis—"Myths and Legends of Japan"—and R. Gordon Smith—"Ancient Tales and Folklore of Japan." Children love to read about Princess Blossoming Brilliantly Like the Flowers on the Trees, and Princess Long as the Rocks, about Prince Fire Shine, and Prince Fire Shade, and the other delightful characters with strange names. The story of "The Magic Sword, the Glittering Jewel and the Heavenly Mirror" is perhaps an especial favourite.

A good example of the legendary narrative is that of Hachiro Tametomo the Archer, told in English by Madame Ozaki in her "Warriors of Old Japan " and given here much condensed.

HACHIRO TAMETOMO THE ARCHER

Hachiro was the eighth son of an illustrious family. As a child he gave promise of being a very strong man, and as he grew older this promise was more than fulfilled. He early showed a love of archery, and his left arm being four inches longer than his right, there was no one in the realm who could bend the bow better or send the arrow farther than he could. He became the most skilful archer in all Japan.

By nature Hachiro was a rough, wild lad who did not know what fear meant, and he loved to challenge his brother, Yoshitomo, to fight. As he grew older he grew wilder still, so that even his own father found him unmanageable. One day a learned man came from the palace of the Emperor to give the boy a lecture. In the course of his talk he spoke of Kiyomori, an enemy of the house, as a clever archer. At this Hachiro laughed aloud in scorn, and told the learned man that he was both foolish and ignorant.

This rudeness was so contrary to the rules of Japanese courtesy that it made the lecturer very angry, and when his discourse was finished he rebuked the boy sternly for his behaviour. When the boy's father heard what had happened he, too, was angry with his son for daring to dispute with one who was his elder and superior, and refused to keep him any longer beneath his roof, sending him away to the island of Kyushu.

Now Hachiro did not mind his banishment in the least. On the contrary, he felt like a hound let loose from the leash, and rejoiced in his liberty. Free to do as he liked at last, his thirst for conflict became so great that he could not restrain himself. He challenged the men in all the neighbouring provinces to match their strength against his, and in the twenty battles which followed he was never defeated. He was like the silkworm eating up the mulberry tree, for just as the worm devours one leaf after another, so Hachiro fought and fought, one after another, the inhabitants of all the provinces anywhere around, till he had them all

ARMOUR AND WEAPONS OF ANCIENT WARRIORS.

X : Prose, Poetry and Plays

under subjection. By the time he was eighteen the boy had thus mastered the whole western part of Japan, and had made himself chief of a large band of outlaws noted for their reckless bravery.

This band became so powerful that the Government decided to interfere and put a stop to the outlawry. A regiment of soldiers was sent against them, but without effect: Hachiro could not be brought to surrender. As a final resort the Government, hoping thus to bring the son to bay, arrested Hachiro's father, and severely punished the old man for being the parent of an incorrigible rebel.

Although Hachiro was so rude and undisciplined by nature, there was hidden deep in his heart a sense of duty to his father, and on this his enemies had counted. He was greatly distressed at what had happened, and feeling that it was inexcusable to let his father suffer for his own misdoings, he gave up, without the least hesitation, all the western lands which had cost him such hard fighting. Then, taking with him ten men, he went to the capital and sent in a document signed and sealed in his own blood, asking the pardon of the Government for all his former offences and begging for the release of his father. When those in authority saw his filial piety, they could not find it in their hearts to treat him with severity, so they merely rebuked him for his lawlessness and set the old man free.

Soon after this a civil war broke out in the land, for two brothers of the late Emperor aspired to sit on the Imperial throne. Hachiro and his father fought on one side, while his elder brother, Yoshitomo, fought on the other. Hachiro was not yet twenty years of age, but was more than seven feet in height. His eyes were sharp and piercing, like those of a hawk, and he carried himself with pride and noble bearing. He was consulted about the tactics to be used in a great battle, and if his advice had been followed, the history of Japan might have been quite different. As it was, the enemy won the victory.

On seeing the foe approaching the gate where he was stationed, Hachiro exclaimed, "You feeble worms, I'll surprise you!" and taking his bow and arrow he shot a samurai through the breast. The arrow was carried in alarm to the general. It was made from strong bamboo and the metal head was like a chisel—it looked more like the arrow of a demon than a man, and the general retired in fear from before the gate.

When Yoshitomo came up, however, he was not afraid, but cried out, "What a wicked deed you commit to fight against your elder brother!" To this Hachiro answered, "It is wrong for me to take up arms against my brother, truly, but are you not an undutiful son to take up arms against your father?" The elder brother had no words to answer this, and Hachiro knew that he could kill him as he stood there. But they were brothers, born of the same mother, and he felt that he could not do it. Yet he could not resist raising his bow and arrow and taking a good aim at the helmet which Yoshitomo wore, shooting his arrow right into the middle of the star that topped it.

In the end Yoshitomo's forces were so much greater than Hachiro and his father were taken prisoners. The older man was put to death, but Hachiro's courage aroused sympathy, even in the hearts of his foes. It seemed a pity to kill so brave a man, and so they set him free. But to prevent his using his wonderful skill against them they cut the sinews in both his arms, and sent him to the island of Oshima.

The simple island folk recognized in him a great man, and he led a happy life among them. One day, while standing on the beach thinking of his many past adventures, he was seized with a desire for more. So, stepping into a boat, he set out on a voyage of discovery. He came to an island which was inhabited by people with dark red faces and shocks of bright red hair. Landing, he went up to a large pine-tree and uprooted it with as much ease as if it were a weed, brandishing it above his head and calling aloud, "Come, you demons! Fight if you will! I am Hachiro Tametomo, the archer of Japan. If you will be my servants and look up to me as a master in all things, it is well—otherwise, I will beat you all to little pieces!" He could have done it, too, because his arms were as strong as ever, notwithstanding the sinews had been cut. So the inhabitants prostrated themselves before him, and he took possession of the island. Later, however, he returned to Oshima.

Now the island of Oshima has always been free from smallpox, and the reason is that Hachiro lived there. One day a little man, no bigger than one foot five inches, came floating in on the waves, sitting on a round straw mat.

"Who are you?" Hachiro asked.

"I am the germ of smallpox," answered the pigmy.

"And why have you come here to Oshima?"

"I come to seize hold of the inhabitants!"

"You would spread the hateful pestilence—Silence! I am Hachiro."

At that the smallpox microbe shrank and shrank until he was the size of a pea, and then he floated away forever, as mysteriously as he had come.

On hearing of this, the Minister of State decided that Hachiro was becoming too powerful and popular a hero. When the young man saw the soldiers approaching the island, he seized his bow and, pulling it to the shape of a half-moon, sent an arrow that upset the boat and pitched the soldiers into the sea. After thinking the matter over, however, he decided that if he fought against the Government it would bring disaster upon the islanders who loved him, and it would be better to die at the height of his glory. So he committed hara-kiri and thus saved himself from all dishonour and the people of Oshima from further trouble.

Of a different sort altogether is the legend of the "Theft of the Golden Scale," so charmingly rendered into English by Mr. Brownell.

THE THEFT OF THE GOLDEN SCALE

Daredesuka was a *ronin* bold, and Eikibo was a beautiful *geisha*. One day Daredesuka asked Eikibo to be his wife, a request that *geishas* will generally accept, for it puts them in the highest of the four classes of society, ranking almost as well as the nobility. But Eikibo only laughed and said, "Such promises are like the little flies that live a day and then no one knows what has become of them!"

Daredesuka cried, "It is not so! Give me some test, for I must have you know I speak the truth. Shall I bring you pearls from the deep sea, or golden scales from the dolphins on Nagoya Castle? Only say the thing, and I will do it, for you must believe me."

Eikibo looked at him and said merrily, "Yes, I must believe you if you bring me a dolphin's golden scale from the ridge of the fifth story of the tower. I know Nagoya well, for I am there every year. Yes, I should know you spoke the truth if you brought the scale!" And she laughed again, for to the *geisha* the parents of a truthful man are not yet born. Then she added, "*Sayonara*! My call-time for the Full Moon Tea-house over the river has arrived. I beg your honourable pardon, I must go now. Next month I shall be at the great *matsuri* at Nagoya, where I am to dance. Bring me the scale, and I shall know your heart!"

Two nights later he was in Nagoya.

Now Daredesuka was a wonderful man with kites. He had made large ones when he was with his old lord, and had once dropped a line far over a junk that was blowing out to sea, and so saved many lives. He decided that he would use a kite to get the scale that Eikibo had declared would tell if he spoke true. Secretly he went to work and made a kite so large that he was sure it would carry the weight of his body. He found another *ronin* to help him in his strange plan, and on a stormy night, in wind and rain and clouds, he went up with his kite, and secured a golden scale from the ridge of the fifth story of the tower. But the tool he had used in prying it off was wet and slippery, and it fell from his hands to the ground far beneath him. The guards' attention was attracted. At the fatal moment a rift in the clouds let the moon shine down, and they discovered the kite. So it happened that when Daredesuka reached the earth they caught him with the golden scale. But because he was a *samurai* he was allowed to commit *hara-kiri,* and performed the act serenely before the State officials.

Eikibo did not do the fan dance at the *matsuri* in Nagoya, for on the morning of the day on which she was to appear, an old priest found her body on Daredesuka's grave.

At first it seemed that the opening of the country to foreigners was to be a death-blow to the old Japanese forms of art and literature. Translations of American and European books have become very common, and Western ideas permeate their work. But side by side with the newer forms, the classic writings are again coming into vogue.

Paradoxical as it may sound, much of the classical Japanese literature is Chinese. This is especially true of the older works, but it holds good only in less degree today. Chinese has always been the written language of the students, and of the higher classes in general, while Japanese was considered fit only for the common people, much as English was regarded down to the time of More's "Utopia." But while written in Chinese characters, much of this literature is distinctly national in spirit and feeling, and belongs as much to the country as does that written in the native tongue. Only within recent times has the common language of the people been used for writing books and scholarly treatises.

Previous to the introduction of the Chinese ideographs in the early Christian centuries, the Japanese had no written language. A knowledge of these ideographs places all Chinese literature at the service of the

X : Prose, Poetry and Plays

Japanese scholar. There are over eighty thousand characters, and three ways of writing as well as of pronouncing each, but one finds that most people know only about five or six thousand.

The great classical period, corresponding perhaps to the Elizabethan Era, covers about five hundred years, from the eighth to the twelfth centuries. During this time history, romance, and poetry flourished. The Japanese record of ancient happenings, dealing with early history and mythology, dates back to 712 A.D. and is sometimes called the Bible of Japan. The romances, many of which were written by women, described the Court life of the tenth and eleventh centuries. Most of the verses were written in the short *tanka* form, but longer ones, comprising groups of these stanzas, were common.

In later times Bakin (1767-1848) became famous for his novels. One of these—the "Tale of Eight Dogs"—contains no less than one hundred and six small volumes.

In spite of the fact that Kozo Ozaki was born less than fifty years ago, he is regarded as the Father of Japanese Literature. His work may be likened to that of making a stone palace from a prehistoric cave, for he simplified and unified the language, which was a mixture of the scholarly speech of the stage with the modern vulgar tongue. Ozaki was a perfect type of the gentleman of Old Japan. He was an artist as well as an author, and also an orator, people flocking to hear him speak. A group of young writers was formed in his time, but he was distinctly the leader. His stories were mostly of love. Among the seventy volumes published before his death (at the age of thirty-seven) "The Confessions of a Lover," "Three "Wives," and "The Golden Demon" are especially well known. Among his most noted contemporaries were Rohan Koda and Kyoka Izumi, the latter of whom was termed the Japanese Maeterlinck.

Today Osaki Batsume is one of the most prominent writers. He was born in Tokyo in 1867, and is said to have taken George Meredith as his model. One of his best known works is "Botchan," which is on the order of "Tom Brown's School Days." Much satire, and much philosophy, is found in his books, but he shows little sympathy with the follies of this life. His local colour and descriptions of social life are excellent, and he attacks the imperfections of his day with good effect. He is considered the master writer of modern times.

Many writers and books might be mentioned, but I want to speak of Dr. Nitobe, whose "*Bushido*" and "Japanese Nation" are known the world over. His wife is a charming American woman, and he has been exchange professor with America. I quote two of his essays that I especially like.

HEART AND CONSCIENCE

In thy sweet tremulous voice whisper in my ears what thou fain wouldst have. And the Heart confided her secret of love to Conscience. Said he in harsh tones of rebuke, "Thou most foolish one! Thy love is born of flesh. Thou shalt never behold the face of thy beloved. Thou art utterly corrupt." The poor Heart wept its bitterest; but her sobs stern Conscience heeded not; they reached the ears of the angels only.

THE SOUL'S QUEST OF GOD

Oft have I asked the question, O God, who art Thou? Where art Thou? And each time the answer comes in softest voice, Who art thou that askest Who I am? What thou art, that I am, and what I am art thou. And where art thou that askest where I am? Where thou art, there am I—and where I am, there art thou.

In worshipping God we worship ourselves, and in worshipping ourselves we worship God. The real self is within us; the essence of the Ego is divine. We clothe it in the rags of flesh and of fleshly desires, until the divine self is hid; and we call that self which does not strictly belong to it.

Japanese poetry differs very largely from anything with which we are familiar. It has little if any rhythm, as we understand rhythm. The *tanka* was for many years the only form of verse known. It has five lines and thirty-one syllables, which are arranged 5-7-5-7-7. This is an unusual metre to our ears, and translators are obliged to change the verses somewhat in order to make them sound more familiar to English readers. The following poem by the late Emperor is typical:—

THE NEW YEAR PINE

"Atarashiki
Toshi no hogigoto

X : Prose, Poetry and Plays

Kiku niwa ni
   Yorodzu yo yobo-o
   Noki no matsu kaze!"

"While New Year celebration fills my mind and heart,
I seem to hear above the palace eaves apart,
Winds calling midst the pines my garden doth adorn;
The voice of countless generations yet unborn!"

                      By Meiji Tenno.
               Translated, by Mrs. Douglas Adams.

Japanese classical poetry consists of poetical ideas expressed in flowery language and packed into the regulation metre. It abounds in word-plays and all sorts of puns, but is absolutely free from any trace of vulgarity. In those early days philosophy, religion, and satire were not considered fit themes for poetic treatment.

There is an even more Lilliputian form of verse than the *tanka*, called the *hokku*, which contains only seventeen syllables, often with little or no rhyme. An example of this form given by Lafcadio Hearn is known as "Vagabondage," and is a good example of much in little: "Heavily falls the rain on the hat that I stole from the scarecrow." Two others of quite a different trend are particularly exquisite: "What I saw as a fallen blossom returning to the branch—lo! it was a butterfly." "So lovely in its cry—What were the cuckoo if it laughed?"

The Japanese believe that if the beauty suggested in the five lines of a *tanka* verse cannot be fully appreciated by the reader, there is something hopelessly deficient in that reader. They do not believe in "smothering the soul with many words."

Perhaps what strikes one most in connection with the classic verses is the dates at which they were written, for many that have come down to us were composed a thousand years ago. Indeed, Japanese poetry is older than Japanese history, and tradition says that there were many versifiers even in the days of the mythological Emperor, Jimmu Tenno. At any rate, Japan had a literature of its own long before the Northmen found America!

In the old days only nobles, Court officials and church dignitaries wrote poetry. The lower classes were not supposed to know anything about the art. Love and "picture" poems were popular, and it is wonderful what perfect thumb-nail sketches were composed. It has been said that "the predominating feature, the under-current that runs through them all, is a touch of pathos. . . . It shows out in the cherry blossoms which are doomed to fall, the dewdrops scattered by the wind, the mournful cry of the wild deer on the mountain, the dying crimson of the fallen maple leaves, the weird sadness of the cuckoo singing in the moonlight, and the loneliness of the recluse in the wilds.

"The souls of children are often pictured as playing in a celestial garden with the same flowers and butterflies they used to play with while on earth. It is just this subtle element of the childlike disposition that has helped to discover the secrets of flowers and birds and trees, has enabled them to catch their timorous fleeting shadows and to hold them, as if by magic, in a picture, on a vase, or in a delicate and wistful poem."

"'Do not say anything unkind, but compose a poem. Is your best-beloved dead! Do not yield to useless grief, but try to calm your mind by making a poem. Are you troubled because you are about to die, leaving so many things unfinished? Be brave, and write a poem to death. Whatever misfortune or injustice disturbs you, put aside your resentment or your sorrow as soon as possible, and write a few lines of sober and elegant verse for a moral exercise.'" Thus Hearn translates from an ancient writer, and then goes on to say:

"In the olden days every form of trouble was encountered with a poem. Bereavement, separation, disaster, called forth verses in lieu of plaints. The lady who preferred death to loss of honour composed a poem before piercing her throat. The *samurai* sentenced to die by his own hand wrote a poem before performing *hara-kiri*. Even in this less romantic era of Meiji young people resolved upon suicide are wont to compose some verses before quitting the world."

These three little love-poems, which have been translated into English by William Porter, were written during the tenth century—the first one in 961 A.D. by the Imperial Adviser, Asa-Tada.

> "To fall in love with womankind
>   Is my unlucky fate:
> If only it were otherwise,
>   I might appreciate
> Some men, whom now I hate."

X : Prose, Poetry and Plays

The second, by Kanemori Taira, was composed in 949 A.D.:

"Alas! the blush upon my cheek,
　　Conceal it as I may,
Proclaims to all that I'm in love,
　　Till people smile and say—
Where are thy thoughts today?"

The last one was written in the same year by the minister of the Kawara district of Kyoto:

"Ah, why does love distract my thoughts,
　　Disordering my will!
I'm like the pattern on the cloth
　　Of Michinoku hill,
All in confusion still."

Japan has not been without her women poets. Lady Horikawa, who wrote this bit of verse, lived in the twelfth century and was in attendance on the Dowager Empress Taiken. The poem is dated 1142, and, like the others, was translated by Mr. Porter.

"My doubt about his constancy
　　Is difficult to bear;
Tangled this morning are my thoughts
　　As is my long black hair.
I wonder—does he care?"

The Empress Jito lived in the seventh century. She was the daughter of an Emperor and became Empress on the death of her husband, the Emperor Tennu. During her reign *saké* was first made. She wrote:

"The spring has gone, the summer's come,
　　And I can just descry
The peak of Ama-no-kagu,
　　Where angels of the sky
Spread their white robes to dry."

Daini-No-Sammi, who was the daughter of a poet, composed this pretty verse:

> "As fickle as the mountain gusts
>   That on the moor I've met,
> Twere best to think no more of thee
>   And let thee go. But yet
> I never can forget!"

Old age seems a favourite subject. Tsure Yuki Kino was a nobleman at Court and one of the great classical poets. He died in the middle of the tenth century.

> "The village of my youth is gone,
>   New faces meet my gaze;
> But still the blossoms at the gate,
>   Whose perfume scents the ways,
> Recall my childhood's days."

Jealousy is the theme of many of the verses:

> "Where many a tree
>   Crowns Takasu Hill,
> Does my wife see
>   My vanishing sleeve
>   And so take leave?"

Of the many picture poems, this is considered one of the best:

> "Out of the East,
>   Over the field,
> The dawn is breaking—
>   I turn to the West,
> And the moon hangs low!"

Another picture poem is by the late Emperor:

X : Prose, Poetry and Plays

"Kie nokoru
 Matsu no kokage no
Shirayuki ni
Ariake no tsuki!"
"At dawn, how cold the waiting moon doth shine
On remnants of snow beneath the pine!"

By Meiji Tenno.
Translated, by Mrs. Douglas Adams.

That the poetry of Japan is not without its humour is shown by the following comic song, which deals with a subject of universal interest:

"In the shadow of the mountain
 What is it that shines so?
Moon is it? or star? or is it the firefly insect?
 Neither is it moon,
Nor yet star. . . .
 It is the old woman's eye—it is the eye
Of my mother-in-law that shines!"

Modern poetry is read by everyone, and composed by everyone. Poems are written on tablets and hung or suspended in the houses; they are everywhere, printed on all useful and household articles. I quote a poem called "The Beyond," which was published in a recent issue of the Japan Magazine. It shows not only a change of form, but of theme as well.

"Thou standest at the brink. Behind thy back
Stretch the fair, flower-decked meadows, full of light,
And pleasant change of wooded hill and dale
 With tangled scrub of thorn and bramble bush,
Which men call life. Lo! now thy travelled foot
 Stands by the margin of the silent pool;
And, as thou standest, thou fearest, lest some hand
 Come from behind, and push thee suddenly
Into its cold, dark depths.

A JAPANESE STAGE.

> "Thou needst not fear;
> The hidden depths have their own fragrance too,
> And he that loves the grasses of the field,
> With fragrant lilies decks the still pool's face,
> With weeds the dark recesses of the deep;
> March boldly on, nor fear the sudden plunge,
> Nor ask where ends life's meadow-land.
> E'en the dark pool hath its own fragrant flowers."

The two young poets, Horoshi Yosano and his wife Akiko, are known as the Brownings of Japan. Yosano was editing a small magazine of verse not long ago when the poetess Akiko sent him one of her maiden efforts for publication. A meeting followed, and in spite of poverty—for poets are poor in Japan as elsewhere—they fell in love and were presently married. They went to France, and were made much of by the young poets of Paris. Yosano is something of a radical, impatient of poetic conventions and thoroughly in harmony with the new spirit of Japan. The power of Akiko's work is suggested in a poem of hers called "The Priest."

> "Soft is thy skin:
> Thou hast never touched blood,
> O teacher of ways
> Higher than mortal:
> How lonely thou art!"

The Japanese drama has not held so high a place as have the other forms of literature, for the stage was regarded for many years as nothing more than a rather common and even vulgar means of amusement. The classic drama, represented by the *No* dances, was partly religious and had more prestige, but there have been few good dramatists. The stage is of interest, however, because it is the only place left where one may study the manners and customs of long ago.

To give a brief summary of this art—the Japanese drama, like the ancient Greek, and the English also, had its origin in religion. In the very earliest days there were crude religious dances and songs. Later, popular tales of history and legend, mixed with poetry, were dramatized.

Minstrels often recited these to the accompaniment of the lute. Marionette dances accompanied by songs were also popular. Since these performances were regarded as beneath the consideration of the nobility, the *No* performance with a chorus came into existence for their benefit. After the earlier form had become debased and vulgarized the *No* dances kept their ancient ceremonial character, and continued to be performed before Shogun and *samurai,* and even before the Imperial family. They developed into something very like the classic drama of Greece. The actors were masked, the plays were held in the open air with no scenery but with elaborate costumes, and had a religious quality which they have retained to the present day. As the *No* is very long, comedy pieces were introduced, like the "interludes" of the pre-Elizabethan stage, to offset the classical severity. The actors have always been of a better class than the *kabuti,* or players for the common people.

Takeda Izuma is one of the most celebrated play writers, having dramatized the story of the Forty-Seven Ronins, as well as other historic tales. Chikamatsu is sometimes called the Shakespeare of Japan; his best work is a play in which the expulsion of the Dutch from Formosa is used as a theme. He was a prolific writer of rather a sensational order. Samba, who has taken the name of Ikku, is one of the best dramatists of the present time, and is renowned throughout Japan.

Hitherto myths, legends—religious or secular—and folklore, as well as passages from Japanese history, have been the material used for plays. Today, however, novels are dramatized as with us, and many plays are translated. Western dramas are having a great vogue at present.

Whether the plays are original or not, the author's name frequently does not appear at all. When Miss Scidmore, the author of "Jinrikisha Days," asked a great tragedian who wrote the play in which he was appearing, the star was puzzled and said that he did not understand. A bystander explained that it was based on newspaper accounts of various catastrophies, made into some sort of scenario by a hack-writer, with the stage-effects planned by the manager and the dialogue written by the actors—each of whom composed his own lines! No wonder the tragedian was puzzled by the question. As a rule, however, the dramatic author has entire charge of the production—he writes the play, arranges the scenes, and consults with the leading actor and proprietor.

CHAPTER XI

AMUSEMENTS

AS the traveller's first idea on reaching land after a long voyage is to enjoy himself, I am going to suggest several forms of amusement. Perhaps I had better begin by trying to answer what is sure to be his first question—"Where is the best tea-house with the prettiest *geisha* girls?"

We found that the most celebrated *geishas* were in Kyoto, where the dancing is classic, a model for the rest of the country. Here were also the best-trained *maikos*, or little dancers. The Ichiriki, or One-Power, Teahouse, which we visited, is one of the most famous in the country, for here in the long-ago Oishi, leader of the Forty-Seven Ronins, resorted in order to mislead the emissaries sent out to watch him by pretending dissipation and cowardliness. There is a shrine in the tea-house to the revered hero.

The place is very typical, with its clean-matted rooms and its tiny garden with miniature features of rock and water, its lanterns and stepping-stones, its gnarled trees and clumped bamboo. At the entrance to this tea-house we removed our shoes and passed over the soft mats into the simple, pretty rooms, open to the air and overlooking the lovely garden.

It took some time for the little entertainers to gather, for they are not used to haste. In the meantime we sat on mats while tea and *saké* were served by the naisan, or maids, who shave off their eyebrows in order to make themselves plainer and so set off the beauty of the dancers. They came slipping in and falling upon their knees before us, bowing low and presenting the tiny cups for drinking—all a matter of much ceremony and etiquette when politely done.

Finally some wee *maikos* came shuffling in with their quaint dress and hair make-up, their whitened faces and painted lips, and knelt among us in picturesque attitudes. These *maikos* are girls of from ten to thirteen years of age who are learning to be *geishas*. Following them came the *geishas* themselves—the older dancers—and then the musicians began to tune and twang their instruments, and to chant the monotonous songs that tell the stories of the dancing.

Our eyes grew big with wonder and delight as the figures were taken up in turn, one after another—movements grotesque, but oh, so dainty and quaint! Such posturing in adorably awkward attitudes! Such sliding with tiny feet turned inward, heads and hands at all angles, eyes askew! To one to whom their dancing has become familiar, it is all so fascinating and fanciful, so full of delight and grace and meaning!

Tomiji and Kanoko, both *maikos*—dear tiny figures in gay garments and huge *obis*—danced the Story of the Stone Bridge. One of them was a peony, and the other was a lion! Then a *geisha*, Harikiku, or the Spring Chrysanthemum, danced the Story of the Spring Rain, which has a theme like that of Romeo and Juliet, as old as the hills—only now one of the lovers was a nightingale while the other was a plum.

So they postured and made picture after picture, and when it was over, came and sat among us to help pass the tea and *saké* and cake and fruits that had been so daintily prepared. After that there was more dancing, and we took our leave amid much laughter and many *sayonaras* and wishes for a speedy return from our cheery little entertainers.

The *geishas* of Kyoto dress in more subdued colors than they do elsewhere. An American woman would be impressed by the cost of some of the kimonos, for no expense is spared in making them as beautiful as possible. The designs are carefully thought out, and an artist is selected to execute them. After the work is completed the stencils are usually destroyed, so that the pattern may never be duplicated.

These girls are the professional entertainers of Japan. They can be called to private houses, as well as to tea-houses, to help pass the time with their dancing and singing, and are cultivated in all the arts and graces that may add to their ability to please. Thus a *geisha* not only sings and dances attractively, but she is a trained conversationalist as well. She is not necessarily immoral, as Westerners often imagine. It is not uncommon even today for a girl to die by her own hand because she loves a man who, for some reason, cannot marry her. Many Japanese believe, however, that *geishas* are dangerous, designing and hard-hearted creatures, related to fox-women—a kind of goblin-ghost believed in by the ignorant.

GEISHA GIRLS AT THE ICHIRIKI TEA - HOUSE, KYOTO
(In the corner is inserted a geisha girl's visiting-card, *actual size*)

The *geisha's* songs are usually of love, the universal theme, and are sung to the notes of the *samisen*. They correspond to our classic love songs, but are much more popular among the lower classes than any music is with us, unless it be rag-time! The sentiment and phrasing are often fairy-like in their delicacy and charm, but, of course, much of this is lost in translation. The following is one of the chief favourites—it depicts "a lover, when the landscape is white with snow, going to the window to look out before he takes his departure." His lady-love seeks to delay his going, and this is the song:

"In vain thy cloak do I hide, Love,
    And in vain to thy sleeve do I cling;
Wilt thou no longer abide, Love,
    Nor give me for Winter, fond Spring?
I push back the window so slightly,
    And point to the snow-burdened land:
    O Love, wilt thou leave me thus lightly,
And choose the cold snow for my hand?"

The little quip at the end which turns this one from a love song to a tribute to the moon has doubtless teased many an ardent wooer:

"In the wide, wide world
    Of woes and tears,
Let us find a narrow spot
    To live together,
You and I,
    Until the world
Is quite forgot,
    O my sweet—
Moon that shines
    In my little window!"

Perhaps the best known tea-house in Tokyo is the Maple-Leaf Club. We dined there one evening when there was a fine full moon, and the lovely, mysterious little garden was like a dream in the glorious night. The meal was served on the lacquer service by dainty *geishas* as we sat

XI : Amusements

on the soft mats, while delightful dances were performed before us. Our favourite was the spider dance, in spite of its name, but we enjoyed them all, and even the music of the *samisen* and *koto*, which many foreigners do not care for. This house is famous for its excellent dancing and its pretty girls.

One feature of the meal which is characteristic of a Japanese dinner we could have easily dispensed with—that was the live fish, which was served to us still breathing, with a knife in its side, to show that it was perfectly fresh.

Theatre-going in Japan is a source of endless enjoyment. There is a big and quite beautiful opera house in Tokyo where the national plays, both old and new, as well as European opera with Japanese words, are given. Here the combination of East and West is very interesting. The audience, although for the most part wearing Japanese clothes, sits in seats instead of on mats. It is said that when the first European opera company came to Tokyo and the leading lady took her high notes, the audience was so convulsed with laughter that the manager had to pull down the curtain.

The English plays and the light operas given by the Japanese strike one as amusing. It always seems strange to see Orientals in European dress, and one never gets used to their ballet on account of their queerly shaped legs, which have been made crooked by ages of sitting upon them.

A sample program of a performance given at the Imperial Theatre in Tokyo, "Daily from 5th January, 1913," at 4.30 p.m., names five plays: 1. "The Soga Vendetta," a musical drama in one act, laid in the twelfth century; 2. "Muneto," an historical drama in four scenes, representing Kyoto in the eleventh century; 3. "Maria de Cronville," a musical pantomime in four scenes, Paris in the reign of Louis XIV; 4. "The Woman Hater," a modern farce in two acts, the settings representing the garden of a hotel in Kamakura and a room in a "hospital for mental diseases;" and 5. "The Merry Ferry," a musical drama in one scene, representing a ferry landing in Yedo in the eighteenth century. It would be an exacting taste which did not find something to satisfy it in a generous bill like this!

Most of the theatres are still quite Japanese. They are built of wood and so flimsily as to be full of draughts. The stage extends across one side of the square auditorium, whose sloping floor is divided into boxes two yards wide by low railings, which can be used as bridges by patrons arriving late or departing early. There is one gallery with boxes in front and room behind where the lower classes may stand. The actors enter the stage by means of two long raised platforms called "flower-paths," which extend across the auditorium—they receive their name from the custom of strewing the way of a popular actor with blossoms when he appears. These paths have been given up in the Imperial Theatre, as have also in some cases the little "supers," dressed in black in order that they may be considered invisible, who were of great service in perfecting the details of a stage-picture. But the old methods are still used in most of the theatres.

When an actor wishes to disappear from the audience he may leave the stage by the flower-paths, he may vanish into the wings, or—more simply still—he may hold up a small curtain in front of him and so accomplish the desired effect.

The revolving stage is used oftener in Japan than it is in Europe, to say nothing of America, where it is practically unknown. It allows quick changes of scene, for one setting may be arranged out of sight in the rear of the stage while another is in use before the audience. Instead of having the curtains lowered between the acts, the audience is often allowed to see the stage turn, which is interesting.

The plays usually begin at half-past four in the afternoon and last until eleven in the evening. A play may run for several days, or there may be three or four at one performance. During the intermissions the audience goes out and gets dinner at one of the score of restaurants in the building.

Although stage people are looked up to a little more than formerly, they are still regarded as a rather low class. Madame Sada Yakko is perhaps the best known actress of the new school, for she met with great success, not only on the Parisian stage in 1900, but later in America as well. Danjuro, Kikugoro, and Sadanji, the greatest actors of the Japanese stage, are all dead. Today the best are Sojuro and Sawamura, who take women's parts, and Koshiro Matsumoto, who takes men's.

On a previous visit we spent a day at the Theatre Nakamuraza, which was then the finest in Tokyo. Danjuro, who was playing there, "supported by a strong company, including the great comedian Tsuruzo," was the favourite actor of the time and delighted a large audience. I do not feel competent to judge his acting, as I saw him only once, but critics say that

AN ACTOR OF THE PRESENT DAY.

he was much like Henry Irving, and one of the world's greatest artists of the old school. There is a marked difference between good Japanese acting and the inferior article, the former is so much more natural, with less that is grotesque and ranting.

The founder of the Japanese drama is supposed to have been a woman—O Kuni, a priestess of the temple at Kitzuki. She was as beautiful as she was pure, and was skilled in the dances which are supposed to delight the gods. One day, however, she fell in love with a "wave-man"—a *ronin*—and fled with him to Tokyo. Here her dancing and her beauty soon made her famous. Not satisfied with this, she and her lover—who was also her devoted pupil—became actors, and were the first to put secular plays on the stage. While still quite young the "wave-man" died, and O Kuni left the stage for ever. She cut off her wonderful long hair and became a Buddhist nun, spending the rest of her life writing poems. From her day until recent times women have not been allowed to appear on the stage, men taking all the parts as in the plays of ancient Greece and old England. Today, however, women often take part with the men, as with us.

The old plays are very interesting and well done, the costumes being superb and the scenery excellent. The characters consist for the most part of *samurai* and *daimyos*, two or three of whom are either killed or commit *hara-kiri* during the performance. While their postures mean little to our eyes, to a Japanese every movement has its significance. When the actors pose and stamp around and finally kill themselves, the audience weeps in sympathy. The speeches are in the scholarly language, which only the better educated (very few of whom are women) can understand. This fact accounts for the large amount of sensational action which is considered necessary to hold the attention of the common people. One result of the many historical dramas given in the theatres is that the lower classes know and revere their national heroes.

In the early days of the theatre masks were much used. They were made to express sadness, hatred or amusement, and the actors chose them to fit the part they had to play. Often they portrayed the faces of well-known persons, and these were especially popular. If the actors wished to represent divinities or devils they had masks coloured black, red, green, or gold, often with real hair on them. The custom of masking on the stage was given up at the end of the seventeenth century.

XI : Amusements

One day we went to a native theatre and sat cross-legged in a box for over three hours, watching with real interest the exciting legendary romance of the famous Forty-Seven Ronins, whose story is told in another chapter. This was a very long play which had already taken twenty days, from eight in the morning till five in the afternoon, and would require three days more to finish it. The dialogue was, of course, quite unintelligible, but the play was nevertheless very interesting, for there was always a lot of action. The hero was truly superb—by a glance of his eye or a threatened blow he could knock down a whole stage-full of men! There was a very realistic suicide, with spurting blood and many gurglings. The acting was a trifle exaggerated—at times even grotesque and absurd—but I could follow the thread of events quite easily.

Some clever tumbling and acrobatic feats were introduced after the play, and a really funny funny-man, but to me the most amusing thing was to see an assistant come out on the stage after some especially violent scene and proceed to mop the perspiration from the actors' faces, walking coolly off again when his errand of mercy was accomplished.

The costumes and stage-effects were rather showy. There were no drop-scenes or flies. The people sat on the floor in their little stalls, and drank their tea or *saké* and nibbled their cakes, coming and going as they wished.

The monkey theatres, where monkeys take the parts of men and women, should not be forgotten. The apes seem to enter into their roles with great spirit and energy. They are dressed in complete costumes to represent farmers, nobles, or two-sworded *samurai*, and they weep and rant and slay each other through the length of a classic play in the most natural manner. Their performance of comedy, tragedy, and drama generally, is absurdly human. There are men behind the scenes who tell the story of the action that is going on, but the monkeys themselves do everything but speak. Now and then, however, they forget their cues and the action stops till they are prompted. One "high officer," who came on to the stage on a big black dog for a horse, caused much confusion by refusing to dismount and kill his enemy, because the enemy, being a very well-trained monkey, insisted upon falling dead anyhow. These theatres are very small and can easily be moved about from place to place, like a Punch and Judy show.

Once while we were in Tokyo there came to town "The Royal Australian Circus," which gave two performances a day to crowded houses—or rather tents. As if the idea of a circus in the heart of Japan were not a sufficiently striking contrast, they pitched their tents, each with its familiar ring and sawdust, almost within the shadow of an ancient temple. For a few yen you got a box with red cotton trimmings and watched "Mr. Merry-man" get off his jokes in cockney English and Yokohama mixed. The show itself was poor, both in quality and quantity, and peanuts—the fundamental element of a proper circus—were wholly lacking.

Moving-picture shows are very popular in Japan as elsewhere. Once, when we were lunching at the hotel in Yokohama, a very pretty American woman made up as a Japanese came into the room, attracting a great deal of attention. We were quite unable to make out the situation, but were afterward told that she belonged to an American moving-picture company and had just come in from rehearsal.

Everywhere the "movie" is taking the place of the story-teller, who used to hire a room and tell over and over the tales of love and adventure which the people enjoy. Only the more prosperous can afford to see the *geishas* dance, but crowds flock to see them on the screen. They also see their native plays acted quite as realistically as on the stage, where the actors might as well be dumb since they do not speak the common language.

Perhaps for the first time the kinematograph has been of use in making history instead of simply recording it. When the Crown Prince of Korea was taken to Japan to receive his education, rumours were circulated among the Koreans that he was badly treated and was in reality a prisoner. There was great danger of an uprising in his behalf, but the Japanese Government hit upon the happy expedient of having the young man followed through a whole day's routine by a man with a moving-picture camera. .When his subjects saw their Prince looking well and happy, learning his lessons and playing games with his friends, their fears were allayed and trouble was averted.

Mr. Arnell and Mr. Arnold, of the Embassy, took lessons in Japanese acting, and Mr. Arnell was able to make up extraordinary faces and to kill himself, apparently in the greatest pain. Of course he dressed in costume, and with his *tabis* on he would make his big toe stand up in true Japanese

MR. ARNELL AND MR. ARNOLD IN JAPANESE PLAY.

style, and would slash with his sword very realistically. Mr. Arnold, in one of the plays they learned together, took the part of a girl named Cherry Blossom; he did it very well indeed.

The English and American colonies often give theatricals: a performance of the "Merchant of Venice" at the opera house was excellent. We enjoyed it, and the Japanese students flocked to see it.

Sports of various kinds are occasionally indulged in. The annual fall exhibition, at which L. was present during one of his earlier visits, takes place late in October. The sports were held in the compound of the University grounds, which was beautifully decorated in honour of the heir-apparent—the present Emperor—then a good-looking little fellow about ten years old, who sat on a green baize chair on a raised platform, surrounded by chamberlains and officers. There were obstacle races, and the 220 on a turf track was run in 27 seconds, the 440 in 60½ seconds. A race between professors created great amusement, and a sprint between champions of the different schools was enthusiastically followed.

"The annual fall meeting of the Nippon Race Club," wrote L. during his visit in 1889, "was held the last of October. This is quite a successful club, and is the racing association at Yokohama. They have a pretty course out behind the Bluff, pretty from an aesthetic point of view only, however, for it is a bad track with a regular Tottenham Corner near the finish. The meeting proved to be great fun and quite exciting. The runners are limited to China and Hokkaido ponies—little brutes between 12.1 and 14.1 hands—and though the time is slow the finishes are generally close and exciting. In one race, the Yokohama plate, one mile and three-quarters, the three leaders finished within a nose of each other. The great interest is, of course, in the betting. There is always a tremendous amount of gambling in the Orient, and these meetings prove exceptional opportunities for this spirit to exhibit itself.

"The second day's racing was graced by the presence of His Imperial Majesty [the late Emperor] and his suite, and so was the great day of the meeting, and a great day for Yokohama also. The Emperor seldom leaves his palace, but his earthly half—for he is still considered half divine by the people—is fond of horses and of horse-racing, and he makes this one of the occasions on which he does exhibit himself. He was very ceremoniously treated. After the last race he was driven around the track in his carriage of State, surrounded by lancers, for the benefit of the

XI : Amusements

thousands who had come out to Negishi Hill to pay their respects to their sovereign."

Near Uyeno Park in Tokyo there is a racecourse, but it is not so popular as it was a few years ago, for the Japanese are not horsemen. The horse of Nippon is thoroughly a beast, and stubborn, and this fact created variety and interest when L. visited the riding-school. The French method was used in those days—hands out in front, body bent forward—and they retained the old custom of short stirrups and knees elevated toward the chin.

The grounds of the school were good. There were about seventy horses, but L. said that only a few half-breed ones were passable, for the thoroughbred Japanese ponies were bull-necked, mule-hoofed, and had miserable quarters. Since those days, however, horses from Australia and Arabia have been introduced, and although they are said not to thrive very well in Japan, they have improved the stock considerably.

A typical amusement of the country is wrestling. The professional wrestler is a man of no mean rank, standing far above merchants, farmers, and actors in the social scale. His family has probably been devoted to wrestling for generations, and he has been trained from childhood and fed on special food to make him big and strong. If he is a famous fighter his patron, who is doubtless some great nobleman, is very proud of him, and the people of his province look upon him as little less than a demi-god.

Although the ladies all go to bull-fights in Spain, very few go to wrestling-matches in Japan. Foreign women are apt to consider it a brutal sport, somewhat on the order of our prize-fighting, because the wrestlers are so fat and dreadful looking. But there is no fist-fighting, and the skill is so great that I found it very interesting. You can always tell the wrestlers when you see them, because they wear their hair done in old-fashioned style, somewhat resembling the queue of the matador.

The history of wrestling goes back to the first century B.C., for it is an ancient as well as honourable profession. It began as a Court function for the entertainment of the nobility. Political issues of great importance are said to have been decided in the ring in the early days. The sport took on a religious aspect during the first half of the seventeenth century, when the priests began organizing matches in the temples to raise money for divers "pious purposes." In time many abuses crept in. There was much bitter feeling between contestants from different sections of the country, and so much foul play that the Government put a stop to all public performances. Not until 1700 A.D. were public matches again allowed, and then only under restrictions which made it safer for the contestants. From that day to this, wrestling (*sumo*) has been very popular with all classes.

In Osaka we saw some fine matches where the wrestlers of the East met those of the West. People gather from all over the country to witness these contests, which generally take place in the middle of the summer.

There are wonderful matches in Tokyo also, which continue during the month of February. Formerly they took place under a large circus-tent, but now they are held in a huge arena, shaped something like a bull-ring, only not open to the sky. The ring in the centre is very small and raised on a platform beneath a canopy. A light is thrown on the contestants as they come swaggering and waddling down the aisles to meet in the centre, mount the stage, and take grotesque postures that show to advantage the muscles of their legs and arms. When they first come in they wear their gold-embroidered aprons, which are very costly. Of course these are taken off when they fight. The referees sit at the corner under a canopy, while two wrestlers try to throw each other out of the ring.

Each bout is preceded by elaborate formalities. The wrestlers pray to their gods, and show themselves off to the spectators. Then they squat, rub their hands, turning them palm outward toward the people, take a cup of water, and scatter salt as a sign of purification. This done, they take positions on all fours, facing each other, till, at a psychological moment, they attack. If one starts his attack before the other, however, it doesn't count, and they swagger back to the sides and rinse their mouths and scatter more pinches of salt. Between the bouts much betting goes on.

Viewed in the dim light, through the smoke of the many little pipes in the audience, the scene was stranger than anything else I have ever witnessed. The wrestlers use such skill, and the excitement is so great when one of them has won, that the cheering is as good as at a football game at home. We saw one bout where fifteen thousand on-lookers became frenzied with excitement, because a "number one" champion was thrown out of the ring. On certain days the wrestlers appear all dressed up in their ceremonial clothes and give a dance.

A WRESTLER.

Ordinary wrestling, or *sumo*, must not be confused with the more scientific form known as *judo*, or more commonly, *jiu-jutsu*, which has been introduced to some extent in our own country. Here weight and strength count for little in comparison with skill and adroitness. While ordinary wrestlers are perfect mountains of men, some of the cleverest exponents of *jiu-jutsu* are quite small. Mr. Harrison, in his "Fighting Spirit of Japan," tells an amusing tale of a contest between exponents of the two systems, to decide which was the better. "At the very commencement of the struggle the big man picked the *judo-ka* up and, holding him high above his head, asked triumphantly, 'Now, where are you?" Apparently not a whit perturbed by this turn of events, the *judo-ka* answered, 'Oh, this is just where *judo* comes in! The moment you attempt to throw me down, I'll kick you to death!' Terrified out of his wits by this awful threat, the fat man, still holding the *judo-ka* above his head, rushed out into the street, shouting loudly for help."

Jiu-jutsu is not practised publicly as is *sumo*, for it belongs to the upper classes. The matches are not advertised or reported in the papers. Its history goes back to mythological times, and it ranks with fencing as an art. Hundreds of young men get up at three o'clock on winter mornings and practise until seven in order that they may become proficient in this difficult exercise.

The foreigner in Tokyo usually feels that he has not "done" the city unless he has seen the sights of the gay quarter—the Yoshiwara—which is very gay indeed and as naughty as it is gay. There is nothing exactly like it outside Japan. It is impossible to see the place in a jinrikisha, so one must thread the crowded streets as best he can on foot. Girls in superb kimonos sit behind barred windows like dolls displayed for sale in a shop. The condition of these girls is much better than formerly. The Salvation Army has done a wonderful work for them, and not long ago the Government allowed all who wished to leave the houses.

When other entertainment fails, there is always a *matsuri*. This is a great holiday institution among the lower and middle classes—a fair held in the streets or in the open spaces about a temple—for, like the drama, the *matsuri* traces its origin to a religious rite. The most popular of these fairs is held near the great Buddhist temple known as Asakusa Kwannon. The long street leading to this temple is very gay with the shops on either side filled with wonderful toys. In various booths in and about the temple

THE *NO* DANCE.

there are many entertainments in full swing—tea-houses and theatres and "movies," fortune-tellers and jugglers—all jumbled up together. It is a strange mixture of things sacred and secular. Murray says that even many years ago this temple was so popular that they had notices prohibiting smoking, and warning people not to take their afternoon naps there.

Every *matsuri* has its fortune-teller. I found one sitting in a little booth—an aged, bald-headed old man with horn spectacles which did not in the least conceal his piercing eyes. He asked my age, and muttering continually, lifted the divining-rod to his forehead. After looking at me through a magnifying-glass he proceeded to separate the packets of rods and finally, by means of an interpreter, he said:

"You will be married in two years, and have three children by the time you are thirty!"

I bowed gravely and thanked him, telling him that he was a wonderful soothsayer—a verdict with which he seemed to agree perfectly. It may be mentioned, however, that I am over thirty, and have been married many years, with no children.

Great reliance is placed on fortune-telling by the Japanese of the lower classes. I have seen a mother with a sick child shake the curiously lacquered box of sticks which the priest of a temple has in his charge, hoping to get help. She exchanged the numbered stick that fell out for a slip of paper which had a prescription printed on it, and then went out to buy the medicine with a sublime faith that it was just what her baby needed for its recovery.

Fortune-telling is not confined to *matsuris* or to temples. One hears the calls of the prognosticator in the streets at night. There is also a very elaborate system of foretelling the future, based on the colouring and formation of the head and features, which a few men of a higher class practise with quite wonderful results.

To these amusements, which any one may enjoy, I add two other forms of a more serious nature which are of great interest, although the foreigner rarely has time or opportunity to see them during a hurried visit. They are the *No* dance and the *cha-no-yu*, or tea-ceremony.

The Japanese nobility rarely attend the public theatres, but they do attend—and even take part in—the *No* dances, which are not really dances, but high-class theatrical performances. Why a play should be called a dance is hard to explain, unless one remembers that this is Japan, where they begin a book at the wrong end, wipe with wet towels, saw and plane toward themselves, shoe their horses with straw, and even have their compass-needles pointing to the south! The Japanese world is "topside down" to us, but I suppose ours is just as much so to them.

We were fortunate enough to see an excellent *No* dance which was being performed in a private house. The performance was given in honour of an ancestor of theirs, who had died two hundred years before. It was a very aristocratic audience—the upper class people are easily distinguished, as they are more intelligent and stronger looking, as well as more refined, than the middle and lower classes. The play was given in a very dignified and ceremonious manner, and the acting was of the highest order, but to one unacquainted with the language and the meaning of the various postures even the best *No* dance is apt to prove tedious. The *No* is further described in the chapter on literature.

An even more serious form of entertainment, and one well worth the attention of those who have longer to stay in the country and who wish to make a study of the customs, is the *cha-no-yu*, a ceremony which has almost the force of a religious rite.

Viscounts Kadenokuji and Kiogoku took us to one of these tea-ceremonies at a private club house—Hosigaoko—in Sanno. This was the most wonderful piece of house-building I have ever seen—the polish on the floor, the fitting of the frames, the joining, was simply perfect. Some of the porch boards were forty-five feet long and as smooth and polished as glass.

A very small room of four and a half mats (nine feet square) is held sacred for the ceremony. The entrance is made through a door which is only a couple of feet square—a custom remaining from the time when visitors were so received lest they hold swords hidden in their robes. The guests, who should be five in number, sit down in a row, the Japanese sitting on their feet in ceremonial manner; foreigners, however, are allowed to cross their legs, tailor-fashion, for one is expected to remain without moving during the whole affair.

This *cha-no-yu* is a relic of the old days when ceremonies were invented to pass away the time, and is the most formal mode of entertainment. It is taught as a fine art and accomplishment by various schools, which differ in regard to small details of etiquette. The master who performed it for us, Nakamura, is the most famous teacher in Tokyo.

The rite consists in making a bowl of tea. Even the tiniest motion has its own particular meaning, and is performed most solemnly and religiously. As in all Japanese ceremonials, it is done very slowly, requiring three hours for its completion. Certain implements are used for the *cha-no-yu* alone, and these are of the finest make. It is part of the performance to pass them around for the guests to examine, and it is etiquette to admire them. The tea-making is followed by a formal dinner, in which the guests get a chance to air their knowledge of strict social laws, even as to what to eat, and how much. The exit is made, after it is all over, by crawling out through the hole of a door.

CHAPTER XII

BEAR-HUNTING AMONG THE AINUS

ON the northern island of Hokkaido (or Yezo) is to be found the Ainu,[7] and with him the grizzly bear which he hunts, kills, and yet worships. The winter climate of Hokkaido resembles that of Canada, and Bruin thrives there, growing to a large size—sometimes ten feet, it is said.

Mr. Arnell of the Embassy went up there in March, reaching the hunting-grounds six days after leaving Tokyo. His party consisted, besides himself, of Major Wigmore, Lieutenant Keyser, and Mr. J. A. Fenner. They had engaged, besides a guide apiece, six Ainu men and three women to meet them at Kushiro and carry their baggage. The women were found to be "stunning walkers" and, with others of their sex, to be not "bad-looking except when tattooed with a green moustache." I will give the story of the hunt in Mr. Arnell's own words.

"Choosing between drenching and freezing," he says, referring to the heavy rains in Tokyo, "I prefer the snow-clad peaks of Hokkaido.

"We reached Kushiro, the terminus of the railroad, three days after our departure from Tokyo. We were met by our faithful Ainu, who had consumed gallons of distilled spirits while waiting for us, and made us lose a day waiting for him to recover. We finally succeeded in marshalling three sleighs, each about the size of a Japanese mat, and seating ourselves in a squatting posture, started up the frozen river.

"The snow was about a foot deep at Kushiro, but increased in depth as we approached the mountains, where it varied from three to five feet. It took us three days to reach the hunting-grounds. After we left the river the road was very uncomfortable. As long as we kept to the centre, progress was good, but whenever the sleigh happened to go one foot too far either side, over we went,—driver, horse, passengers, baggage! Spills

---

[7] The Ainus are quite distinct from the Japanese, both in appearance and language, and are gradually being supplanted by them.

of this kind were frequent, and relieved the monotony of the journey. We spent two nights at inns in lumber-towns on the way.

"We had telegraphed ahead to the last town, Teshikaga, and a courier was dispatched to collect the Ainu beaters, who were waiting our arrival. There we held a council of war with the warden of the Imperial forests—the dwelling-place of His Majesty's ursine subjects.

"We also tried out our showshoes, oval frames of mulberry wood, without which locomotion was impossible. There was not time to make perfect fits, so we had to make the best of ready-made ones, all of which were baffled by the Major's avoirdupois.

"An interesting bird had been shot at this camp the day before our arrival; it has no name, but is known as 'the bird which appears only every six years,' and is distinguished by having its legs above its tail-feathers, so that when it waddles on dry land, if it ever does waddle, its tail forms the head of the procession. It is probably related to the penguin, but is different from it in that its beak is long and straight like a crane's. Strange to say, on our return to Kushiro by river a week later Mr. Fenner shot another of the same species, and with the waters of the Kushiro we christened the fowl *Avis rara Fenneri!*

"On the day after our arrival we continued our journey by sleigh to the shores of Lake Kutchare, which is in the heart of an uninhabited forest and has a circumference of over twenty-five miles. Here we separated into two parties—the Major and Fenner, Keyser and myself. Across the frozen surface of the lake rose the ghost-like summit of Mount Shari.

"'Bears, bears!' whispered the Ainus, pointing to the peak with their hairy fingers.

"After dining on salt salmon, corned beef and hard-tack, we put on our snowshoes and set out across the lake, accompanied by the aborigines carrying our baggage. Keyser and I, the 'lean detachment,' struck for the higher spurs of the mountain, while the Major and Fenner, the 'fat brigade,' fixed their gaze on the lower slopes.

"Keyser and I—hereafter designated simply as 'we'—reached the foot of the mountain as night set in, and, to our keen disappointment, found a dilapidated hut made of pine boughs; we had yearned to spread our skin-lined sleeping-bags under the starry heavens. (As it turned out, however, the roof of the hut was sufficiently starry, for the night was spent in receiving falling lumps of melting snow.) With the remnants

THE HUNTING PARTY.

of the walls we built two fires, one for the wild men, and the other for ourselves; while I boiled the coffee and the mush, Keyser fried the bacon and the spuds. For dessert we had raisins and chocolate.

"The rest of the evening we spent in council of war with our braves. With our clothes on, our guns by our sides, and our Colt six-shooters in our bags, we resigned ourselves to dreams of the morrow's chase, while the Ainus spread themselves around us like the crust on a pumpkin pie. The fires soon died out, and we were awakened about four in the morning by the murmurs of frozen feet, and passed the remaining wee small hours struggling between romantic sentiments and cold—very cold—facts. At half-past five the hairy men relighted the fires, and at six I jumped from my bag like a dum-dum from an automatic; I set the mush and coffee to boiling, and was soon followed by Keyser with the spuds and bacon.

"We decided not to wash for three days, for a bath is inconvenient with all your clothes on, and the Ainus considered it bad luck anyway. At seven we put on our snowshoes, and armed with a can of pork and beans, a biscuit, a flask of brandy, a kodak, a Winchester high power self-loading rifle, and a Colt six-shooter, we set out with one guide and one packman each.

"Our course first lay along the shore of the lake for about a mile, after which we entered the snow-laden pine forest, where each step through four feet of snow felt like a ton. After emerging from the majestic pines, we started the climb, now erect and now recumbent, until at last from the middle of the mountainside the country lay like a conquered army at our feet.

"'Where are the bears?' we asked. The Ainus pointed to the misty summit above us. 'Whew!' we said, and went on.

"The bears live in holes which are practically invisible, among the spurs of the mountain, and it is no easy matter to approach their lair. The attack is usually made under conditions that might easily give Bruin the first fall.

"At one o'clock we sat down on the spur beneath the peak and taking out our lunch we fletcherized the brandy, and fed the beans to the Ainus and the dogs. With our stomachs full, we clicked a charge into the chamber, with four reserves in the magazines, and scanned the horizon. 'A bear hole!' whined the Ainus—but alas, of last year!

XII : Bear-hunting among the Ainus

"We reached the summit; the day's work was done, but the bears were none the worse for it, so far. Separating, we commenced the descent, Keyser down one valley, I down another, reaching camp about six o'clock. I forgot to say that one of the Ainus shot a hare, which provided an entree for our menu that evening. The other courses were identical with those of the previous dinner, which happily relieved us from the necessity of mimeographing fresh bills of fare.

"At nine o'clock we were tired, but not discouraged, for our expectations had been fully realized. We aligned ourselves for the night, regardless of race or previous condition of servitude, and were soon oblivious of the crackling of the snow, for the thermometer continued to drop until the Hour of the Rat. The men of the wild snored, but it sounded like the murmuring of the pines, and only added to the romance.

"Next morning we were up again at six, and, after eating, set out with our previous equipment, except that we left our revolvers behind; we had discovered that they impeded the hip movement, and in the event of a race would leave us far behind the bear. Fearing that the animals would be intimidated by the size of our army, we decided to separate into two detachments, Keyser with his guide and packman and I with mine. He climbed one valley, and I another, with three valleys between us.

"My ascent was even more difficult than that of the previous day, but I went with a knowledge of what was before me. I ate two quarts of snow at each halt, and the anticipation of the next meal cheered me on. We reached a broad open slope just below the summit at one o'clock. The wind cut like a newly honed razor, but my alcoholic luncheon afforded me all the comfort of a winter hearth.

"The dog did not stop as usual to eat my pork and beans, but trotted up the glassy incline for a little exercise. In about five minutes he returned like an arrow from a bow, his tail seeking refuge between his legs, his voice pitched in a minor key.

"'Shut up, you fool!' growled the Ainu, thinking the pup had been frightened by a shadow.

"But the yearling only struck another key and continued his descent, evidently expecting us to follow. We decided to see whether there was any cause for his alarm, and followed his tracks to the side of a tree. The dog watched us from a safe distance, growling his disapproval. Lo and behold!—there was a circular hole in the snow, some six inches in diameter. The edge of the hole was brownish, and no more evidence was needed that the inmate was there and had already risen on his hind quarters to receive us.

"It had started to snow in thick flakes. There were no rocks on which to seek refuge, and the soft snow fastened us at each step. I stamped a foothold at a distance of seven feet from the hole—the nearer the safer, the Ainus said, for we could not afford to let the bear evade us. I was directed to stand sentinel, with the stock of the thunder-stick against my shoulder, while the savages, singing in their native dialect, ran down the slope to fetch a tree.

"They were soon back with a trunk about eight feet long, and took up their position above the hole. The old Ainu unfastened his girdle and tied it to one end of the pole, which he placed in the snow over the aperture. The guides had only one gun between them, and that a single-loader, so the young Ainu decided to go in search of a club in case my shot should fail to tell and we should be drawn into a fisticuff with the enemy.

"No sooner had the hairy youth gone than his square-jawed uncle pulled the girdle, driving the tree into the den just before Bruin's nose. Claps of ursine thunder followed. The beast rose to his feet with a heavy thud. Next moment the snow scattered as if raised by a snow-plow, and a broad head with flashing eyes and bared teeth emerged, and gave me a glance that ran down my back-bone. He had not got out beyond the shoulders, however, before I buried a .401 calibre soft-nose bullet in his left ear, and close on the tracks of that came a round lead ball from the savage's blunder-buss.

"My Winchester makes a deep impression on animal tissue at a distance of one hundred yards, deep enough to make a bear forget that he is alive, so the impact at a range of seven feet was tremendous. When the bullet struck the head it swung to the opposite side, as if hit by a fifty-pound sledge-hammer. There was a pause of fifteen seconds, and the huge form made another plunge, which was evidently the death struggle, but giving the advantage to the doubt I pulled the trigger again; there was no response, and I found that a bamboo leaf had choked the bolt. In about five seconds, however, I was able to restore the gun to working order by ejecting the cartridge in the chamber, and then popped two more peas into the waning intellect of the brute. The Ainu's lead must have gained admission, as he stood a foot nearer than I did, but we failed to locate

MR. ARNELL, AND AINUS.

it at the autopsy. My bullet—a pancake of lead with splinters of nickel-steel—was lodged in the right jaw, having passed through the brain from the left ear.

"The next step was to skin and quarter the bear, but before doing so my Ainus insisted on paying their last respects to the spirit of the departed—a spirit which was to hover over them for all time to come, for the moment my bullet entered the ear of the bear he had taken his place in the pantheon of Ainu gods. The savages spread his feet and placed his head in position, then they arranged several branches in a row before him, and kneeling on the snow, with bowed heads, they rubbed their hands and muttered fervent prayers.

"They prayed, 'O bear, we thank thee for having died! We humbly beseech thee to permit us to kill another bear as we have killed thee. We pray that this happy event may not be far off, and that when we meet thy brother or sister, thy aunt or uncle, or other kin, whatever his or her kinship may be, thy kin may not bite or strike us, and above all, dear bear, that he or she may not evade our poisoned arrow or our leaden bullet. O bear, we beseech thee to be always near, and to oversee our welfare in this land, where since the advent of the Japanese the number of bears is rapidly decreasing, so that we poor Ainus are day by day being deprived of the pleasure of our forefathers. O bear, again we thank thee for having died!'

"After the prayer meeting had closed the young Ainu crawled into the wintry home of the deceased. But the cub which we expected to take back to Tokyo was not to be found. However, on skinning the bear we did find two lead bullets which told the story—the cub had been killed the previous year, but the mother had escaped. It seems cruel to have taken her life, but when one knows that she had killed at least ten horses during her career, and would have continued to slaughter two per annum for the rest of her days had she been allowed to live, she forfeits the sympathy of the wise. The forests of Hokkaido are strewed with the bleached bones of horses taken from the pastures by marauding bears. Wherever we made our headquarters we were visited by owners of pastures, who were often accompanied by the Chief of Police or the provincial Governor, earnestly requesting us to come to their assistance.

"Having justified my act, I shall resume the story. The first part which the Ainus dissected was the stomach, which is dried and powdered

XII : Bear-hunting among the Ainus

and serves as a panacea for all ills; this was the occasion for a short prayer and was sanctified by repeated touching of the bear's nose. After the skin had been removed, the meat was cut into six portions and was buried in the snow until next morning. The skin itself was rolled into a scroll weighing about sixty pounds, and was placed on the back of the young Ainu. The head of the bear faced outward, and the packman looked like one of the itinerant showmen who used to ply their trade along the Tokaido in the days of the Shogun, with the mask of a long-nosed hobgoblin fastened to his back.

"We descended the mountain as if shod with skees and were soon crossing the lake on our way to camp. When the *menoko*—female children, a generic term for Ainu women—spied us at a distance of half a mile they burst into a weird chant, clapping their hands and jumping up and down, keeping it up until we reached the place where they stood.

"Keyser had already returned with an empty bag. The Major and Mr. Fenner joined us that evening, having deserted their camp after vain efforts to traverse the soft snow which covered the lower hunting-grounds, on which they had worked; later their *menoko* followed with their baggage. The evening around the campfire was very merry as we ate our bear meat and watched the Ainus perform their devotions.

"The ground had been cleared to make, a space for the altar. On this the bearskin was placed with the head pointing outward. Each Ainu knelt before the head, and as he rubbed his hands—now and again raising them to his forehead, after lightly touching the nose of the bear—be murmured a prayer similar to the one made on the mountain. One grey-bearded patriarch continued his fervent invocation more than five minutes, then, having finished, he knelt in front of me, and after a solemn salaam exclaimed, 'Hurrah, hurrah!' With this the introductory service came to an end.

"Meanwhile the barbarians had been boiling their bear meat and, the services over, they started to make way with it, their eating continually interspersed with rubbing of hands and mumbling of prayers.

"Next day Keyser and Fenner went out again in search of bear, but I decided to rest on my oars for one day, and so did the Major, who had become completely disgusted with the snow. We spent the day in talking and eating,—three meals on bacon and two on bear. All the comfort and luxury of a cozy home seemed to be concentrated between our mud floor and snow roof. At noon four carriers, who had gone up the mountain early in the morning, returned with their loads of meat.

"In the evening, after every one had assembled in camp and Keyser and Fenner had reported that no tracks of bear had been seen, preparations for the grand mass were begun. The Ainu to whom the hunting-grounds of the mountain belonged removed the hide and meat from the skull. Ordinarily he would have left the nose, but as I wished it for purposes of mounting he reluctantly consented to cut it off. The skull cleaned, it was placed on the altar.

"The ceremony then opened and continued for over an hour, every Ainu present taking part. While the mumbling of prayers, rubbing and raising of hands, and occasional touching of the missing nose, were going on, the cartilaginous soles of the bear's feet had been boiling, to the accompaniment of intermittent chanting by the women, and after being cut into two-inch pieces were arranged on sticks in front of the skull. After another invocation the elastic tid-bits were removed and eaten with much loud smacking. The meat was put through a similar ordeal, and the services were followed by a grand feast, which lasted till after midnight and was characterized by a great deal of mirth, despite the absence of distilled spirits, which the Chief of Police had prohibited. To us its absence was a blessing, but to the simple barbarians a curse, for they imbibe spirits as we drink water—in fact, it is the principal cause of the gradual extermination of the race.

"We went to bed before the dark-skinned Mohawks, but got up with them at sunrise. During the night sleet had begun to fall, and as we could not tell how long it might continue, we decided to break camp and re-cross the lake, as soon as we had seen the funeral services.

"The place chosen for the last rites was the top of a snow-covered knoll beside the camp, where a palisade was built of bamboos and fir branches, decorated with the ceremonial sticks with the skull of the bear in the centre. The men—for apparently the Ainu women do not take part in funerals—then proceeded to the place in a line, and arranging themselves before the palisade, invoked the spirit of the king of the forests in loud prayers, to the accompaniment of the usual rubbing and raising of hands. We were clicking our cameras meantime, which added a musical touch to the solemnity of the occasion, but the snow showed no traces of our tears.

KAGOS (SEDAN-CHAIRS) FOR MOUNTAIN CLIMBS.

"Ordinarily the skull is left on the palisade for years and years, but I needed it to mount the head of my trophy, so I negotiated with my guide for its surrender. He readily consented, but when the women learned my intention they made a terrible fuss, and with tears in their eyes begged me to leave their god undisturbed. I was finally allowed to take the skull, if I promised to see that it was not abused on the way to Tokyo, and if, after my return, I would have it placed on the altar of my parlour, paying it due reverence for all time to come. The parting between the women and the skull was quite pathetic, and would have moved a soft-hearted man to mingled emotions. I have fulfilled my promise, and the mounted skull now adorns the dais of my drawing-room, with its nose pointed toward all believers in the omnipotence of the bear.

"The services over, we shouldered our lighter baggage and started on our snowshoes across the lake, followed by the packmen. The ice had begun to melt in places, as the lake is full of hot-water springs, so we had to select our route with care. The women and the bearskin were left behind, as there was some sort of a memorial service still to be held, for which our packmen returned that evening. It was to have been a primitive bacchanalia, but as the Chief of Police had ordered the only two human habitations within miles not to sell any *saké* or *shoohu* to the worshippers, they must have passed a merry night on icewater.

"After crossing the lake we walked about five miles farther to a hot sulphur spring, where we were given a fairly comfortable room by the Japanese landlord. The hot springs were excellent, and we took three baths each, one for every day we had hunted. We woke bright and early to find the sleighs waiting to take us back to civilization, and contrary to our expectations, the Ainus appeared at the appointed hour with the skin. Paying them off, we bade them farewell until the scarcity of bear meat in Tokyo should necessitate our return. As parting gifts we distributed among them most of our remaining cans of corned beef, Boston baked beans, sweet corn and strawberry jam. From the manner in which the bear meat was treated by the recipients in the Capital, I fear we shall have to find some other pretext than its scarcity for revisiting the sylvan wilds of The Highway of the Northern Seas—Hokkaido. They said it tasted granular, and fed it to the dogs, cats and chickens!"

CHAPTER XIII

MOTORING AND CRUISING

PARTIES of tourists usually land at Yokohama, rejoining their steamer a few days later at Kobe. After a little sight-seeing in Yokohama they generally take a train to Kamakura and stop at the island of Enoshima. If there is time, they continue on to Miyanoshita. They take in Tokyo, Nikko, and Kyoto, with perhaps a few hours in each, and then go on to Kobe. In the limited time this all has to be done by train, which, in the present condition of the roads, is a quicker and surer method of travel than any other. *Kurumas* (jinrikishas) can be used for side trips, or *kagos* (sedan-chairs) for mountain climbs. Trolley cars are a convenience in the cities, and often take one to quite remote places in the country as well. The rates are lower than in the West, and special cars can be hired for a moderate amount.

For those who have longer to stay, the motor offers a delightful way of seeing the country as well as many opportunities for getting off the beaten track and having adventures. Because the roads are narrow and the bridges frail, the motorcycle, rather than the automobile, is after all the ideal method of travel, for it takes one into really out-of-the-way places which could not be reached in a larger machine. Of course this pastime is only for men, and for men who are willing to rough it, at that. If a woman is at all inclined to be nervous she had better not try motoring in Japan, even in a car, except on well-known roads.

The traveller with sufficient time at his disposal also finds various trips to be made by steamer, such as the one through the Inland Sea, which is described in this chapter.

Motoring is just beginning to be popular in Japan. Many of the roads are not bad except in spots, and the scenery is usually beautiful. During the rainy season the country roads are very disagreeable,—often almost, if not quite, impassable. Only in a city like Tokyo or Yokohama is it worthwhile for the resident to have a car the year round.

The best touring months are in the spring and autumn—in March, when the plum blossoms are finishing and the cherry blossoms beginning, and in April and May. In June comes the rain. The heat during July and August is very severe, then come the typhoons, and rain again in September. When the maple leaves are turning, later in the autumn, there is another happy moment for the motorist. Although the winters are not really disagreeable, there is a cold wind, and the Japanese inns are damp and chilly.

A short machine is necessary, as well as a skilful chauffeur, for the turns are often very sharp, especially at the bridges. These bridges, by the way, are treacherous and need to be strengthened for motor-traffic. They were built for the use of a 'ricksha or—at the most—for a horse and two-wheeled wagon. Gasoline may now be procured in many places, and road-maps are also to be had. It is important to take someone along who can speak Japanese, and to provide food for the trip, if one does not like the native dishes. Hot tea may be had almost anywhere.

In taking a motor trip one would naturally start at Yokohama. At first glance this city seems thoroughly Japanese, but, on knowing it better, I have found it to be in reality very European and not at all typical of the country or its people. It is rather a laughing-stock among the Japanese themselves, who call things "Yokohama" as a term of derision. Most foreigners live on the "Bluff," which overlooks the bay. Some of the houses in this section are fascinating, for they are surrounded by gardens and command wonderful views. Some glimpses of real Japan may be caught in the native quarter of the city, but coming back to Yokohama after having been into the interior gives one the impression of having left Japan behind.

A trip which is easy and comfortable for ladies may be made from Yokohama to Miyanoshita. It takes several hours each way, with a day added if one goes on over the Hakone Pass. L. and I took this trip while the plum-trees were in bloom.

From Yokohama to Kamakura much of the way was through the paddy-fields, which reminded me of trips on the narrow roads between the canals of Holland. We passed some strange new pagodas on a hillside, erected lately in honour of the Fire-God—a terrible creature carved on a rocky cliff and painted in colours. We also passed a succession of little places famous for the "plum-viewing," with their small tea-houses all

THE BUDDHA OF KAMAKURA.

ready for the viewers. There were camellia-trees in bloom, too, and the paddy-fields were beginning to show faint greens where the farmers were pottering about in the carefully cultivated land.

Kamakura is sunny and warm, by the sparkling sea. Many invalids go there, especially in winter—foreigners often rent the native houses. The big Buddha, surrounded by plum-trees, has twice been washed by tidal waves. The silvery branches with their white blossoms looked as if they had been sprinkled with snow, and the delicate perfume in the air was delicious. The Buddha is said to have stood there in the wind and rain and sunshine for seven hundred years. It is perhaps the finest large piece of bronze in the world; it has eyes of pure gold and a great silver boss on its forehead that looks like a full moon, while on its head are eight hundred curls. "These are the snails that kindly coiled themselves on Buddha's head when by thinking too much in the hot sun he might have been sun-struck."

We visited another shrine at Kamakura, where there is a huge trunk of cedar carved into a Kwannon—she is the goddess of pity and humility. It is said that once upon a time an illumination was seen over the waters, and on going to find out what caused it some fishermen discovered the figure of this goddess, carved in wood, which they brought ashore and set up for all to worship.

It is told of Kwannon that "in her boundless love she divided herself into many bodies and renounced the joy of Nirvana that she might bring peace and happiness to others." She is often compared to the Christian Madonna, and is considered the goddess of mercy, as well as the protector of dumb animals, especially of horses and others that work for man. She is variously depicted in Japanese art—sometimes with a thousand hands, in each of which is an answer to a prayer—sometimes with eleven faces, "smiling with eternal youth and infinite tenderness." A remarkable piece of embroidery which was brought to the Embassy to sell at a huge price showed Kwannon as the divine mother, pouring forth from a crystal vial holy water, each bubble of which contained a tiny child.

Osame told me that Kwannon was the daughter of a king of the Chow dynasty who sentenced her to death for refusing to marry. The executioner's sword broke without inflicting a wound, but her spirit went to hell, which, however, she straightway turned into a paradise. The king

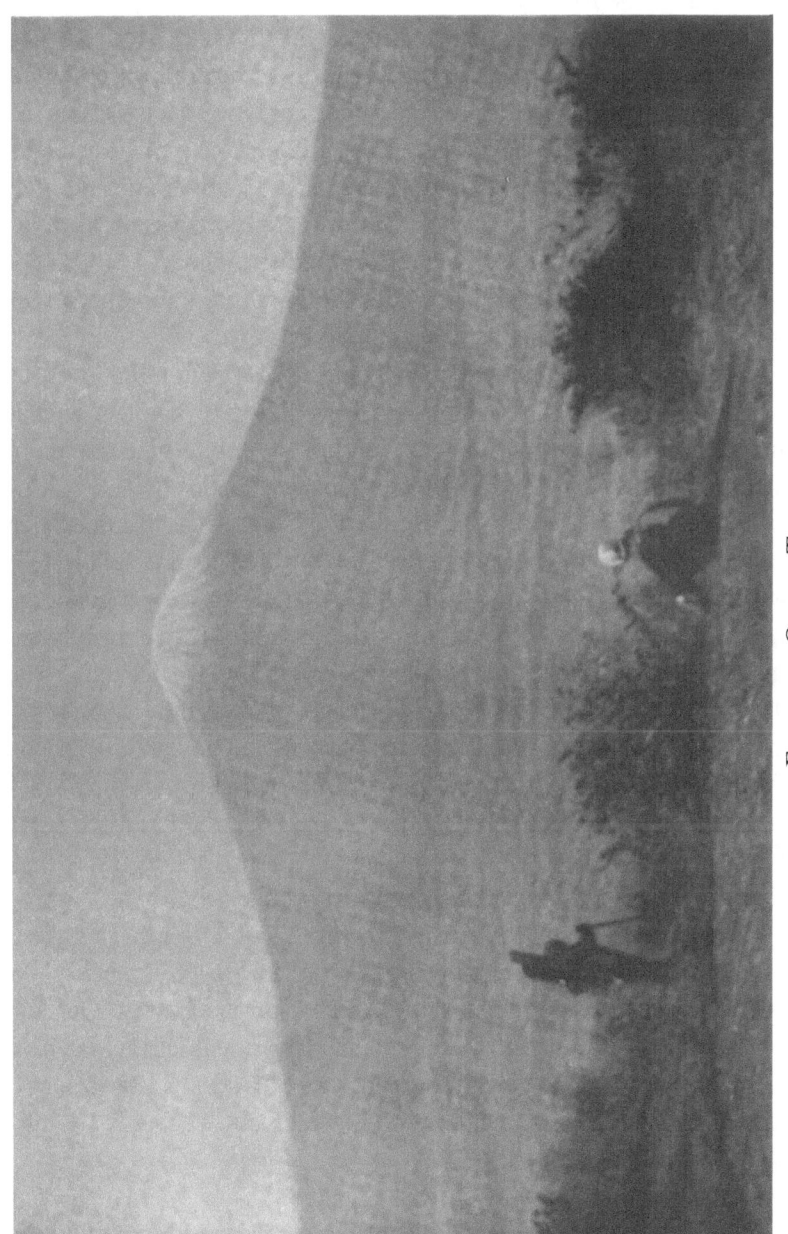

Fuji from Otome-Toge

of the infernal regions hurried her back to earth and turned her into a lotus flower on the island of Pooh-to.

While we were standing at her shrine, which is on the side of a pine-clad hill looking out over the sea, there came a sad funeral procession led by men carrying a big wicker birdcage. When I asked about it, Osame said that birds were kept in it and were set free at funerals to typify the release of the soul. There was the usual gold paper, and the coloured paper lotus flowers. The unpainted carved box, or coffin, shaped something like a palanquin, was borne on the shoulders of four men. The widow was clad in white, which is the mourning colour. Following the mourners came men, bringing trees and plants to set out on the grave.

En route from Kamakura to Miyanoshita we motored over the old Tokaido road—the great highway from Tokyo to Kyoto—with its crooked pines on every side and its views of the bright blue sea and of enchanting Fuji, so often represented in Japanese art.

On the way we passed the wonderful island of Enoshima. Here Benten, goddess of the sea, has her shrine, for the island is said to have arisen from the deep at her coming. She is one of the seven goddesses of luck, and is likewise referred to as the divinity of love, beauty and eloquence. It is customary for people who are in love, or for those who, on the contrary, wish to be divorced, to go to Enoshima and pray to Benten. She is said to have descended from the clouds and, entering a cavern where the sea king dwelt, to have married him out of hand. He was a dragon who devoured little children, but her good influence put an end to his sins. She is depicted as having eight arms, and as riding upon a dragon. Her shrines are generally found on islands.

I had always felt that Fuji was much overrated, but on this day it certainly wove its charm about me. Mayon, in the Philippines, is as beautiful in shape, but it never has any snow on its summit. Our own snow-capped Mt. Rainier is truly superb, but its shape is less symmetrical than Fuji's. Snow-capped and perfect in line, Fuji seemed to rise out of the sea in its mist, a great, beautiful ghost-mountain. Seeing it, I felt the Spell of Japan as never before.

So many things have been said about Fuji, and so many poems have been written, that it would be impossible for me to invent anything new in regard to it. It is called the "Supreme Altar of the Sun" and the "Never-dying Mountain." It is supposed to hold the secret of perpetual

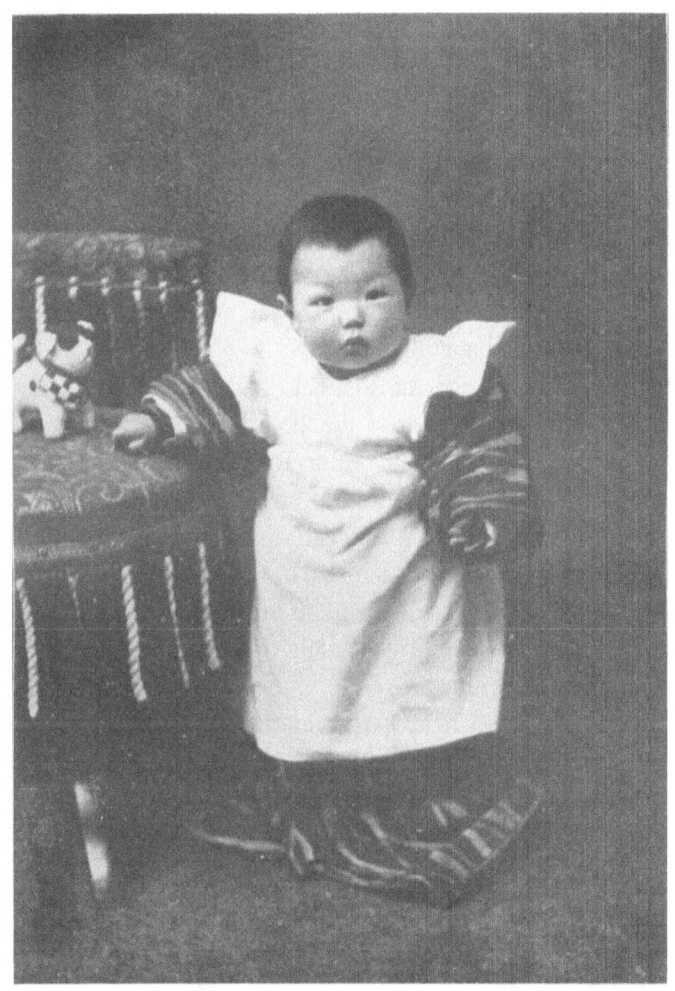

"LOOKED WISELY AT SOME PRESENTS WHICH WE HAD FOR HIM."

life, and miracles are said to have been performed there. It is likened to a white lotus, and to a huge inverted fan. Sengen, the fire goddess, and Oanamochi, "Possessor of the Great Hole," dwell there, while near the shrine of the God of Long Breath is a spring of healing for the sick.

Miyanoshita is one of the most famous summer resorts in Japan. It is two thousand feet above the sea, and is surrounded by mountains as high again. The climb up there in the motor went well; the air was fine and clear, and the hot sulphur baths at the hotel refreshed us. This hotel is excellent. It overlooks a beautiful valley, picturesque and green in the foreground, and shading off into that pale blue of distance which makes a Japanese panorama so complete. Around us rose high hills, ravined and grotesque, with here and there the roofs of tiny tea-houses peeping through the trees. As I looked from my window the tops of the mountain opposite were all big and grey, like elephants' ears. The view down the valley to the sea made me think of the wonderful Benquet Road in the Philippines.

In a tea-house garden near the hotel were many-coloured carp dashing about in the clear sulphur water. The long-tailed cock of antiquity is now rarely to be found, but there was one in this same garden, and also a minor bird which spoke quite as clearly as our parrot at home.

We went over the pass to Hakone. The road was difficult; the bridges were often shaky, and occasional small landslides delayed our progress. We were rewarded, however, by the sight of a charming lake some seven miles in length, with mountains stretching down into it, and Fuji-San beyond, hiding his lovely head in the clouds. The Emperor has a summer palace at Hakone, built in European style.

When we came down from Miyanoshita in the motor, it was a beautiful morning, and a beautiful ride it was, too, down through the valleys and out on to the plain, along the Tokaido with its avenues of cryptomerias, and across the paddy-fields.

I am told it will soon be possible to go by motor from Yokohama to Miyanoshita by another route—over the new military road when it is finished, across by Otome-Toge, and over the Hakone Range into the valley this side of Fujiyama to Gotimba.

Another trip from Yokohama is to Mishima. We did not try this ourselves, but the account of it given by a writer in the *Japan Magazine*, from whom I quote, shows some of the difficulties to be encountered on the road:

THE WONDERFUL AVENUE OF CRYPTOMERIAS.

"It was on the stroke of ten, on the nineteenth of April, when three of us, with a chauffeur, pulled out of the E. M. F. garage on the Yokohama Bund in the new twenty-five h. p. Studebaker. Kozu was reached at noon, and twenty minutes later we turned off the beaten track—from a motoring point of view—at the terminus of the Odawara-Atami light railway.

"Here the real interest of the day's run began. The road to Atami, though rather narrow, has a good surface for the most part, and runs along the coast, now almost at the sea level, now winding over the hills, from which a magnificent panoramic view of the Odawara Bay far below is obtained. From the heights the coast with its white line of surf can be followed by the eye beyond Enoshima on the one side, and on the other side a succession of capes, merging in the haze, end in the dim vista of Vries Island. A halt of some thirty minutes at a roadside rest-house near Manazuru to have lunch and enjoy the beautiful scenery passed all too quickly. Atami was reached at 2.30 p.m.

"So far the road presents no particular difficulties, but good care must be taken, and a little backing is required to get around two or three sharp turns. After a short halt to inspect the radiator and to see whether the tires were well inflated, we started on the long climb."

The motorist had gone over the road on foot, and it had seemed quite possible to negotiate all the curves without backing, but this did not prove true in actual test. The curves were for the most part of the real hairpin variety and came in such never-ending series that count of them was soon lost. On more than half of them it was necessary to back at least once, before getting round.

"Nevertheless," he resumes, "we were making good and steady progress until within about a mile and a half from the top of the ridge, when the gasoline began to get too low to reach the engine against the incline and the cant of the car on the turns. From this spot on, the last mile resolved itself into a trial of patience and muscle in manoeuvring the car round each corner to a sufficiently even—or uneven—keel for the gasoline to run to the engine until the critical point of each turn was surmounted. The last two corners were negotiated in the dark, with the writer sitting on the gasoline tank and the chauffeur blowing into it to force the gasoline into the carburetor. At eight in the evening we arrived safely at Mishima.

LAKE BIWA.

"Taking the above experience as a basis, it can be safely asserted that passengers on a motor car would not run any risk at all on this road, as there are no unprotected banks over which they could fall, as on the Miyanoshita road. It also makes one of the most beautiful trips out of Yokohama, for as one gradually rises above Atami the magnificent panorama of land and sea displays itself before one's eyes in ever widening circles. In our case we reached the Daiba Pass too late to enjoy the splendid view of the hills on the one side, and of the ocean with a fringe of foam along the shore down below, though the breakers could be distinctly heard."

We often motored from Yokohama to Tokyo. The road-bed is comparatively good, being hard and smooth, but it is very narrow, with constant traffic, and there are so many children running across that speed is impossible. Although the distance between the two cities is about twenty miles, the street is like one long village with its rows of houses on either side. It was endlessly interesting, with its procession of carts and wagons with their picturesque loads, and its groups of little, scurrying children in many-coloured kimonos clacking about on their clogs. There were continuous rows of small open shop-fronts with their wares set out in pretty array, and we had hurried glimpses of clean matted interiors and quaint gardens and temple entrances. Every now and then we would cross one of the queer, humped-up little bridges and look down upon the thatch-roofed cabins and high poops of the sampans congested in the river beneath. About an hour and a half is allowed for the run.

Once on this road we stopped at Osame's home—a perfect plaything of a house about two inches big, with an artistic bamboo fence and wicket, a tiny entrance-place, and little six-mat rooms. The wife prostrated herself repeatedly, and offered us tea and cake with many protestations which Osame translated. Their baby was brought in, and looked wisely at some presents which we had for him.

There are a number of one-day excursions from Tokyo for cars, and still more one- and two-day trips for motorcycles. The roads about Tokyo are good, but with a car one is likely to strike mires or bad bridges or ferryboats that are too small. These difficulties can generally be overcome, however, and they make the trip both varied and amusing.

A short expedition from Tokyo, and one comfortable for the motorist, is to the prehistoric caves—Hyaku Ana—near Konosu. These are some

XIII : Motoring and Cruising

two hundred cave-dwellings that have been uncovered on the side of a cliff. They have long, low entrances, and vary from tiny holes to caves ten feet square and high enough for a man to stand in. The pieces of jewelry and pottery which have been found there are small help in reconstructing the life of the troglodytes—"earth spiders," the Japanese call them—who may have lived there some thousands of years ago.

Another trip from Tokyo[8] is to the Boshu Peninsula. The tourist will have an excellent opportunity of getting a few glimpses of unfamiliar Japan without going very far afield. The road follows the seashore most of the way and offers a great variety of scenery—pine-clad hills, rice fields, pretty gardens, and fishing villages with the ocean breaking on rocky cliffs. There is little chance for speeding, as the highway is often narrow and passes through many tunnels with sharp curves, but the trip was made without any trouble by Mr. S.'s large fifty h. p. Clement-Bayard.

Mr. S. and friends started from Tokyo after tiffin, and spent the night at Inage, a small village two miles from Chiba, where there was a quiet inn. Next day, they drove along the coast southwest to Tateyama, which is a popular bathing resort, reaching there in time for tiffin. The views along the way, both of the hills and of Tokyo Bay, were very fine. They went on to Katsu-ura for the night, passing Mera, which is an important fishing village at the extreme tip of the peninsula, built on a cliff near a lighthouse. It was here that the *Dakota* was wrecked in 1909. Part of the way the volcano on Vries Island is to be seen.

Near Katsu-ura is the birthplace of the famous Buddhist saint, Nichiren. He was born in 1222 A.D., and became a priest at the age of fifteen. His doctrines being considered unsafe, he was sentenced to death, but the executioner's sword was broken by lightning, and orders came from the Regent to release him. Various well-known temples have been erected in his memory.

Next day the return trip was made by way of Ichinomiya, Hamano, and Chiba. The entire excursion can be made in two days, and with an extra day one could also take in Narita, which has a very interesting temple and is well worth visiting.

Mountaineering by motor is also possible in some parts of Japan. A successful trip was made from Tokyo over the Torii Toge not long

---

[8] For this, and several other notes on motoring, I am indebted to the *Japan Magazine*.

ago, although the road left much to be desired, being narrow, tortuous, and often washed away in places—between Azuma-Bashi and Narai it was especially bad. This pass gets its name from the massive granite *torii* at the top, and is over four thousand feet above the sea. The road over the Shiojiri Toge, which is thirty-four hundred feet high, is so well engineered that it was found possible to get to the top on middle gear. The views along the way are said to be of the finest, and the "Kame-ya" at Shimono-Suwa, a very comfortable hotel with natural hot baths and an obliging landlord.

One motorist found difficulty in garaging his car, and it had to be left under the wide eaves of the roof of the hotel. The ingenious landlord, however, borrowed a huge sheet of thick oil-paper and covered it all up snugly and securely from the weather, as well as from the attentions of a crowd of boys who had gathered round.

"I found the boys troublesome everywhere," this traveller writes; "they were not content to look, but must finger everything. On one occasion they turned an oil-tap and lost me half a gallon of precious oil which could not be replaced. . . . After this I tied up the oil-tap every night and took the wires off the accumulators, for on another occasion I found that a boy had switched these on." Such hints may prove useful to the prospective motorist.

The road from Tokyo to Nikko is good, except at one point, where it crosses a river. Next to Miyanoshita, this is the most popular excursion, for the temples are glorious and the hotel is good. We did not hear whether the road from Nikko to Chuzenji was passable.

The Japanese have a saying that you must call nothing beautiful until you have seen Nikko. L. says nothing is beautiful after you have seen Nikko. It is supreme, the climax. In 1889 he journeyed three hours to Utsunomiya, and then five hours by *kuruma* to Nikko, through the wonderful avenue of cryptomerias, with the foliage meeting overhead. This avenue is said to extend for fifty miles. When the temples at Nikko were being raised, some three hundred years ago, many nobles presented portions of them; but some, poorer than the rest, for their share planted these trees as an approach to the temples.

L. was not disappointed in going there on a later visit, for the great trees still stood solemnly above the gorgeous temples, and peace and religious quiet were to be found there as always. On the other side of

AMA - NO - HASHIDATE.

the rushing river, however, there was a change, for hotels and European comforts had been provided.

I am not sure whether one can motor from Tokyo to Fukushima or not, but, in any event, it would be worth trying. We went there on a former visit, staying at a Japanese inn, sleeping on mats in comforters. Next day we went on, part of the way by train, part by jinrikisha, to the "eight hundred and eight islands," the most fascinating place in the world. We took a boat and went in and out among the islands until we came to Matsushima, a little fishing town which is considered the first of the Sankei—"the three finest views in Japan"—on account of its exceptionally beautiful sea view. The islands are covered with queer, stunted pines, among which quaint temples are to be seen. Even now in the stillness of the night I can hear their bells, like a mysterious, musical moan.

The following condensed account of a trip by motorcycle from Tokyo to Kyoto and beyond may be of use to the traveller. The distance is about three hundred and forty miles. Three and a half gallons of petrol were consumed, which is more than would have been used if the second and third days' ride had not been in the teeth of a gale. The machine was a 2¾ h. p. twin-cylinder Douglas with free engine clutch and two-speed gear. A lightweight of this sort has proved most suitable for Japan, for there are dozens of occasions—lifting in and out of boats, up steps, pushing over stony river-beds—when one is glad of its lightness. One never wishes for more speed. Allowing time for rest, food, and casual stops, not over a hundred miles can be made in a day with any pleasure.

On this expedition the cyclist went by way of Kozu and stayed over a day at Shizuoka. It is fifty-five miles from there to Fukuroi, where he lunched, and then continued on to Maisaka for the night.

"From Maisaka," he says, "one can cross over the Hamano Lagoon to Arai by ferry, one can take the train over the bridge, or make the circuit of the lagoon. As there was a strong gale blowing the ferry did not put out, so this night was spent at Benten-jima, a pleasant little bathing resort at the mouth of the lagoon."

Next morning, he left Arai at nine o'clock. About two miles out there was a very stiff hill, which is frequently mentioned in pictures of Tokaido travel. The ascent commenced immediately after a sharp turn out of a village street, so that it was impossible to get a good start. The

ANCIENT TEMPLE NEAR NARA.

view over the sea from the top was splendid, however, and the run down to Toyohashi among slopes blazing with azaleas proved delightful.

At Atsuta, fifty-five miles from Toyohashi, the cyclist left the Tokaido and passed through one of the suburbs of Nagoya. This is the third city of Japan, Tokyo being the first and Osaka the second in size. It is famous for its potteries and especially for its castle, which has a keep typical of the ancient feudal times and often shown in Japanese art. The castle is in fairly good preservation and is one of the best specimens of architecture in the country. The central building is a massive structure one hundred and fifty feet high, surmounted by two golden dolphins, which may be seen from a tremendous distance glistening in the sun. One of them was exhibited at Vienna in 1873; on its way home it was lost with the ship, but was finally recovered at great expense.

After Nagoya, Kano was reached. Here one turns to the left, without entering Gifu, and proceeds along the Nakasendo—the great highway that connects Tokyo and Kyoto by way of the mountains while the Tokaido runs nearer the coast. Maibara, on the shores of Lake Biwa, was reached that evening at eight o'clock; from there it was a straight run to Kyoto.

Lake Biwa, the largest piece of fresh water in Japan, is about forty-five miles long. It is surrounded on all sides by hills and is supposed to have been produced by an earthquake early in the third century before Christ.

It is also possible to go from Tokyo to Kyoto by way of Atami, but it is not a very good trip. Those who try it generally get on the train at Kozu and get off again at Gotimba—a method much easier for a motorcycle than for a car, of course.

There are a thousand things to do and see in Kyoto, but if one is there in cherry blossom season one must not fail to see the glorious old cherry tree so widely renowned. Near it is the Mound of Ears. Osame told me that long ago, after a great battle in Korea, the returning victors brought with them their enemies' ears and noses, instead of the heads, to show how many Koreans they had killed. These trophies were buried in a mound to commemorate the battle.

A trip was made from Kyoto to Ama-no-Hashidate—another of the "three finest views"—by way of Suchi and Kawamori. For some miles the road out of Kyoto is bad; there is a long climb before Kameoka and

XIII : Motoring and Cruising

a steep, long, but well-graded pass between Sonobe and Kinokiyama. The whole of this day's journey lay through beautiful, well-wooded country with glimpses of the Yuragawa as one rode along its left bank, then over a splendid hilly coast road into Miyazu—a distance of about ninety miles in all.

The return was made by way of Shin-Maizuru, where one turns to the right after getting into the broad main street and soon reaches the coast again near Takahama. From there on to Obama the scenery would be hard to surpass with its views of the coast and of the wooded hills inland covered with azaleas, wisteria and other brilliant flowers. The road from Imazu skirts the western shores of Lake Biwa and is very narrow and bumpy until within ten miles of Otsu. Indeed, the roads, after leaving the coast, are often so narrow that there would be no pleasure in taking a car over them.

L. and I found most of the roads around Kyoto good. A few of them present difficulties, such as the one from Kyoto to Kamazawa, but from this point they are again fine, though many hills and dangerous spots are still to be met with. On a former visit we went in 'rickshas to the foot of these hills, passing green fields of rice and reaching the Harashiyawa River, which flows rapidly into the plain. We took a flat-bottomed boat and were towed and poled up the swift water between the steep, wooded banks, where it was very lovely. We had tea at a tea-house on the bank, and watched the fishermen in boats, and looked out over the pleasant landscape in the sunset glow of crimson and gold before the purple shadows fell across the plains.

From Kyoto to Otsu, which is on the shore of Lake Biwa, is about an hour's ride by rail. There one takes a small steamer up the lake to Nagahama, where, after a tiffin of carp with rice and *soy* at a tea-house, one may take a train again for Nara.

One may also go from Kyoto to Nara direct by *kuruma*—a day's journey. There are interesting temples to visit on the hillsides along the road—popular shrines where thousands of pilgrims with jangling staves, and holiday-makers taking tea and cakes, enjoy themselves simply in their beautiful surroundings. We passed among them, beneath the great gates guarded by fantastic demon gods, green and red and blue, and into temples, gorgeous but often dilapidated and dusty, past pagodas and through long avenues of stone lanterns. At Nara we saw the Golden

Pavilion and the Silver Pavilion, the summer places of retired princes. There are entrancing gardens with little ponds filled with goldfish, tiny bridges and imitation mountains, the "wash-the-moon" cascade, and the platforms where warriors used to sit and look at the moon—those fierce, two-sworded warriors of other days.

The old temples of Nara have stood there silently for over a thousand years, beneath the gaze of that huge, ungainly bronze Buddha who looks down with half-shut eyes, one hand held up in benediction, the other resting on his knee. He sits on his open lotus flower beneath the tall, solemn cryptomerias,—this wonderful Dai Butsu, the largest in all Japan.

We wandered through the groves and the park where the dainty wild deer are so friendly. On the hillside above is a temple to Kwannon, over a thousand years old, standing out from the dark green of the pines. Farther along is a Shinto temple, low and with galleries and many lanterns. Here we saw priests praying—shaven-headed *bonzes* in their robes—at whom pilgrims were tossing coppers. Beyond is the Wakamiya, where, for a consideration, some priestesses perform a dance called *kagura* while priests chant and play the flute and the tom-tom. As we went by, we saw a veiled priestess dancing there in true Eastern style. At the foot of the slope is a five-storied pagoda, black with age, for it dates back to the eighth century.

Nikko and Nara! The one a place of some three hundred years, gilded and coloured—the other ancient, and sombre, and impressive.

From Nara to Osaka you pass more old temples, where they say an eye of Buddha is secretly guarded. Osaka is sometimes called the Venice of Japan, on account of its many canals and bridges. The castle here must have been by far the most magnificent in the country before it was destroyed by fire. The moats and foundations that remain are splendid specimens of masonry.

From Kyoto to Kobe is a ride of two and a half hours in the train. The road skirts the hills which bound Kyoto, passes Osaka, and follows some rivers that flow higher than the level of the country—indeed, the road runs through tunnels under three large streams!

The terracing of the land is very marked along this route. Japanese methods of farming and irrigation require that the land shall be level, and so the country is all plotted off into little irregular terraces. The ground is saturated with water, which stands to a depth of several inches around the

A VIEW OF MATSUSHIMA.

growing crops. Paddy-fields are really ponds of standing water, while a farm is a marsh, the house alone rising above the surface. Farmers, while taking in their rice or plowing their fields, work with the water and thick black mud up to their knees.

Kobe is the foreign name applied to Hyogo, the treaty-port. It is next to Yokohama in commercial importance. The foreigners in Kobe—English, German and American—have a very pleasant club, and pretty bungalows on the hills back of the town. A beautiful waterfall and the Temple of the Moon are not far away.

Maiko, in the province of Harima, is one of the most enchanting spots in this part of Japan. It is near the upper entrance to the Inland Sea, not far from Kobe. Nothing can be more fairy-like and mysterious than the spreading, twisted trees on the white sand there in the moonlight. *Maiko* means dancing girl, and the place gets its name from the effect given the ancient pines when the wind blows the sand into shifting scarfs about them.

Lake Shinji, on the northern coast, is also one of the most interesting places in the country and one seldom seen by foreigners. Ogo-Harito is famous for its giant rocks washed by the sea into strange and fantastic shapes. It is the female spirit of the west coast, while Matsushima is considered the male spirit of the east coast.

If one has time, Yahakii should be seen, for it is a very strange valley with its enormous conventional terraces made by nature. At the bottom of the canyon is a swift river, and temples are perched here and there on high crags. Koro Halcho, in the province of Kii, is very beautiful, especially in the spring when the gorge with its deep cliffs is made lovelier still with wild flowers. A motorcyclist would find inviting trips in Hokkaido, where the roads are not bad, though it is rather difficult getting there. Over on the other coast, from Nazano to Navetta, and around Kamisana, there are good roads.

Our trip through the Inland Sea, from Kobe to Nagasaki, was one of the most delightful experiences that we had in Japan. We chartered a boat at Kobe, after an extravagant comedy of errors. L. went on board at midnight to examine it, and the agent did not discover until after the business was finished that it was not the boat which he intended L. to see at all; but the captain was too quick for him, and seized the opportunity to make a good bargain.

JAPANESE JUNKS

It turned out very well indeed for us. The steamer was of two hundred tons burden, one hundred and fifty feet long, with very comfortable cabins—two small ones in European style and one large one extending entirely across the boat, with mats in native style, where Japanese passengers may lie side by side on their comforters. We took our own supplies, and had a very good cook until he went off one night on a spree.

We went aboard one evening, and sailed at daybreak next morning, being awakened by the rattling of the chain and the churning of the propeller. Soon we were gliding out of the harbour between the shipping, just as the sun came up out of the Eastern Ocean, chasing the shadows down the hillsides and bathing the shore in a glorious crimson. We turned Hyogo Point and headed for Akashi Straits, to enter the Inland Sea, passing palisades like those on the Hudson.

All day long we went through the archipelago of green and yellow islands. At first the sea was glassy, then gently ruffled, and junks and sampans with queer sails glided by. Toward evening we passed into even narrower passages and straits, and the moon rose, all silver in the twilight sky, while we turned many times, now to the right, now to the left, finally coming to anchor off the twinkling lights of Onomichi. We landed after dinner and walked through the little town, then sat out on deck and sang in the flooding moonlight.

When we left next morning it was to pass more promontories on beautiful islands, lovely mountains rising behind, and picturesque shores fringed with tiny trees all green and purple in the haze. In the afternoon the clouds and rain that crossed our path only added to and varied the loveliness of the approach to Hiroshima.

During the day we had an unsurpassed panorama of Japanese scenery, with grotesque, broken islands fringed with pine, and ravined mountains dipping down into the calm blue waters, on which the quaintest and most unreal of sampans and junks were idly floating. We felt as if we were passing through a miniature ocean with its islands and old-world villages constantly appearing and disappearing in the rising, shifting mist. No wonder the Japanese believe in ghosts and in Bahu, the Eater of Dreams!

As the sun went down we rounded the enchanted island of Miyajima—the third of the "three finest views"—and glided into the bay before the famous temple. When it grew darker the four hundred lanterns of bronze and stone along the water's edge were lighted for us.

THE GREAT *TORII*

The Spell of Japan

The temple itself is built on piles, and the *torii* stands far out from the shore. We were sculled across the still waters in a sampan. The tide was at its highest, and the hundreds of little lights were reflected in its glassy surface. Slowly we drifted beneath the great *torii* to the temple entrance. Once more the Spell of Japan stole over us.

The sunrise next morning was too beautiful for words. We appeared to be coming out from a rosy dawn into a grey, dim future, as the sun came up through a pearly mist and the little clouds rose in wreaths about the tops of the strange mountains, making pictures such as the art of Japan loves to depict. Tiny straw-sailed boats appeared and disappeared mysteriously. It was all very silent and lovely.

Later in the day we climbed the hill behind the temple, then came down and bathed, having tea at a delightful little tea-house, taking tiffin ashore beneath the tiny-leafed maples near a brook; we went aboard in the late afternoon, and, hoisting anchor, steamed away.

Next morning we saw the sun rise at Moji. We passed Shimonoseki and then steamed out into the China Sea, keeping the picturesque shore of Kyushu in sight all the way. We picked our course through the outlying islands and the swirling straits of Hirado, and reached Nagasaki late at night. Contenting ourselves with one look at its twinkling lights, we retired. Morning showed us once more its beautiful harbour, the mountains range on range behind it, and the city itself on either side, the houses rising above each other on long terraces to the summits of the hills on which Nagasaki is built.

Near us a big ship was coaling—a wonderful sight to one who beholds it for the first time. It was surrounded by countless barges upon which were swarming crowds of Japanese—men, women and children. Forming a long line that reached from the barges up a ladder into the ship's hold, they handed baskets of coal from one to the other, so that a continuous stream poured steadily into the ship. The strangeness of the costumes, the unusual sight of women doing a man's work—many of them with babies strapped to their backs—added to the interest of the busy scene. Down in the hold, where the heat must have been suffocating, they plodded on, men and women, clad chiefly in coal-dust. All day long they worked away with happy smiles, the babies bobbing up and down on their mothers' backs, doubtless wondering what it was all about. The sight reminded me of the passage in the Æneid, where the poet speaks of the ants as "tiny toilers of giant industry," and describes them carrying crumbs in their mouths to the common storehouse in a seemingly never-ending line.

As we steamed out of the harbour, the green hills rose steeply from the water with houses and shrines peeping through the trees, backed by a still higher range of hills which were finally lost in the blue distance or broke off into crags and cliffs.

Chapter XIV

FLOWERS, INDOORS AND OUT

"If one should inquire of you concerning the spirit of a true Japanese, point to the wild cherry blossoms shining in the sun."

The poet Motoori.

THE Spell of Japan owes no small part of its potency to the abundant flowers, which weave about the land an ever-changing veil of bright colours and exquisite textures. First appear the fragrant plums, earliest of the "One Hundred Flowers," and the freesias, and the wonderful display of cherry blossoms in March and April, then the wisteria and azalea, the iris and the peony, "the flower of prosperity"—in China it is called "the queen of flowers"—in July the lotus, and in the autumn the chrysanthemum, "the long-lasting plant." Of all these the cherry and the chrysanthemum are the most famous.

The plum, an emblem of chastity, is enjoyed chiefly by the intellectual. There is only a breath of flower on the gnarled stock, a mystery of white or pink or red, which requires close study to find delight in the manner in which the blossoms scatter irregularly on the beautiful, twisting branches, silvery with lichen.

This charming little poem by Sosei refers to the plum as the herald of spring:

"Amid the branches of the silv'ry bowers
The nightingale doth sing: perchance he knows
That spring hath come, and takes the later snows
For the white petals of the plum's sweet flowers."

The cherry, being gayer and more profuse, is more popular with the people. It is called "the king of flowers," and especially represents abundance and vitality. It is therefore a fitting symbol of the national

XIV : Flowers, Indoors and Out

population. When the cherry is in blossom, the Japanese make excursions to view particularly beautiful trees, and as they feast and float in their pleasure boats, they enjoy even the fluttering petals, whether seen in the bright sunlight or the pale moonbeams. So high an official as a Prime Minister will take a day's journey for the sight of a cherry tree in bloom.

A Japanese of the olden time has beautifully pictured the blossoming cherry trees: "When in spring the trees flower, it is as if fleeciest masses of cloud faintly tinged by sunset had floated down from the highest sky to fold themselves about the branches."

The wisteria is an especial favourite with foreigners, no doubt for the reason that we seldom see in America drooping clusters of such length— the length of an umbrella, as the Japanese measure. It is believed that this flower attains great size and beauty if the roots are nourished with the rice wine of the country, and there is at Kameido a tree producing unusually fine blossoms, at the base of which visitors are accustomed to empty their wine cups.

Everyone is familiar with the beautiful and varied colours of the Japanese iris, as the bulbs are shipped to all parts of the world. The peony often measures nine inches across, and some of the tree peonies have petals of a lovely silky sheen and texture. It is sometimes called "the plant of twenty days," because it is said to keep fresh for that length of time. In art, it forms a constant decoration on temple and palace walls, and it is supposed, like the lotus, to have medicinal properties.

The lotus is not used for festivities or rejoicing in Japan, but for sacred ceremonies and funerals. As it is a Buddhist flower, and as Buddhism started in India, it is sometimes called the national flower of India. It grows wonderfully, however, on the castle moats in Tokyo.

In its season the chrysanthemum pervades the country. It blossoms in every garden, it grows by the roadside, and it stands in every tiny shop. Each loyal son of Dai Nippon has a flower upon which he may rest his eye and with which he may delight his artistic and patriotic sense. The sixteen-petalled flower is the crest of the Emperor, and no one else is allowed to use that as a design, although the blossom is often reproduced in decoration with fewer petals. The people go on pilgrimages in order to gaze with semi-religious awe upon "the long-lasting plant;" the Emperor gives a chrysanthemum party; and the season of this most decorative of flowers is made one of general rejoicing.

A Japanese Flower Man

XIV : Flowers, Indoors and Out

The chrysanthemum has been cultivated in China for more than two thousand years, says Dr. Bryan in the *Japan Magazine*, and there is evidence of its being cherished in Egypt a thousand years before it is mentioned in China. "Whether it came from Egypt to China, or vice versa, it is impossible now to determine, but the Chinese like to regard it as a product of the Far East. Confucius mentions it in 500 B.C., under the name of *liki*. From China it was brought to Japan, where it has reached its highest development.

What the lotus was to Egypt, the fleur-de-lys to France, and the Tudor rose to England, the chrysanthemum is to Japan. The flower is single, yet many. It is a unity in variety, and a variety springing from one undivided centre. The Japanese call it "binding flower," for just as its petals bind themselves together on the surface, so the Emperor and the people are forever bound together in indissoluble union. It was probably chosen as the most natural and artistic emblem of the sun, but both this and the cherry blossom, like the Emperor and his people, are considered children of that luminary, whose orb resplendent stands for the country as a whole. Many a maiden of Japan is named after "the binding flower," and its use is very typical of Japanese art and life.

At one chrysanthemum show we saw nine hundred blossoms on a single plant, and the flowers were arranged to form figures of warriors and ladies of long ago, from the fairy tales of Old Japan. At Dango-zaka, a place of professional gardens, an exhibition is held each year, for which visitors are charged two *sen*[9] a peep. Here we saw wonderful figures made of flowers—one of an elephant and his rider being thirty-six feet high. In the grottoes and rockeries of the garden were other life-like figures. It was a sort of "Madame Tussaud's" with the characters in flowers instead of wax. On revolving stages were rocks and mountains, horses and men in all sorts of attitudes, brilliant, curious and interesting—all made of flowers. One scene represented Commodore Perry's reception by the Shogun.

The Imperial Chrysanthemum Party has been in vogue at the Japanese Court since 1682.[10] Formerly, as the guests came before the Emperor, a vase of lovely blossoms, to which was attached a bag of frankincense and myrrh, was placed in front of His Majesty, and cups of

---

[9] A *sen* is three-fourths of a cent.
[10] For this description, also, I am largely indebted to the writings of Dr. Bryan.

saké with the petals floating in them were handed around. In the annals of China we read the explanation of this custom:

There was once upon a time, as the story goes, a man who was warned of an impending calamity, which could be warded off, he was told, by attaching a bag of myrrh to his elbow and ascending a certain hill, where he was to drink *saké* with the petals of the chrysanthemum floating in it. The man did as was suggested, but on returning home he found all his domestic animals dead. When he informed his teacher that the plan had not worked, the former replied that the calamity was to have come upon his family, and that by acting upon the warning he had averted it, throwing the vengeance on the animals instead.

The Emperor's Chrysanthemum Party is now conducted in a somewhat different manner from that of the olden time. It is held in the flower palace of the Imperial garden at Akasaka. Upon the arrival of the Emperor and his suite at the main gate, the Japanese national anthem begins, and the guests, who are already in their places, line the pathway on either side, bowing as Their Majesties, the Emperor and Empress, and the princes of the blood, file past. Then the guests fall into line after the Imperial party and follow to the place where the feast is prepared.

The Emperor takes his place on the dais at the head of the marquee, and receives all the representatives of foreign countries and some of the higher officials of the Empire. As each diplomat appears in the Mikado's presence he bows three times, and his felicitations are translated into Japanese by an interpreter who stands near His Majesty. The Empress is seated on a dais slightly lower but very near, and all who approach the Emperor bow also to the Empress. This function over, the Emperor sips a glass of wine, which is the signal for the feast to commence. As soon as the feasting is ended the band strikes up, and His Majesty begins to prepare for his departure. The guests again line up, and bow in farewell as the Imperial procession files out, then they enjoy the view of the superb chrysanthemums.

The Imperial Cherry Blossom Party in the spring is held in the same garden at Akasaka, and is conducted in much the same way, an elaborate feast being laid in a great marquee. The palace in these grounds originally belonged to Prince Kishu, but after the burning of the Emperor's palace in 1873 this one was used as a temporary abode of the Imperial family, and was afterward the residence of the Crown Prince, now Emperor.

XIV : Flowers, Indoors and Out

In the province of Kai there is a hill called Chrysanthemum Mount, overhanging a river into which the petals fall. It is believed that long life is assured by drinking the water. Among the people the custom also survives of placing small blossoms or petals in the cup during the wine-drinking that takes place at the festival on the ninth day of the ninth month.

The Japanese fondness for flowers is not bestowed chiefly on the rare and costly varieties produced by the florist's skill, but are lavished upon the familiar blossoms of every day. Love of nature is shown in their pilgrimages for seeing flowers, picking mushrooms, gathering shells, and even for viewing the moon, which form their favourite holiday excursions. One of the prettiest conceits of the Japanese imagination is that which regards the snowflakes as the flowers of winter, and has added snow-viewing to the list of flower-festivals.

Parties are even formed to rise at dawn and go out to see the morning-glories open. I can testify, too, from my own experience that they are well rewarded, for Japanese morning-glories are worth seeing. One day when our train was delayed at a village, the station master invited us to view the morning-glories in his tiny garden, about twenty feet square. The colours were so beautiful that they were really a feast for the eyes. Some were pale in tint, some brilliant, and some had crinkled flowers and leaves.

Among the Japanese popular names for plants are some interesting ones. The tufted grass that grows on the hillsides has the delightful name of "lion's moustache." The barberry, which grows wild in Japan as it does here, is popularly styled "snake-can't climb-up," on account of its thorns, the idea being that the snake wants the berries, but the thorns keep him off. The little pachysandra, sometimes used here for borders in gardens, bears the high-sounding title of "noble plant." We are surprised at this until we discover that it is very hardy, adapts itself to any surroundings, and blossoms under the unfavourable conditions of early spring. Because of these qualities, rather than for anything striking in its outward appearance, it is called noble. It is also a symbol of good luck, perhaps in recognition of the fact that a person's good fortune comes chiefly from his hardihood, adaptability and power to overcome obstacles.

On one of our visits to Japan we imitated the fashion of the country and made pilgrimages to view the lotus, which was in full bloom in July,

IKE-BANA OR FLOWER ARRANGEMENT.

XIV : Flowers, Indoors and Out

its pink and white blossoms almost covering the waters of the ponds. Again in the autumn, we went on excursions to enjoy the charming colours of the maples. Often we took jinrikishas and went to an inn by a rippling brook, where we spent the day, eating the native food with chopsticks from little lacquer trays, and looking out from the balcony of polished wood upon the bright, sharp-pointed leaves dancing in the sunshine.

At the various festival seasons of the year, different flowers and plants are used, either alone or in combination with others. For instance, the pine and the bamboo appear among New Year decorations; the iris is the flower of the Boys' Festival; fruits and berries are used on the first day of the eighth month. Such occasions as the coming of age of a young man, a promotion in rank, farewell gatherings, death anniversaries, poetry meetings, tea ceremonials and incense burnings, all are adorned by their appropriate flowers.

Japanese flower arrangement differs fundamentally from that of the West, and includes much more than the mere massing of a cluster of blossoms of beautiful colour and texture, set off by a sufficient number of leaves of some kind. *Ike-bana*, as they call their art, considers the flower as a mere detail and of little beauty apart from its proper place on the stem. In addition to grace and beauty of line and an entire absence of crowding, it requires the expression of the thought that what you have before you is not simply cut flowers but a growing plant—which must always have an uneven number of branches. Buds and even withered leaves are used as well as flowers, in order to suggest the natural mode of growth. By keeping the stems together for a few inches at the base a strong plant is indicated, springing from the surface of the water, which is supposed to represent the surface of the earth.

As we learn the rules of *Ike-bana*, we do not wonder that it has been the study and diversion of philosophers, generals and priests. The three branches with which the arrangement starts are named Heaven, Man and Earth. Heaven, the longest branch, must be one and one-half times the height of the vase and must stand in the centre of the cluster. Man should be one-half the length of Heaven, and Earth one-half as long as Man. These sprays are bent into the desired curves before they are placed in the vase. Finally, but with great care, every leaf or flower that hides another must be ruthlessly cut off.

"THE TABLE DECORATIONS... ARE ESPECIALLY INTERESTING."

XIV : Flowers, Indoors and Out

By the use of special flowers and the varying disposition of the sprays the season of the year or the particular occasion for which the arrangement is designed may be indicated. For example, unusual curves of the branches suggest the high winds of March; white flowers are used at a housewarming, or they signify water to put out a fire; evergreens or chrysanthemums are used when a youth comes into his property, to express the wish that he may long keep his possessions.

Following out the Buddhist idea of preserving life as long as possible, the Japanese make their vases with a wide mouth, so that the water they contain may be exposed to the air. This makes it necessary to support the branches, and various kinds of holders have been devised for this purpose. Both vases and holders are made of basket-work, porcelain, bronze and bamboo, and according to their shape they are called by such names as "Singing Mouth," "Crane Neck," and "Rampant Lion." Hanging baskets in the form of boats, too, are popular, and receive names like "Cloud Boat" and "Dragon-head Boat." In summer low, shallow vases are used, which suggest coolness by the extent of water surface exposed.

According to the law of *Ike-bana*, vases should be nine-tenths filled with water in spring and autumn, in hot weather they must be brimful, in winter only four-fifths full, and even less in very cold weather. Pebbles may cover the bottom of the vase in imitation of a river-bed, both white and black ones being used. An effective arrangement is to place three large stones on top of the small ones—quite a high rock to represent a mountain, a second flat one, and a third between the others in height.

The Japanese love to decorate their houses with flowers, but we might say on entering, Where are they? Why, in the most honoured place of all! On the raised platform of the alcove, perhaps beside the image of some god, stands a large vase with a few carefully arranged branches of flowers, or maybe of leaves alone. These are enough. You feel no need of anything more.

The table decorations made for Europeans are especially interesting. They are often placed directly on the tablecloth. One that we saw contained a conventionalized Fuji in evergreen needles, like a flat print, overhung with cotton wool to imitate clouds. Sometimes miniature landscapes are formed in a box, for anything tiny delights the Japanese, and they spend whole days arranging such things. The Inland Sea is often represented in blue and white sand, with real earth for the shores and the islands, while small pine branches are introduced to look like twisted trees. Boats and fishes are put in the blue sand, and small temples set up on the shore. As every imaginable toy is made by the Japanese, the scene can be varied according to the taste of the designer—I have even seen tiny European ladies imitated, and railway trains and telegraph poles introduced.

In the miniature landscapes which Watanabe devised for us he used dwarfed trees in almost every instance, and imitated water and waterfalls with sands of different colours. For the Fuji of these pictures he sometimes used one of those oddly shaped pebbles that abound in Japan.

On Washington's Birthday Watanabe surpassed himself in this sort of decoration. He represented Washington City by a diminutive Capitol and White House and Washington Monument, set in a park-like arrangement of gravel drives and avenues of tiny trees. Among these appeared absurd little equestrian monuments and decorative detail of various kinds. As he had never been in America we asked him how he had pictured it so correctly. He answered that he found a photograph of the Capitol in a book, and took it to a friend, who made models of the buildings for him. He also had arranged a large cherry tree (which, because it had artificial flowers, appeared to be in full bloom), into which the proverbial hatchet was stuck.

The Japanese art of landscape gardening arose from their fondness for nature, which led them to reproduce in miniature the scenery visible from their homes. No doubt Chinese influence had its effect upon this art, as upon many others, through the medium of the Buddhist priesthood.

Among the earliest examples of landscape gardening were the temple groves of Nara. From the twelfth to the fourteenth centuries gardens took on a freer form, more like that of the present time, but the dried-up water scenery was used, showing the hollow of a lake dry, as if in time of drought, sometimes combined with the bare mountain. In the fifteenth century, when the tea ceremony was introduced, a special form of garden was devoted to its use, while at the same time the art of flower arrangement flourished. Soami, about 1480, and Enshiu, a hundred years later, are among the best known landscape artists. "The Rocky Ocean," "The Wide River," "The Mountain Torrent," and "The Lake Wave" are fanciful names given to different styles of gardening.

A Japanese garden is generally enclosed by a bamboo paling, often in some pretty design, which may surround the house as well. There

XIV : Flowers, Indoors and Out

should be one high point in the garden, which dominates the whole, and it may contain a miniature mountain, dwarf trees, stones, and a tea-house with a gateway at the entrance. If possible, there should be water with a bridge over it, and a cascade to bring luck.

From the varying arrangement of these features, we find hill gardens, flat gardens, finished, intermediary or rough gardens. On our place in Brookline, Massachusetts, we have a Japanese hill garden. The flat effect is especially popular in Japan, with its gravel walks and stone lanterns in different sizes and designs; but whichever style is chosen, it must be so planned as to present its best appearance from the house.

No garden is complete without one or more lanterns, which are placed, if possible, by the water, that their light may be reflected in the pond. The stone basins for washing the hands vary in style, and so, too, do the gateways; these sometimes have thatched roofs, which provide shelter, and can be made very attractive. There are twisted dwarf trees here and there, of course, and variously shaped stepping-stones set in regular order along the narrow paths. Low bridges, usually without railings, cross the tiny pond, in which there are often double-tailed goldfish and carp which rise to the surface when you clap your hands. Some enclosures even contain gaily coloured pheasants, ducks and storks.

Curiously shaped stones are carefully selected for the garden, each one having a name and a meaning attached to it. Standing upright in the centre should be the high "guardian stone." You may look for the "worshipping stone" in the foreground or on an island; you will find the "perfect view" on the hillside or in some prominent place; you discover the "water-tray stone" on the pond shore, and the "shadow stone" in the valley between two hills. Next to the "worshipping stone" is the "seat of honour," which is flat and horizontal. The "snail" is the most important stepping-stone.

Trees as well as stones have rank in the miniature landscape. The principal tree is the largest, and is as a rule either a pine or an oak. One in a secluded corner with thick foliage to afford shade is called the "tree of solitude." The "perfection tree" should have fine branches. Around the waterfall is planted the "cascade circuit," consisting of low bushes; and in the background is the "setting-sun tree," which is turned westward in order to screen the garden somewhat from the rays of the sun, and is often a maple that will light up the place with its own glow in the autumn.

A Japanese Garden, Tokyo

XIV : Flowers, Indoors and Out

In the literature of gardens we read of male and female cascades and rocks—just as of male and female styles of flower arrangement—the big one being the male, the smaller one nearby the female. The flowering tree is also considered a male, the plant in the same pot a female.

The dwarf trees, that looked so strange when we first saw them, soon became to us one of the delightful features of gardening in Japan. These, as well as the gardens themselves, originated in the love of nature, the Japanese wishing to have about them reduced copies of trees which they admired. As the demand for these pigmies has greatly increased in recent years and the process of dwarfing is slow, Japanese florists have discovered a way of making them by a speedier method. When they find old, stunted trees that have taken on unusual shapes—those that have become gnarled and twisted by growing among rocks are especially good for this purpose—they cut them back very closely, root and branch, then leave them to grow for a time in the soil. After this they take up the plants carefully without disturbing the earth immediately about the roots, and place them in pots. Trees even one hundred years old have been successfully treated in this way.

But this is not "real dwarfing," which was described to me by my Japanese gardener. For this process, if you wish to keep the tree very small, it is raised from seed sown in a pot. After the seedling has made the growth of the first year, it is taken up, and the earth is carefully shaken off the roots and replaced with soil adapted to the special needs of the tree, which is allowed to grow for two or three years. Then it is time to begin trimming it into shape, and here the same symbolic arrangement is followed as in *Ike-bana*, based upon the three main branches, Heaven, Man and Earth. Root-pruning must also be started after the growing season is over, and the larger roots cut away, leaving only the finer ones. If the branches run out too far in one direction, their growth is stopped by cutting off the roots on that side. A tree that is to be kept very small is not repotted until the roots have filled the pot; one that is to make a larger growth is transferred at an earlier date. By scraping off the top of the soil occasionally and putting on fresh earth repotting may be postponed for eight or ten years according to the kind of tree.

Dwarf maples from seed are ready for sale in two or three years; seedling pines require from five to ten years to fit them for the market, and plums four or five years. Lately, however, it has become the custom to graft the plum, cutting back the tree until only a contorted old stump is left, and grafting upon this. We had two such trees at the Embassy, which were simply old stumps filled with plum blossoms, one cluster pink and the other white, diffusing their perfume all over the house. They were very beautiful with a plain gold screen for a background.

All kinds of evergreens, oaks and maples, the plum and some other flowering trees, bamboos and every sort of flowering shrub, and some vines, such as the wisteria and the morning-glory, are all used for dwarfing. Plants having thorns are never treated in this way, neither are they used in the decoration of shrines nor in real Japanese flower arrangement. For this reason the large, fine roses in which we take such delight, had never been cultivated in Japan until perhaps forty years ago, when the first one was brought from Holland, and the method of cultivation was also borrowed from the Dutch.

In gardens, these diminutive trees are carefully shaded from the rays of the afternoon sun, and special pains are taken to keep them well watered. When the temperature is above ninety degrees, they are watered three times a day—at eleven in the morning, and at two and five in the afternoon. If they are used as house plants, the care of them is a dignified occupation, in which even nobles and princes may engage in their own homes. As the use of ordinary fertilizers might be disagreeable to these exalted personages on account of their bad odour, a pleasant and economical way has been found of supplying the small quantity of nourishment needed from eggs. After an egg has been broken and the yolk and the white removed, the shell, with the small amount of albumen that adheres to it, is taken in the hand and the broken edge touched here and there to the soil of the pot, leaving on each spot a tiny drop of white of egg. This process, repeated from day to day, furnishes the little tree with all the nutriment it requires. Milk is also sometimes fed to these plants by the Japanese, who have discovered that it gives brighter colours to the flowers.

We visited a charming exposition of pigmy trees in Shiba. Many gentlemen of Tokyo had sent their tiny plants and miniature vases, *hibachi*, lacquers, books and jades to decorate the doll-house rooms. These playthings are in many cases of great antiquity and value, and lovely in quality and colour; as much pains and taste are required to arrange these little expositions as to decorate the large rooms of a palace.

XIV : Flowers, Indoors and Out

On account of our visit the gardener had taken particular trouble, and he showed us all the fairy articles with loving hands and words. There were microscopic trees an inch high and landscapes two inches long, which were a real delight, so exquisite were they. Such trees are really works of art, and some of them indeed as valuable as gems. About us, in pots of beautiful form and colour, were the dwarf trees of fantastic shape—stunted plum in fragrant bloom, white and pink, and gnarled trees hundreds of years old with blossoming branches springing out of seemingly dead trunks.

The Arsenal Gardens in Tokyo are said to have been formerly the most wonderful in the country. Kora-kuen, their Japanese name—literally translated, "past pleasant recalling,"—probably means "full of pleasant remembrances." They were designed some three hundred years ago with the object of reproducing in miniature many of the most renowned scenes in the Island Empire. In front of the pavilion, however, is a lake which is copied from a noted one in China called Soi-ko. Beyond the lake rises a wooded hill, on which stands a small, beautifully carved replica of the famous temple Kiyomisu at Kyoto. Lower down the hill is a little stream spanned by an accurate copy of the well-known bridge at Nikko; further on is the shrine of Haky-i and Shiky-sei, the loyal brothers of Chinese legend. An arched stone bridge leads to still another shrine, and from this a path through a thicket of creepers conducts to a lake covered with lotus and fed by a stream which forms a lovely cascade. Another path crosses little mountains through thick foliage of bamboo and pine, passes the artificial sea with its treasure island in the centre, and leads over bridges, by waterfalls and around temples.

In these gardens the Japanese most perfectly realized their desire to transfer the features of a natural landscape to their immediate surroundings; here were magnificent trees of great size, lakes and streams and mountains in miniature, and a wide jungle of grass and bamboo. Through the noise and dust and dilapidation due to the encroachments of the Arsenal workshops, one can still catch a glimpse of the underlying plan and imagine the ancient beauties of Kora-kuen.

Chapter XV

THE ARTIST'S JAPAN

"The great characteristic of Japanese art is its intense and extraordinary vitality, in the sense that it is no mere exotic cultivation of the skilful, no mere graceful luxury of the rich, but a part of the daily lives of the people themselves."

Mortimer Menpes.

AT every turn of the head the artist in Japan discerns a picture that delights his eye—a quaint little figure dressed in bright colours standing by a twisted tree, a fantastic gateway through which he sees a miniature garden, or the curving roof of a temple, half hidden among the trees.

As architecture is always more or less affected by climate, the Japanese, in their land of earthquakes and typhoons, have put up low wooden structures, using cedar or fir principally, because they are plentiful. The laws require that houses shall not exceed six *kin*, or fathoms, in height, but allow warehouses, or *godowns*, which are more substantially built, to be carried up much higher. If by any chance a house has two stories, the second is very low. When I asked the reason for such a law in China, where they have a similar one, I was told the wind gods did not like tall buildings, but I was also assured that it was partly to keep missionaries from building high churches. In Japan, I think it is probably on account of the danger of earthquakes.

Owing to the rainy seasons in spring and autumn, the houses have no cellars and are set on low piles. The summers are very warm and the winters are fairly cold, so the *shoji*, or sliding screen, without windows, was no doubt developed for that reason. Every house can be thrown open in summer and closed tightly in winter. As fires are frequent, no house is expected to last many years, and therefore the Japanese store their valuables in fire-proof *godowns*.

XV : The Artist's Japan

The "Flower of Yedo" blossomed gloriously the other night, for hundreds of the tiny fragile houses went up in smoke, and thousands of people were made homeless. These Flowers of Yedo are the conflagrations that time after time spread through wide districts of the Capital with startling rapidity and leave nothing behind. Two days after the fire, little houses and fences of fresh new wood were springing up, for the people have been accustomed from time immemorial to these "Blossoms of the Flower."

In olden times the roofs were covered with thatch, but the danger from fires is so great that this has been replaced on many houses by tiles. In China it is said that the fashion of curving the roofs of buildings originated in order that the devil, when sliding down over them, might be tossed up again; in Japan, there are also curving roofs and—in the interior of the country—upon the outer walls there are drawings of the god Jizo, who carries a large sword in both hands to ward off misfortune.

In Japanese dwellings the kitchen is at one side of the front door. The rooms seldom have more than one solid wall, the others consisting of paper screens. In this solid wall there is always a *toko-noma*, or alcove, raised about a foot above the floor of the room and perhaps two feet deep. It should stand opposite the entrance, and is the most honourable place in the house. Here, where the *kakemono*—a perpendicular, panel-shaped picture—is hung, and a rare porcelain vase of flowers may stand, is the seat of honour. At one side of the *toko-noma* is a cupboard—the place for the "honourable" book—and above this is a drawer where the writing-box is kept, also the wooden pillow. In some houses a square hole is found under the mat, in which a fire is built for warmth or for cooking purposes. Where there are none of these "fire holes," prettily decorated jars of charcoal, called *hibachi*, are used.

The *shoji* is often adorned with paintings or made of beautiful carved wood. The hammered brass, the lacquered and polished wood, and the superb ceilings add much to the beauty of the homes of the rich.

Wood carving, both inside and out, is such a feature of the houses as well as the temples that it deserves mention here. At the entrances to fine places and also on the slanting roof over the doorway of the house itself superb carvings are often seen. So many designs and colours are introduced, especially on temple gates, that full scope is given to the

A CARVED PANEL.

XV : The Artist's Japan

imagination and taste of the artist. The famous cat, for instance, on one of the gates at Nikko, is so wonderfully carved and so life-like that it is said to frighten the rats away. Bahu, the Eater of Dreams, and the phoenix and other imaginary animals also appear in Japanese wood carving.

Temples are built on rising ground because the people believe that the gods are pleased with high places. The old castles and temples are finer architecturally than other buildings, the former, which were built upon hills or beside great rivers, being extremely picturesque. They are many-storied, pyramidal structures, with curving roofs and gables projecting over each story. The buildings generally stand in three enclosures, each surrounded by a wall or moat, and cover a large extent of ground. The innermost, chief castle, is a large, square tower, three or four stories high, in which lived the lord in feudal times. The gentlemen of the household dwelt within the second enclosure, and in the outer one the soldiers and servants had their quarters.

In the erection of castles and pagodas which have stood for many centuries, the Japanese have shown not only their skill as architects but also their knowledge of the principles of construction. Castles and the sides of moats are built of huge blocks of stone, some of those at Osaka being over thirty feet long and fifteen feet high, but the walls, slanting from base to apex, are really pyramids, which are supported within and bound together by enormous timbers.

Among the most interesting of these old structures are the castle at Nagoya and that at Kumamoto, in Kyushu; the castle of Himeji is the most perfectly preserved. Kumamoto was built in its present fashion in 1607, and in the Saigo rebellion of 1877 it held out successfully against a large force of rebels, showing no lack of strength in its construction. The castle at Osaka, one hundred and twenty feet high and commanding an extensive view over the River Temma and the surrounding country, was once the finest fortress in the East, but has since been partially destroyed in various sieges.

Pagodas—which are really towers with a series of curving roofs—are very striking in appearance and most artistic. Some of them have stood for seven hundred years or more, and many of them are kept upright by an exceedingly ingenious device. In the centre, suspended from the top by one end, hangs an immense log, the lower part of which is surrounded

THE CASTLE OF HIMEJI.

XV : The Artist's Japan

by four other logs of the same size, firmly bolted to it. The base of this enormous structure is about an inch from the earth at the bottom of the pagoda, so that it forms a mighty pendulum, which in case of earthquake sways sufficiently to keep the building stable.

When we discover that in Japan every person is an artist, we wonder at the universal deftness and skill in handiwork, until we learn that Japanese calligraphy is itself a fine art. Every character is an exercise in freehand drawing, each stroke of the brush, which is filled with India ink, being made by a quick movement of the forearm without support for the wrist.

The methods of Japanese painters are very different from those of Western artists. They begin work with a burnt twig, often on a piece of prepared silk, afterward using the brush with India ink and water colours. Each one values his own special cake of India ink very highly. They do not draw directly from the object, but study it for hours in every detail, and then draw from memory. After a picture is well thought out, its execution may require only five or ten minutes.

Japanese artists have conventional types of beauty, as the Greeks had. A woman must have a forehead narrow at the top, eyebrows far above the eyes, eyelids scarcely visible, and a small mouth. A man should have greatly exaggerated muscles, and arms and legs placed in almost impossible attitudes. Their pictures abound in bold, sweeping lines—the touch of power—and perhaps for that reason, they have great admiration for Michel Angelo's work.

Although we may know the colour prints of the Japanese better than their paintings, it is nevertheless true that their leading painters rank among the great artists of the world. Pictures were painted for the aristocracy; the colour prints, which cost but a trifle, were made for the common people. Painting was introduced into Japan by Buddhist priests, and some of the finest masterpieces are shut up from the world in the temples of Buddha. Many of them, however, have been reproduced in the beautiful series of wood cuts published by the Japanese Government. America has two collections of the original paintings which are finer than any in Europe—that in the Boston Museum of Fine Arts, and the Freer collection in Detroit.

Painting, as a fine art, has existed in Japan for twelve centuries. The oldest picture recorded is said to have been done on the wall of a temple at Nara in the early part of the seventh century. The ninth century was the first great literary and artistic era of Japan, when Kanaoka lived, who is called the greatest master in the whole history of Japanese painting. His works included not only Buddhistic figures but also animals, landscapes and portraits.

Tradition has it that the peasants in the neighbourhood of a certain Buddhist temple were greatly troubled on account of the havoc wrought in their gardens by the nightly visits of some large animal. Setting a watch, they discovered the intruder to be a magnificent black horse, which took refuge from his pursuers in the temple. They entered, but no horse was there, except one superbly painted by Kanaoka. As they stood beneath the picture, drops of sweat fell upon them—the horse was hot and steaming! Then one of the peasants caught up a brush, and painted into the picture a halter which fastened the horse to a post. This was effective; he never again foraged in the peasants' gardens.

The earliest purely Japanese school was the Tosa, which originated in the tenth century. A glorious artistic period covered the three centuries from the eleventh to the fourteenth. It was in 1351 that the great Cho Densu was born, who has been styled "the Fra Angelico of Japan." By some critics he is ranked with Kanaoka himself. Although he was a Buddhist priest he did not confine himself to religious subjects, but was equally great in other lines.

The Kano School was founded in the fifteenth century. This was the period of the masters of landscape painting, among whom Sesshiu is the most famous. His landscapes are full of grandeur and dignity, but it is said his figure paintings must be seen before his power can be appreciated. He went to China for study, but to his disappointment could find no artist who could teach him anything he did not already know. Then he said, "Nature shall be my teacher; I will go to the woods, the mountains and the streams, and learn of them." As he travelled through the country in carrying out his purpose, he found Chinese artists came to study with him. The Emperor of China engaged him to paint a series of panels on the walls of the palace in Peking, and on one of them, as testimony that the work was done by a Japanese painter, he depicted the peerless Fuji.

In the seventeenth century arose the Ukioye, or Popular School, of which Moronobu and Hokusai were the great artists. They are perhaps even better known for their prints. The Naturalistic School, more like

XV : The Artist's Japan

European work than that of the earlier artists, was founded by Okio in the eighteenth century. To this group belonged Ippo, a fine landscapist, and Sosen, one of the famous animal painters of the world, particularly known for his pictures of monkeys.

Yosai, who died in 1878, was the last great Japanese painter. He studied in all the schools, and combined some of the best characteristics of each. Since his death there have been clever painters but no great artists.

Like many other things in Japan today, her art of painting is in the transition stage. There are two schools, the conservatives, who cling to the art of ancient days, and the progressives, who believe that they must borrow fresh conceptions from the Western masters, and feel that want of reality has been a defect in the old Japanese work. However, in copying Western methods, they are introducing vulgar subjects, from which Japanese painting has generally been free. At the art exhibitions of 1913 there were ninety-three who entered oil paintings; this alone shows the great change in their work. While the Japanese painters of today cannot escape the influence of European art, it is to be hoped that they will not lose the delicacy of treatment, the subtle suggestiveness, and the grace and sweep of line that belonged to the old masters.

To my mind the most interesting things for Europeans to collect in Japan are the prints, which first came in vogue about 1690. The Japanese have, in these, added a charm quite their own to every thought which they have received from other nations. The conditions under which the artists worked in olden times were most favourable, for they lived under the protection of the great *daimyos*, were supplied with the necessities of life, and were free from care.

Mr. Keane, of Yokohama, is an authority on old prints, of which he has made several collections. "We lunched one day with him at his home in the upper part of his office building on the Bund, in Yokohama. (When foreign merchants first went to Japan they always lived over their places of business.) The view over the sparkling harbour and away off to the horizon, where little fleets of slanting-sailed sampans were working their way up the Bay of Yedo with the sunlight striking their sails, was really superb. Mr. Keane stores his prints in a safe, but for the enjoyment of his guests he took them out on the day of the luncheon. They were so much finer and more interesting than the common, every-day prints of the dealers that they quite took our breath away.

VIEW OF MOUNT FUJIYAMA.—PRINT BY HOKUSAI.

XV : The Artist's Japan

Of American collections, that of Mr. William Spalding, in Boston, is particularly good, including, as it does, some beautiful rare figures in black and white by Matabei, the father of the Ukioye school of painting, from which the art of colour printing is derived. Mr. Spalding has hand-coloured prints by Moronobu, some of which are in orange-red and old rose. In some cases the paper of the old prints takes on a beautiful yellow autumn glow with age, which adds to their beauty. The colours yellow, black, orange and green were introduced about 1765. For the orange-red and old rose red-lead (*tan*) was used, hence the prints of this kind were called *tan-ye*, and are of great value today. Moronobu was a wonderful draughtsman, and his figures in black and white are greatly prized.

Masanobu and Kiyonobu were prominent among the early artists, but the perfection of technique in prints was reached under Kiyonaga.

Utamaro, who became the leading print designer of his day, lived in the latter part of the eighteenth century, when the art of making these wood cuts was at its best. Unfortunately his whole life was a career of dissipation; his father disowned him, and he was finally put in prison for libelling the Shogun. Soon after that, his health gave way, and he died at the age of fifty-three. Toward the end of his life, however, he was so popular and so overwhelmed with commissions that in his endeavour to fulfill orders his later work degenerated. Utamaro's style was copied by his pupils, and his signature was so often forged that it is difficult to pick out his prints. His chief works were pictures of *geishas*, in which the long lines of the kimonos are much admired. His were the first colour prints to reach Europe through the Dutch.

Toyokuni was another master of the same period, whose favourite subjects were actors in character. In this sort of print and in his technique he was unsurpassed.

Hiroshige—two of whose pupils took his name—lived at the beginning of the downfall of Japanese colour printing. He was a prolific worker, and his wood cuts are delicate and seldom show strong contrasts. He is especially noted for landscapes, and did views of the Inland Sea, of snow scenes, and of mists and rains, in very delicate pastel colours. Eight famous views of Lake Biwa, as well as several sets of the Tokaido, were done by this artist. Heads by Sharaku with a silver background are very striking, and have lately become the rage in Paris. They certainly have strength and individuality, but they are hideous beyond words. He was especially fond of doing actors, and the faces are full of expression.

Hokusai, whom Whistler called "the greatest pictorial artist since Vandyke," is placed by European critics at the head of all colour-print designers, but in Japan is considered second-rate. For one reason, the Japanese cannot forgive the vulgarity of some of his subjects. We might well apply to him the name given to the school of art of which he is the best example—Ukioye, "Mirror of the Passing World." He was born in 1760, and started as an engraver, but became a book-illustrator at an early age. At eighteen he went into the studio of Shunsho as a pupil, but his work was so original and so unlike his master's that he was soon expelled. After that, he was so poor that he peddled in the streets of Tokyo.

Later, Hokusai collaborated with the successful novelist Bakin for many years. The famous set of prints of a hundred views of Fuji, the series of the waterfalls of Japan, the noted bridges, the scenes in the Loochoo Islands, as well as the views of the Tokaido, were all done in the latter part of his life. Hokusai used strong colours, and produced fine work. He was most unfortunate in having all his original studies destroyed by fire, and as he was careless about money matters he died in poverty. Just before his death—in 1849—he said, "If fate had given me but five years more, I should have been able to become a true painter."

Entirely green and entirely red prints, I was told, were rare. I never saw but one wholly green print in Japan, but that sold for a small sum, so perhaps I was misinformed as to its value. I was also told that the prints entirely in red were made to amuse the lepers in olden days, so were destroyed afterward, hence few exist, but as I find some collectors never heard of this story, again I am in doubt. The triptychs are particularly valuable today. The long strips—the pillar prints—were made for the poorer classes, the *kakemono* for the nobles. Both paintings and prints are usually in one of two shapes, either the *kakemono*, or long scroll, or the *makemono*, the horizontal picture. The former are not framed, so they can easily be rolled and stowed away when not wanted for decoration.

The blocks on which the prints were engraved were made of cherry wood, both sides of which were used for economy's sake. The design on thin Japanese paper was pasted on the block, face downward, then the wood was cut by the engraver. Black ink was used in the first stages of the reproduction. Proofs were then taken by hand-pressure and pasted on other blocks, one for each colour. "'Each of these colour-blocks was then cut in a manner to leave a flat surface of the correct form to receive the pigment proper to it; and the finished print was the result of a careful and extraordinarily skilful rubbing on all the blocks in succession, beginning with the key block.'"[11]

Some of the great Japanese painters designed prints, others did not. Often it is difficult to distinguish by whom a print was designed, notwithstanding the signature, because artists sometimes gave their own name to their favourite pupil. For this reason and many others, beware of the print-dealer.

The highly developed artistic sense of the Japanese has found expression in various ways, but their deftness and delicacy of touch has led them especially to the production of small objects that delight the collector of curios. There is the *netsuke* in endless variety; the *inro*, or small medicine chest; the ornamental sword-hilt; minute wood carvings; besides bronzes and porcelain in shapes innumerable.

Collectors will show you with great pride their *netsuke*. These were worn as ornaments attached to the cord of the tobacco pouch to prevent it from slipping through the sash. The *inro* and the pocketbook were also worn in the same way. The oldest and most valuable *netsuke* were made of the heart-wood of the cherry, which becomes a rich brown colour with age, and some were beautifully carved.

A very old wooden *netsuke*, which was presented to us, represents the goddess Uzume-no-Mikoto, popularly known as Okame. She was so beautiful that she could not be pictured. As it was impossible to reproduce her charms, a face was chosen to represent her that in no way was a likeness, but was sufficiently individual never to be mistaken. She is made very fat in the cheeks, and sits in the shade of a mushroom.

Netsuke are also found in ivory, bone and jade. Many are images of gods and goddesses, and some are humourous figures. A beautiful ivory one that was given us is in the form of a turtle, which signifies long life, but on the underside is one of the seven gods of luck with his shiny bald head.

During the sixteenth and seventeenth centuries the *inro* was worn as an ornament, and no man of taste would consider himself well dressed

---

[11] Quoted from Mr. Arthur Morrison, in J. F. Blacker's "The ABC of Japanese Art."

without it. This led many of the great artists to design them. Among the well-known inro artists were Jokasai, Iizuka and Saiihara-Iehidayu, but there are so many others who are noted in Japan that it is impossible to give them all here. Some of the finest specimens of their work are found today in the Imperial Museum in Tokyo. Many of these are of lacquer, minutely and exquisitely carved, those in gold lacquer and dark red being the most valuable.

There are lacquer vases and boxes, too, but the fine old lacquers are not easy to get nowadays. Writing-boxes, some of which are in charming designs, are also much in demand for collectors. Some of our writing-boxes are of deeply carved old red lacquer, depicting houses and landscapes. One is of gold and black with tinted maple leaves, exquisite in design. Another has a background of speckled gold, on which are dwarf cherry trees with blossoms of enamel, and still another of gold lacquer is inlaid with mother-of-pearl.

Sculpture, like painting, was brought to Japan by Buddhist priests, and many of the earliest statues were figures of gods and goddesses. These were usually of bronze or wood, not so often of stone. As early as the seventh century fine bronzes were cast at Nara, and over a hundred altar-pieces of that period are still in existence in Japan. To a somewhat later age belongs the colossal Buddha of Nara, the largest statue ever cast in bronze. The Great Buddha of Kamakura, rather smaller but of finer workmanship than that at Nara, is believed to date from the thirteenth century.

Old bronzes are much sought after by collectors, the best dating from the seventeenth century. Vast numbers of gods and goddesses and mythical animals were made of small size to be set up in houses as well as temples. Among these some of the Buddhas and Kwannons are fine. Buddha has many attitudes—sleeping, exhorting or meditating—and all are interesting.

Temple-lanterns, candlesticks, bells and incense-burners were also made of bronze in forms showing great wealth of imagination. The beautiful old bronzes are of several kinds—gold and silver, and many shades of green and brown. The gold bronze takes on a wonderful polish, and can be made in different colours according to the proportions of the metals used in the alloys, varying from a deep-blue violet to a red-yellow or a golden green. The silver bronze has a fine silver-grey tint.

XV : The Artist's Japan

These metals are also used in combination with gold lacquers and with mother-of-pearl and silver, or are encrusted with charming relief designs in enamels.

In the entrance hall of our Washington house is a huge green bronze Buddha, at least ten feet high, with tight curls upon his head, half-shut eyes, and the big ear-lobes, which signify longevity. In the bronze halo about his head are small figures of Kwannon, and Chinese characters decorate his garment. With one hand uplifted, he sits serene and imperturbable, cross-legged on his lotus flower.

Not far from the Buddha is a bronze Kwannon about five feet high, a gracefully draped figure, standing on a large petal of the lotus. About her neck are jewels, and behind her crown is a small image of Buddha, typifying her ever-present thought of him.

We also have a shrine that we prize greatly—a modern shrine, perhaps five feet in height, such as is found in a Japanese gentleman's house. The exterior is of black lacquer, but when the folding doors are open, the interior is seen to be golden. In the centre stands a small Buddha; the wise men—his advisers—sit cross-legged on either side. The carving in this shrine is slightly tinted in colours, mixed with gold, and is indescribably fine and beautiful. A *No* dance is depicted for the entertainment of the Buddha, above which are palaces, people and animals, supposed to represent scenes in heaven. On either side hang two bronze lanterns. On the table before the shrine are the ceremonial utensils, consisting of an incense-burner, two flower vases, and two candelabra. Below is a gong for the devotee to strike, in order to call the Buddha's attention, and nearby is the box containing the holy books.

In feudal days the *samurai* went into battle clad in breast-plate and helmet, gauntlets and coat-of-mail, all of which were adorned by the armourer's skill, but the most beautiful decorations were lavished upon the sword—"the soul of the *samurai*." The *shakudo*—sword-hilt—is a curio that people collect. The inlaying and overlaying and blending of metals that was done on arms and armour in olden times was marvellous, and even the metal-work of today is remarkably clever. Besides the sword-hilt, there was the sword-guard, a flat piece of metal, often in exquisite designs.

Pottery from Korea and porcelain from China, of course, had some influence in Japan. The Japanese are considered very fine potters, perhaps the best in the world, and their old ware is highly prized. The handsome old pottery made in Kyoto and also that of Bizen are much valued by Japanese collectors, and the work of such famous men as Nomura, Ninsei, and others is highly esteemed. Old Imari and Arita wares are considered choice, as well as Satsuma, but all of them, especially Satsuma, are much imitated today.

The Arita, a blue ware, is thought very pretty, but not until after German methods were introduced did it attain perfection. The Seto porcelain, made in the Tokugawa Period, is very well known. Kutani is especially popular in America, and Awada ware is also in demand in the foreign market. The cream-white made today in Kyoto is particularly attractive. Neither the ancient nor the modern Japanese porcelains, however, compare with the old Chinese, some people even going so far as to say that the only things in the Far East worth collecting are old Chinese porcelains.

Incense-burners are made in porcelain and bronze, and are beautifully modelled in the form of gods and goddesses, and of birds and other animals. Curiously enough, besides their office in worship, they were used in playing a game, which consisted in guessing the name of the perfume that was burning.

There are attractive lacquer and porcelain *saké* cups to collect, and so many charming modern things that I will not mention any more, except the wonderful crystal balls, so clear and mysterious that they quite hypnotize you if you look into their depths. The legend called "The Crystal of Buddha" seems to show that these balls were originally introduced from China. I insert the story here in order that we may always be reminded of the delightful mythology of Japan as well as of the treasures of the land. In a few words it is this:

A beautiful Japanese girl became the wife of the Emperor of China. Before she left Japan, she promised to send back three treasures to the Temple of Kofukuji. The Chinese Emperor found her very charming and loved her very much, and when she told him of her promise, he put before her many curios to choose from. She finally decided upon three fairy treasures—a musical instrument which would continue to play for ever, an ink-stone box which was inexhaustible, and the last, in Madame Ozaki's words, "A beautiful crystal in whose clear depths was to be seen from whichever side you looked, an image of Buddha riding on a white elephant. The jewel was of transcendent glory, and shone like a star, and whoever gazed into its liquid depths and saw the blessed vision of Buddha had peace of heart for evermore."

But alas! while the treasures were on their way to Japan, there arose a terrible storm, during which the crystal ball was stolen by the Dragon King of the Sea. A poor fisherwoman at last found it shining in the depths of the ocean. While in bathing, "she suddenly became aware of the roofs of the palace of the Sea King, a great and gorgeous building of coral, relieved here and there with clusters of many-coloured seaweeds. The palace was like a huge pagoda rising tier upon tier. She perceived a bright light, more brilliant than the light of many moons. It was the light of Buddha's crystal placed on the pinnacle of this vast abode, and on every side of the shining jewel were guardian dragons fast asleep, appearing to watch even in their slumber." The fisherwoman stole the jewel, but it cost her her life. In reward for her bravery her son was brought up as a *samurai*, so the wish she had most at heart was gratified.

Chapter XVI

SAYONARA DAI NIPPON

AT the close of the last administration, L. resigned his post, and with real regret we prepared to leave the Land of a Million Swords. We had experienced nothing but the pleasantest relations with the Japanese, nor had we at any time heard of rudeness to Americans.

The day we sailed L. was besieged with people who came to say good-bye. Among those who called were Mr. Sakai and Mr. Yoshida, for the Foreign Office. Mr. Matsui, the Vice-Minister of Foreign Affairs, brought us a superb basket of flowers, while Mr. Nagasaki, Master of Ceremonies at Court, presented us with some orchids from the Imperial greenhouse.

Best of all, as we thought at the time, Mr. Baba, Master of Ceremonies to the Empress, came with a magnificent gold lacquer box from Her Majesty. .We received him in state in the parlour, and with much ceremony and repeated bows he presented the gift, accompanying it with many pleasant messages from the Empress. In return we bowed and expressed our gratitude for the great honour, speaking of our love for the country and our deep regret at leaving, and adding that we should always have the happiest memories of our stay in beautiful Japan. The most gratifying token of appreciation, however, has come to my husband since his withdrawal from the diplomatic service. This is the grand cordon of the Order of the Rising Sun, First Class, conferred in recognition of his efforts to promote friendly relations between this country and Japan.

Many people telephoned to know by what train we were leaving, but we decided to slip away to Yokohama in the motor. We looked for the last time at the Embassy, with its pretty garden, where we had been so happy, and getting into the car were shot out of the porte-cochère and around the circle, waving good-bye to some of the Staff and the servants who stood bowing at the door.

XVI : Sayonara Dai Nippon

At the Consulate in Yokohama L. joined Mr. Sammons, the Consul-General, and went to a luncheon at the Grand Hotel given in his honour by the Asiatic and Columbia Societies, which are composed of the American colony. All joined in drinking his health and in wishing him a pleasant voyage and a speedy return. In answer L. said that during his all too brief stay in Japan he had come to realize the great cordiality and hospitality of the American community in Yokohama and other cities, and this realization made it all the harder for him to say farewell. After adding that each visit to Japan only made him like the country better, he closed by saying that while he was about to cease to be officially the Ambassador from one country to the other, he yet looked forward to being in the future, unofficially, an ambassador between the two, and hoped that he would soon see many of those present at his home, where they would always be welcome.

I went to Mrs. Sammons' luncheon, where she had several ladies as guests. The table decorations were exquisite, in Japanese style. After luncheon Mrs. Sammons took me in her motor to the wharf, where we found L. waiting for us with a number of people who had come to see us off. Everybody cheered as we boarded the launch, which took us to the steamer; there we found baskets of flowers, candies, books, and other gifts awaiting us.

In a few minutes the big ship began to shake and the water to rush by, and we knew that we were off. Soon the sun, a great red disk—fitting national emblem of Japan!—went down in the glow of the dying day. Above the darkness, which settled on earth and sea, rose the mysterious cone of "O Fuji-San," seeming detached from all that was earthly below, a divine spirit of a mountain-top, which slowly disappeared as the night filled the heavens with stars.

As I sat in my steamer chair I had time to think again and again of the land and the people we had left behind. I remembered with pleasure the pretty, gentle women with their laughing, almond-eyed babies riding happily on their mothers' backs, and recalled with admiration the Spartan men, so loyal to their country. Closing my eyes I seemed to see the quaint little streets, lined on either side with paper houses, in front of which gay toys were displayed for sale. Industrious workmen, making curious objects with their deft fingers, sat in their doorways, and painters also, designing fantastic animals of the imagination. Once I seemed to catch the

THE LITTLE APES OF NIKKO.

XVI : Sayonara Dai Nippon

perfume of the plum blossoms, and with it I dreamed of golden temples on the hillside and thought I heard a Buddhist priest muttering to himself, "All beings are only dreaming in this fleeting world of unhappiness."

Mixed in the fantastic medley of this dream passed the animals of the years—the strutting cock of 1912, the stolid bullock of 1913, and in the distance the crouching tiger of the year to come. Then I saw the little apes of Nikko, sitting motionless before me—Mizaru, who sees no evil, Kikazaru, who hears no evil, and Mazaru, who speaks no evil. Above them all flew the H-oo, the guiding bird of good omen, which only appears to herald the coming of peace and prosperity. May he bring them both to Japan!

Many times since, on looking back, it has seemed as if Dai Nippon must be all a dream—a fairy island, perhaps, conjured out of the sea by some mighty giant. I often wonder if it did not truly sink into the sea beneath the red eye of the setting sun.

When I am troubled about this, I get out Osame's letter and read it again. It came to us soon after we reached home, and is very reassuring. In order that you, too, may know that Japan is real, I will let you read it.

"Dear Excellency," he wrote L., "when the first news of your coming to Japan announced I could not feel but the happiest news like from Heaven, and only waited the day might flew to your arriving date. The joy and happiness reached its maximum height when I had the pleasure and delight of meeting you and Madam once more at Kharbin. Three years passed since your last visit and you and Madam had not least changed, like the peerless Fuji towering high above the clouds I wished I had power to show you the appreciation and gratitude I always indebted to you, but it was vain effort.

"However Heaven blessed me that you had an interview three years ago with late Emperor and now again with His Majesty his son, we look up to them like a living God enthroned since 666 b.c. I was so pleased. Now alas you passed away again from Japan at four o'clock on the fifteenth instant. As I left the ship I could not utter a word with the heart-rending unhappiness of parting from you. The launch blew the whistle thrice, and puffing out a great column of smoke she slowly moved away. I saw you fading sight and thanked you for your kindness of watching me until we could not discern each other. And the joy and happiness rolled with the waves following your course. With no sign of encouragement I reached shore and out the dream. I ran to the Post Office to send a cable.

"I hope you are enjoying the best health and the best time. Do not forget this humble Osame, always with you no matter what part of the planet you may travel, and always glad and feel happy to hear.

"Please recommend me to one who come to Japan.

"I hope I may be a little service to you for the rare opportunity and honour in my life. With the best wishes for you and Okusuma, anxiously awaiting to hear I remain

"Your humble servant,
"OSAME KOMORI."

So it ends, and so likewise, respectfully bowing, the "Rustic Wife" makes her last apologies and bids the "Honourable Reader *sayonara*!"

THE END.

BIBLIOGRAPHY

ANDERSON, WILLIAM: Japanese Wood Engravings
ANETHAN, BARONESS ALBERT D': Fourteen Years of Diplomatic Life in Japan
ARNOLD, SIR EDWIN: Azuma, or The Japanese Wife. A Tragedy in Four Acts
AVERILL, MARY: Japanese Flower Arrangement
BACON, ALICE MABEL: Japanese Girls and Women
BINYON, ROBERT LAURENCE: Japanese Art. (In International Art Series)
BLACKER, J. F.: The ABC of Japanese Art
BRINKLEY, F. A.: Japan and China
BROWNELL, C. L.: The Heart of Japan
BURTON, MARGARET E.: The Education of Women in Japan
CHAMBERLAIN, BASIL HALL: Handbook for Travellers in Japan
——Things Japanese
——Aino Fairy Tales
CLEMENT, E. W.: Handbook of Modern Japan
DAVIS, F. HADLAND: Myths and Legends of Japan
DICK, STEWART: Arts and Crafts of Old Japan. (In The World of Art Series)
GORDON, REV. M. L.: An American Missionary in Japan
GRIFFIS, WILLIAM ELLIOT: Fairy Tales of Old Japan
——Hepburn of Japan
——Townsend Harris, First American Envoy in Japan
——The Mikado's Empire
GULICK, SIDNEY L.: The American Japanese Problem
——Evolution of the Japanese
HARADA, TASUKU: The Faith of Japan
HARRISON, E. J.: The Fighting Spirit of Japan
HEARN, LAFCADIO: Glimpses of Unfamiliar Japan. (See also other works by the same author)
HONDA, K.: Japanese Gardens. (In European and Japanese Gardens)
MENPES, MORTIMER: Japan: A Record in Colour
MITFORD, A. B. F.: Tales of Old Japan
MORRISON, ARTHUR: The Painters of Japan
NITOBE, INAZO: Bushido: The Soul of Japan
——The Japanese Nation
——Thoughts and Essays
OKUMA, COUNT SHIGENOBU: Fifty Years of New Japan
OZAKI, YEI THEODORA: Warriors of Old Japan

Pasteur, Violet M.: Gods and Heroes of Old Japan
Porter, Robert P.: The Full Recognition of Japan
Porter, William N.: A Hundred Verses from Old Japan: being a translation of the Hyaku-Nin-Isshiu
Ransome, J. Stafford: Japan in Transition
Scidmore, Eliza R.: Jinrikisha Days in Japan
Seidlitz, W. von: A History of Japanese Colour Prints
Singleton, Esther: Japan as Seen and Described by Famous Writers
Smith, R. Gordon: Ancient Tales of Folklore of Japan
Strange, Edward F.: The Colour Prints of Japan. (In Langham Series of Art Monographs)
Teery, T. Philip: The Japanese Empire

INDEX

A
"ABC of Japanese Art", 239
Abe, Mr., 64
Adams, Mrs. Douglas, 145, 149
Ainus, 25, 173, 174, 176, 177, 178, 180, 181, 182, 184
Akasaka, 29, 52, 216
Akashi Straits, 208
Akashi, General, 12
Akiko, 151
Altai Mountains, 1
Ama-no-Hashidate, 202
Ama-no-kagu, 147
Ama-terasu, 25, 86
Amaterasu-Omikami, 99
Ambassador, American, 28, 29, 40, 58, 59, 62
Ambassador, French, 61
America, 10, 29, 33, 38, 40, 50, 58, 63, 67, 75, 79, 80, 81, 84, 93, 107, 122, 124, 126, 127, 128, 133, 158, 213, 222, 233, 242
diplomatic service in, 29
American Board (of Foreign Missions), 130, 131
"American Japanese Problem, The", 76
Americans, 26, 73, 76, 244
Amida, 109
"Ancient Tales and Folklore of Japan.", 136
Anethan, Baroness d', 106
Anezaki, Professor, 133
Aoyama, 54
Arabia, 165
Arabs, 115
Arai, 200
Argentina, 77, 78
Arita, 242
Arnell, Mr., 162, 173
Arnold, Mr., 162
Arsenal Gardens, 227
   (Kora-kuen), 227
Asaka, Prince, 52
Asakusa Kwannon, 168
Asano, Lord of Ako, 43
Asa-Tada, 146
Atami, 194, 196, 202
Atsuta, 202
Attachés, Naval and Military, 45, 64
Australia, 33, 74, 165
Austria, 29, 37, 64
Ayaha Festival, 99
Azuma-Bashi, 198

B
Baba, Mr., 244
Bacon, Miss Alice M., author, 93
Bahu, the Eater of Dreams, 208
Baikal, Lake, 2
Bakin, 143, 238
Baptists, 130
Bashô, epigram by, 88
Bean Night, 93
Benquet Road, 192
Benten, 190
Benten-jima, 200
Bergson, 133
"Beyond, The", 149
Bismarck, quoted, 26
Biwa, Lake, 202, 203
Bizen, 242
Blacker, J. F., 239
Bluff, the, 164, 186
Boardman, Miss, 10
Boshu Peninsula, 197
Boston, 35, 50, 184
Back Bay of, 35
   Museum of Fine Arts, 233
Boys' Festival, 95, 219

251

Index

Brazil, 77, 78
Brazilians, 29
British, 75
  Islands, 73
Broadway, 39
Brookline, Mass., 223
Brownell, Mr., 72, 141
Brownings, of Japan, 151
Brussels
  last sight of, 1
  palace in, 52
  to Kyoto, 2
Bryan, Dr., 19, 215
Bryan, Secretary, 76
Bryn Mawr, 124
Buddha, 21, 25, 35, 41, 89, 95, 109, 111, 112, 117, 188, 204, 233, 240, 241, 242, 243
Buddhism, 10, 100, 102, 103, 109, 117, 132, 213
Buddhist, 10, 21, 41, 91, 93, 95, 102, 105, 107, 109, 111, 113, 115, 118, 119, 127, 135, 160, 168, 197, 213, 221, 222, 233, 234, 240, 247
Bushido, 102, 117, 118, 119

C

Caldwell, Mrs., 40
California, 40, 74, 75, 76, 77
Canada, 173
Carolingians, 26
Catholics, Roman, 12
Central America, 74
Chamberlain, Professor, translation by, 87, 117
Champ de Mars, 54
Changchun, 2, 4
Chemulpo, 128
Chiba, 197
Chicago of Japan, the, 80
Chikamatsu, 152
Chile, 77
Chinese, 1, 5, 6, 8, 9, 14, 21, 23, 25, 26, 31, 39, 66, 69, 80, 84, 85, 89, 90, 99, 119, 120, 125, 126, 142, 215, 222, 227, 234, 241, 242
Chionin Temple, 19
Cho Densu, 234
Chosen (Korea), 4, 10, 12, 14
Christianity, 12, 126, 131, 132
Christians, 131, 133
Church Roman, 117, 126
Chuzenji, 198
Clement, E. W., translator, 88
Cleveland, 62
Columbus, 84
Confucianism, 10, 103, 132
Confucius, 117, 119, 215
Congregationalists, 130
Copts, 74
Corps, Diplomatic, 53, 55, 61, 106, 107
Court
  (Imperial), 37, 45, 52, 53, 55, 64
  of St. James, 53
  Shogun's, 89
Crawford, Marion, 64
Crown Prince, 35, 52

D

Dai Butsu, 21, 204
Daiba Pass, 196
Daini-No-Sammi, 148
Dakota, 197
Dalny, 9
Dango-zaka, 215
Danjuro, 158
Daredesuka, 141
Davis, F. Hadland, author, 136
Dick, 33
Dickinson
  Mr., 55
  Mrs., 55
Diet, 65, 66
Dolls' Festival, 93, 94
Doshisha University, 132
Dutch, 26, 29, 40, 152, 226, 237

Index

E
East River of Heaven, 98
Eastern Capital, 26
Ebisu, 100
Egypt, 215
Eighty Myriads of Gods, 87
Eikibo, 141, 142
Elizabethan Era, 143
Embassy
  American, 28, 45, 55, 66
  Italian, 37
Emperor, present, 5, 9, 16, 17, 19, 24, 25, 26, 27, 35, 37, 41, 45, 48, 50, 51, 52, 53, 54, 55, 56, 58, 61, 64, 65, 91, 93, 94, 100, 101, 102, 111, 113, 117, 121, 131, 137, 139, 144, 145, 148, 164, 192, 213, 215, 216, 234, 242, 247
Empress
  Dowager, 54, 63, 130, 147
  the present, 48, 51, 52, 53, 54, 55, 56, 58, 93, 94, 128, 216, 244
Engineering College, 124
England, 52, 64, 79, 160, 215
Enoshima, 185, 190, 194
Episcopalians, 130
Eucken, 133
Europe, 1, 26, 58, 61, 64, 74, 75, 77, 78, 80, 82, 85, 126, 158, 233, 237
Europeans, 34, 66, 75, 77, 221, 235

F
"Fairy Tales of Old Japan,", 134
Feast of the Oven, 101
Fenner, Mr. J. A., 173, 174, 181, 182
Festival of the Dead, 98
"Fighting Spirit of Japan, The," quoted, 132, 168
Fire-God, 186
Florin, 76
Formosa, 9, 14, 74, 84, 130, 152
  description of, 13

G
Gare du Nord, 1
Genro, 65
"Gentlemen's Agreement,", 74
Germany, 1, 39, 66, 79, 127
Ghosts of the Circle of Penance, 99
Gifu, 202
Ginza, the, 39
Gion Festival, 97
Go-chiku, 21
God of Long Breath, 192
Gordon, Dr., 68
Gosho Palace, 21, 23
Gotimba, 192, 202
Grand Hotel, 245
Great Bell, Kyoto, 21
Great Britain, 79
Great Council, 59
Greece, 152, 160
Greeks, 76, 117, 233
Greene, Rev. Dr., 131, 133
Griffis, Dr. W. E., quoted, 134
Guiccioli, Marchesa, 61
Gulick, Dr. Sidney L., quoted, 76

H
Hachiro Tametomo, 137, 139, 140, 141
Hakone, 192
  Pass, 186
  Range, 192
Haky-i and Shiky-sei, 227
Hamano, 197
  Lagoon, 200
Harashiyawa, 203
Harikiku, 154
Harima, 206
Harris, Mr. Townsend, 58, 59, 60
Harrison, Mr. E. J., author, 132, 133, 168
Hawaii, 74
Hearn
  (Lafcadio), quoted, 56
  quoted, 95, 107, 145
  referred to, 67, 105

253

Index

Hepburn, Dr., 127, 131
Heusken, Mr., 59, 60
Hideyoshi, 21
Himeji, 231
Hindoos, 115
Hirado, 210
Hiroshige, 237
Hiroshima, 208
Hokkaido, 25, 164, 173, 180, 184, 206
Hokusai, 234, 238
Holland, 186, 226
Honolulu, 130
H-oo, 247
Horikawa, Lady, 147
Horse Day, 91
Hosigaoko (in Sanno), 171
Household, Imperial, 46, 51, 65
Hudson, the, 208
Hyde, Miss, 35
Hyogo, 81
  (Kobe), 206
  Point, 208

I
Ichinomiya, 197
Ichiriki Tea-house, 153
Icliejo-Tadado, 54
Ike-bana, 219, 221, 225
Ikegami, 100
Ikko, 109
Imari, 242
Imazu, 203
Imperial
  Museum, 240
  Theatre, 157, 158
  University, 115, 124
Inada, Princess, 97
Inage, 197
India, 79, 82, 126, 213
  Southern, 109
Indians, 76
Inland Sea, 25, 97, 115, 185, 206, 208, 221, 237

Ippo, 234
Irving, Henry, 160
Ise, 103
Izanagi, 24, 73
Izanami, 24, 73
Izumo, 100

J
Jaehne, 31
Japan Club of Harvard University, 9
"Japanese Empire, The", 19
"Japanese Girls and Women," quoted, 93, 94
"Japanese Nation, The,", 144
Japan Magazine, 75, 149, 192, 215
Jesuit, 26
Jew, 76
Jimmu Tenno, 25, 145
Jingo, Empress, 25, 101
"Jinrikisha Days", 10, 152
Jito, Empress, 147
Jizo, 229
Johnson, Governor, 76
Jokasai, Iizuka and Saiihara-Iehidayu, 240

K
Kadenokuji and Kiogoku, Viscounts, 171
Kagawa, Countess, 56
Kai, 217
Kaka, 107
Kamakura, 157, 185, 186, 188, 190, 240
Kamazawa, 203
Kameido, 213
Kameoka, 202
Kamisana, 206
Kanagawa, 127
Kanaoka, 233, 234
Kaneko, Baron, 9
Kanemori Taira, 147
Kan-in, Prince and Princess, 50, 52
Kano, 202

School, 234
Katsura, Prince, 50, 64, 65, 66
Katsu-ura, 197
Kawamori, 202
Keane, Mr., 235
Kengyu (Aquila), 98
Keum-Kang-San, peaks of, 10
Keyser, Lieutenant, 173, 174, 176, 177, 181, 182
Kharbin, 2, 4, 9, 247
Kiai, 118
Kido, 120
Kii, 206
Kikugoro, 158
Kinokiyama, 203
Kira, 43, 44
Kishu, Prince, 216
Kitzuki, 103, 105, 160
Kiyomisu, 227
Kiyomori, 137
Kiyonaga, 237
Kiyonobu, 237
Knox, Mr., 17
Kobe, 78, 80, 185, 204, 206
Kodama
  Count, 12
  Countess, 10
Kofukuji, 242
Kojin, 95
Kompira, 117
Komura, Baron, 9
Konosu (Hyaku Ana), 196
Korea, 1, 2, 4, 6, 8, 9, 10, 13, 25, 74, 84, 101, 125, 202, 241
  Crown Prince of, 162
  dethroned Emperor and Empress of, 8
  Empress Bin, 8
  history of, 8, 9
  missions, 12
  mourning in, 5
  religions, 10
  southern, 12
Koreans, 9, 12, 25, 126, 162, 202

Koro Halcho, 206
Kosai Maru, 130
Koshiro Matsumoto, 158
Koya-san, 115
Kozo Ozaki, 143
Kozu, 194, 200, 202
Kumamoto, 231
Kushiro, 173, 174
Kutani and Awada, 242
Kutchare, Lake, 174
Kwannon, 188, 204, 241
Kyoka Izumi, 143
Kyoto, 2, 16, 19, 24, 25, 26, 27, 28, 31, 97, 101, 109, 134, 135, 136, 147, 157, 185, 190, 200, 202, 203, 204, 227, 242
  Brussels to, 2
  description of, 19
  geishas of, 153, 154
  prefecture, 24
Kyushu, 137, 210, 231

L

Lancers, Imperial, 45, 54, 164
Landsborough, Mr., 76
"Latin-American A-B-C", 77
Laughing Festival of Wasa, 99
Liaotung Peninsula, 9
London, 2, 41, 53
Loochoo Islands, 84, 238
Los Angeles Times, 76
Lucky Day, the, 91
Luther of Japan, the, 100

M

MacCauley, Rev. Dr., 130
Madonna, 188
Maiko, 206
Maisaka, 200
Makino, Baron, 55
Malay Peninsula, 74
Malays, in Formosa, 14
Manazuru, 194
Manchuria, 2, 4, 9, 74, 85

Maple-Leaf Club, 156
Masanobu, 237
Massachusetts, 66
Masumi Hino, Professor, 132
Matabei, 237
Matsui, Mr., 244
Matsushima, 200, 206
Mayon, 190
McKim, Bishop, 130
Meiji Era, 64, 126
Meiji Tenno, 16, 27, 145, 149
Memorial Temple, 17
Mencius, 119
Menpes, Mortimer, 228
Mera, 197
"Merchant of Venice", 164
Meredith, George, 143
Mexicans, 76
Mexico, City of, 64
Michel Angelo, work of, 233
Michinoku, 147
Middle Ages, 84
Mikado, the, 17, 23, 24, 25, 26, 27, 46, 55, 56, 58, 64, 216
Milky Way, 98
Ming Tombs, 25
Mishima, 192
Misogi, Festival of the, 97
Miwa-Daimyo-jin, 100
Miyajima, 97, 115, 208
Miyanoshita, 185, 186, 190, 192, 196, 198
Miyazu, 203
Mizaru, Kikazaru, and Mazaru, 247
Moji, 210
Momoyama, 16
Mon (entrance gate), 8
Mongols, 1
Moon Festival, 99
Moronobu, 234, 237
Morrison, Mr. Arthur, quoted, 239
Morrison, Mt., 13
   renamed Nii-taka-yama, 13

Moscow, 1, 2
Mound of Ears, 202
Mukden, 9
Murray, 170
Mutsuhito, Emperor, 16, 19, 54
   tomb of, 16
"My People", 19
"Myths and Legends of Japan", 136

N

Nagahama, 203
Nagasaki, 26, 78, 206, 210
Nagasakis, the, 52, 244
Nagoya, 25, 141, 142, 202
   Castle, 141, 231
Nakamura, 171
Nakamuraza, Theatre, 158
Nakasendo, 202
Nara, 97, 203, 204, 222, 233, 240
Narai, 198
Narita, 197
Naturalistic School, 234
Navetta, 206
Nazano, 206
Negishi, 165
New York, 76, 78
Nichiren, 100, 197
Night, Queen of the, 99
Nijo Castle, 23
Nikko, 50, 113, 115, 185, 198, 204, 227, 229, 247
Ninigi, 25
Ninsei, 242
Ni-o, 103
Nippon Race Club, 164
Nirvana, 112, 188
Nitobe, Dr., 63, 102, 119, 144
No, 93, 151, 152, 170
Nogi, General, 9, 107, 117, 119, 124
Nomura, 242
Northmen, 145
Norway, 76
Nowazu, 54

Index

O
O Kuni, 160
O Sawa, 33
O'Brien, Mrs., 56
Oanamochi, 192
Obama, 203
Obi River, 1
Odawara, 194
Ogo-Harito, 206
Oishi, 43, 44, 153
Okio, 234
Okubo, 65, 120
Okuma, Count, 54, 65, 131
Onomichi, 208
Osaka, 80, 134, 135, 136, 166, 202, 204, 231
Osaka Museum, 41
Osaki Batsume, 143
Osame Komori, 2, 248
Oshima, 140, 141
Otome-Toge, 192
Otsu, 203
Ozaki, Madame, 64, 134, 137, 242
  Mr., 64, 65

P
Panama Canal, 73, 78
Paris, 54, 63, 93, 151, 157, 158, 237
Pasteur, 134
Peabody, Professor, quoted, 74
Peace Society, Japanese, 63
Peking, 234
palace in, 8
Peony Hall, 48, 50
Perry
  Commodore, 26, 64
  reception, 215
Pescadores, 9
Philadelphia, 124
Philippines, 33, 40, 55, 74, 130, 190, 192
Phœnix Hall, 48
Port Arthur, 9, 130

Porter, William, translator, 146, 147
Portsmouth, N. H., treaty signed at, 10
Portugal, 77
Portuguese, 13
Presbyterians, 130
President of the United States, 26, 58, 59
"The Priest", 151
Protestantism (of Japan), 109, 126

R
Rainier, Mount, 190
Red Cross, 10, 128, 130
Reese, Mr., 76
Religion, Japanese Bureau of, 131
Riddell, Miss, 128
Rohan Koda, 143
Rokumeikan, 54
Romans, 117
Rome, 76
Room of One Thousand Seeds, 50
Russia, 64, 78, 128
  furs in, 39
  negotiations with, 9
Russo-Japanese War, 13, 80

S
Sada Yakko, Madame, 158
Sadanji, 158
Saghalien, 10, 13
Saigo, 231
Saikyo (Kyoto), 19
Sai-no-Kawara, 107
Sakai, Mr., 244
Sakatani, Baron, 133
Sakon-No-Sakura, 23
Salvation Army, 168
Samba (Ikku), 152
Sammons, Mr. and Mrs., 245
San Francisco, 78, 120
San Joaquin, 76
Sandalphon, 111
Sankei, 200

257

Index

Satsuma, 25
  Lord of, 84
  province of, 124
  ware, 242
Scidmore, Consul-General, 6
  Miss, 10, 152
Secretaries, 28, 40, 45
Secretary First, 29
  First Japanese, 29
  of War, American, 40, 55
Seiryoden, 21
Sengen, 192
Seno, Madame (the Japanese Hetty Green), 70
Seoul, 2, 6, 12, 14
  American colony in, 12
  arrival in, 6
Sesshiu, 234
Seto (porcelain), 242
Seven Gods of Good Fortune, 89
Seyukai, 65
Shakespeare, of Japan, 152
Shamanism, 10
Shanghai, 131
Sharaku, 237
Shari, 174
Shiba Park, 41, 99, 226
  Temples, 41
Shijo Road, 97
Shimoda, 58
Shimonoseki, Chosen to, 14
  passed, 210
  shrine in, 101
  Straits of, 9
  treaty of, 9
Shimono-Suwa, 198
Shinano, Prince of, 59
Shinji, Lake, 206
Shin-Maizuru, 203
Shinmei Feast, 99
Shinto, 17, 19, 89, 93, 97, 101, 102, 103, 105, 106, 107, 109, 113, 115, 117, 132, 204
Shintoists, 103, 132, 133

Shiojiri Toge, 198
Shishinden, 23
Shizuoka, 200
Shogun, 21, 23, 24, 26, 27, 41, 43, 58, 59, 64, 89, 113, 152, 181, 215, 237
Shokonsha, 100
Shunsho, 238
Siberia, 1, 48
Siberian Express, 1
Sierras, Californian, 2
Smith, R. Gordon, 136
Soami and Enshiu, 222
Societies, Asiatic and Columbia, 66, 245
Society of Universal Love, 128
  Asiatic, 131
Sodesuka, Mrs., 72
Soi-ko, 227
Sojuro and Sawamura, 158
Sonnomiya, Baroness, 63
Sonobe, 203
Sosei, author, 212
Sosen, 235
South America, 73, 74, 77, 78
Southern Cross, 13
Spain, 165
Spalding, Mr. William, 235, 237
St. Valentine's Day, 63
Staff, American Embassy, 28, 35, 40, 45, 48, 89
Stars, Festival of the, 98
State Department, 59
Suchi, 202
Suez Canal, 78
Sujin, 25
Sun-Goddess, 24, 25, 46, 86, 103, 115
Susa-no-o, 87
Susa-no-o-no-mikoto, Prince, 97
Swift, Professor, 121
Syrians, 74

T

Taiken, Empress, 147
Tai-kun, 59

Tai-Sho, 16
Takahama, 203
Takasu, 148
Takeda Izuma, 152
Tanabata, Princess, 98
Tateyama, 197
Temma, river, 231
Tennu, Emperor, 147
Terauchi, Count, 10
Terry, author, 19
Teshikaga, 174
Testevinde, Father, 127
Teusler, Dr., 128
Thanksgiving (Japanese), 101
"Theft of the Golden Scale, The,", 141
Throne Room, 51, 53
Toda, Count, 46
Togo, Admiral, 9
Tokaido, 58, 181, 190, 192, 200, 202, 237, 238
Tokyo, 9, 17, 19, 24, 26, 27, 28, 29, 31, 35, 39, 41, 43, 45, 53, 54, 58, 61, 63, 70, 74, 75, 80, 81, 84, 87, 88, 99, 100, 106, 107, 121, 124, 128, 130, 133, 143, 156, 157, 158, 160, 162, 165, 166, 168, 171, 173, 180, 184, 185, 190, 196, 197, 198, 200, 202, 213, 226, 227, 238, 240
  Boys' Guild of, 33
  climate of, 35
  Club, 66, 67
  London to, 2
  Normal School, 119
  University, 133
Tomiji and Kanoko (maikos), 154
Torakichi Inouye, 81
Torii Toge, 197
Tosa, 234
Toyohashi, 202
Toyokuni, 237
Trans-Siberian, 2
"Travels of the Two Frogs, The,", 134

Treasure Ship, 89
Tsuda, Miss, 122, 124
Tsukiji, 29
Tsure Yuki Kino, 148
Tsuruzo, 158
Turkey, 28

U

Ukioye, 234, 237, 238
Ukon-No-Tachibana, 23
United States, 17, 28, 40, 63, 74, 75, 78, 79
Ural Mountains, 1
Utamaro, 237
"Utopia," More's, 142
Utsunomiya, 198
Uyeno Park, 43, 91, 165
Uzume-no-Mikoto (Okame), 239

V

Van Royen, Madame, 40
Vandyke, 238
Vega (star), 98
Venice, of Japan, 204
Vienna, 28, 202
Vladivostok, 2, 14
Vries Island, 194, 197

W

Wadagaki, Prof. K., translator, 115
Wakamegari-no Shinji, 101
Wakamiya, 204
Wallace, Rev. Dr., 130
"Warriors of Old Japan", 137
Waseda, 121
Washington, 35, 63, 87, 222, 241
Washington's Birthday, 63, 222
Watanabe, 33, 34, 63, 93, 222
Watanabe, Count, 46
West River, 98
Western Capital, 25
Whistler, 238
Wigmore, Major, 173, 174, 181

Index

X
Xavier, Francis, 126

Y
Yahakii, 206
Yahashira, Prince, 97
Yalu River, 9
Yamagata, met at luncheon, 9
Yamamoto, 65
Yamato, 120
Yamisaki, 109
Yedo, 26, 58, 136, 157, 228
Bay of, 235
Yezo, 25, 173
Yi
  dynasty, 8
  Prince, the Elder, 8
  Prince, the Younger, 8
Yokohama, 61, 62, 63, 66, 130, 131, 162, 164, 185, 186, 192, 196, 206, 235, 244, 245
  Bund, 194, 235
  United (club), 66
Yorimasa, 97
Yosai, 235
Yosano, 151
Yoshida
  Mr., 244
  Professor, 124
Yoshiwara, 168
Yuragawa, 203

Z
Zen, 118

www.ingramcontent.com/pod-product-compliance
Lightning Source LLC
Chambersburg PA
CBHW020326170426
43200CB00006B/291